The Extraordinary Work of Ordinary Writing

had a light rain last night
has been very warm all day. I have
ville, Colorado; this a.m. I made curt
their Bed.

some a great deal 16. Saturday Exceedingly
of work **BENNETT** made a larg
today of bread. ah
tings up generally. Business in the shop
LACKSMITHS, — only been moderate
is week.

Miners Tools a Specialt

Sunday. 17. Cloudy and r
intended to go down to the farm today b
Jefferson Avenue, near Locus
oked so much like rain that he did
have so much to do that it seems I
idly get a spare moment untill after no
ay) on sunday no matter how well I
work on Saturday. Read a good d
to P.M.

Monday 18 Very pleasant
done my washing and done a lot of ol
ork. I got my Photos tonight they ar
od. we had to fix the Bed cord tonight

Tuesday 19
is has been a beautiful day. I churn
ned and Browned coffee this a.m. en
wed a good deal, Jam and Baby wer
while this P.M. my head aches an
el sick.

Wednesday 20
rained this morning. also thundered &
cleared of about 8 oclock. Has been f
ine. I have sewed a good deal today. Mis
mith and Mrs Laughlin called to day
licite aid for the church.

Thursday 21
ry pleasant. I made Bread. Baked Beans
ed ham today. Sewed some this P.M.

The Extraordinary Work of Ordinary Writing

ANNIE RAY'S DIARY

Jennifer Sinor

University of Iowa Press Ψ Iowa City

University of Iowa Press, Iowa City 52242
Design by Richard Hendel
http://www.uiowa.edu/uiowapress
A portion of the introduction originally appeared in
"Waiting for the Words of Annie Ray" in *Rosebud*, vol. 17 (2000).
A version of chapter 3 originally appeared in "Reading the Ordinary Diary"
in *Rhetoric Review*, vol. 21, no. 2 (2002).
A portion of chapter 4 also appears in the essay
"Inscribing Ordinary Trauma: The Diary of a Military Child"
in *Arms and the Self: War, the Military and Autobiography* edited by
Alex Vernon, forthcoming from Kent State University Press.

The publication of this book was generously supported
by the University of Iowa Foundation.

Library of Congress Cataloging-in-Publication Data
Sinor, Jennifer, 1969–
The extraordinary work of ordinary writing: Annie Ray's diary/ by Jennifer Sinor.
p.   cm.
Includes bibliographical references (p.) and index.
ISBN 0-87745-832-4 (cloth), ISBN 0-87745-833-2 (paper)
1. Autobiography—Authorship. 2. Diaries—History and criticism. 3. Women
pioneers—United States—Diaries. 4. Frontier and pioneer life—United States.
5. Ray, Annie, 19th cent.—Diaries. 6. Sinor, Jennifer, 1969-—Family. I. Title.
CT25 .S554 2002
808'.06692—dc21   2002021138

02   03   04   05   06   C   5   4   3   2   1
02   03   04   05   06   P   5   4   3   2   1

FOR BILLIE SCHUNEMAN

AND ANNIE RAY

Contents

Acknowledgments *ix*

Prologue: Annie's Gaze *xi*

A Note on the Editing *xiii*

Introduction: Stories That Matter, the Matter of Stories *1*

1. A Story of the Diary *23*

Intertext: The Year 1881 *58*

2. Time, Days, and Page *86*

Intertext: The Year 1882 *123*

3. Putting Things to Right Generally *145*

4. Making Ordinary Writing *180*

Notes *211*

Bibliography *225*

Index *233*

Acknowledgments

A text is populated by those who have helped daily in its making. They should be more visible. I have benefited greatly from the time and generous attention of many strong and creative scholars. I am thankful for the support of Anne Ruggles Gere, whose dedication to, and respect for, the writing of ordinary women provided a place to begin thinking about Annie's writing. My thanks also to Ruth Behar — poet, critic, and ethnographer — who encouraged me by word and example to take risks in my writing. Thank you to Pamela Moss for being a paragon of reflexivity in both her conversation and her teaching and to Patsy Yaeger whose work on trauma introduced me to the everyday. I have also benefited greatly from the support of the Institute for the Humanities at the University of Michigan, and the Hunting family in particular, who provided a yearlong fellowship that allowed me to work on this project.

Also, my thanks goes to those in FHE, my writing group at Utah State University, as well as to Kathryn Flannery, Andrea Lunsford, Roxanne Mountford, Margaret Brady, Judy Nolte Temple, Theresa Enos, and to the two anonymous reviewers for *a/b: Auto/Biography Studies*. Each of them enters this text in some significant way. Michael Spooner, editor of the Utah State University Press, helped my manuscript find a home at the University of Iowa Press and for that I am ever grateful. Thank you also to those at the University of Iowa Press for their time and commitment. In particular to Prasenjit Gupta, Holly Carver, and Charlotte Wright.

Making a text requires the love and support of others as well, people who are dear to me. Thank you to Cathy Best, Seunghee Ha, and Rona Kaufman, women who represent all that is good and strong and beautiful in female friendship. With a special thanks to Rona, whose brightness and generosity of spirit has literally carried me at times. Thank you to Elizabeth Dutro, Kathleen Collins, Leslie Jeffs, Kara Plumb, Dave Youn, Rafael Heller, Matt Kaplan, Anne Reeves, Babette Cain, Debbie Minter, Amy Brugh, and Keith and Joline Sinor, who have all, in so many ways and at different times, made my world a better, brighter place.

And to my family, who, like Annie, have not asked to enter my text, yet without whose stories a text would not exist. Thank you seems hardly enough. My parents, Morris and Cynde Sinor, my brothers, Scott and Bryan Sinor, and my aunt, Billie Peterson-Lugo, are my bedrock. In a military family, you learn early on that, unlike houses, friends, states, and schools, your family is the one thing that you will never have to leave behind, making them all the more precious. In addition to tremendous amounts of love and support, they have given me story, that which roots us to our past and shapes our future. I could ask for no more.

Finally, to my poet and partner, Michael Sowder. His love of nature, poetry, and being in this world has infused my soul, nourished my mind, and captured my heart forever. Thank you always.

Annie's gaze

Begin at the end. The last picture I have of Annie Ray is one taken a year or so before her death in 1931; it speaks to the space her writing claims. There are seven people in the picture, including her husband and her great-nieces. The men stand to Annie's left, the females to her right. While the others are dressed in summery whites, straw hats, and cotton dresses, Annie stands engulfed in folds of black satin, a bit of lace clutching at her throat. The way she shrinks into the dark shrubs behind her, already she seems absent, less the center and more the hole. While the others meet our eyes solidly, Annie looks away from the camera. Her gaze extends beyond the frame of the photo, refusing to stop at the edges. In the turn of her head, though, the reach of her eyes, she urges us to remember all that exists beyond what is thought worthy of capturing on film. All that slips past unnoticed, uncelebrated, unmourned.

Annie's gaze reminds me that as a writer I, like the photographer, will fail to account for everything. Even as I recover some, more will be lost. Like the photographer framing this moment, every decision I make in this text results in the loss of alternative subjects, angles, and frames. A sentence runs this way, and therefore not that way. An idea is selected and other protean thoughts remain buried in my writing notebook. A connection is made at the same time a gap is concealed. From the outset, I feel the need to acknowledge all that this book does not capture, all that exceeds my frame. For while Annie's writing, like her gaze, urges me to pay attention to the unworthy and the dull, I cannot help but realize that it is in the act of marking, of remarking, that the ordinary is made.

Annie Ray and her family, circa 1928.

A Note on the Editing

Editing a manuscript diary ultimately accrues into what Ralph Cintron calls a failed expectation. There is no way for me to adequately represent Annie's writing for you. The spacing, the feel of the paper, her handwriting, the doodling — all the things that let us know a real and unprofessional writer is writing this text — are lost in the movement between manuscript and type. These are enormous losses. If only you were to hold Annie's diary, turn the pages, see the way it is disintegrating, its fragility alone would encourage a more careful, halted reading. Instead I have transcribed her text for you, reined in the margins, centered the entries on the page, made even more order than the one she imposed. I have tried to do so as carefully as possible, but my footprints remain.

I have maintained Annie's spelling, spacing, and punctuation. I do not write "[*sic*]" every time her grammar or spelling is unconventional. For example, she always writes "untill" for "until." I only note with "[*sic*]" those moments when I think a reader might consider Annie's choice in wording or punctuation a mistake on my part. I have also tried to maintain Annie's spacing. This is difficult. As you will see in chapter 2, Annie uses spacing strategically, so it is important that her original spaces be kept intact whenever possible. However, I do not maintain her line breaks. This means that, at times, I have to exaggerate the space so that the reader knows a space exists and not simply the end of the typed line.

Anything that Annie writes in the margins I have placed between /slash/ marks. My definition of margin is anything beyond the body of the day's entry — meaning anything above, below, or beside. My own editorial comments are in [brackets]. Annie has coded parts of her diary. For example, Annie notes the beginning of her menstrual flow with an asterisk, which I have rendered * in the text. I also believe that she tracks the times she and Charley have sexual intercourse with a small flower, rendered /❀/ in the text. There are also codes that I have been unable to decode. These include some numbers at the ends of entries and some abbreviations, as in "T.D.s lost."

. . .

The diary begins in 1881 and proceeds for four years. At the time of the first entry, Annie is working at the Granger's boardinghouse for her keep. Her husband, Charley, is spending the winter in Leadville, Colorado. He is an itinerant blacksmith and often leaves during the winters to shoe horses for miners in Colorado, leaving Annie alone for months at a time. In a few years, he will open his own blacksmithing business in Bridgewater, a town in the southeast corner of what is now South Dakota. Annie's brother, Robbie, and Charley's brother, Walter, enter Annie's days, as does her father. Her mother died months before she marries Charley. It is a great loss.

Because part of the experience of reading ordinary writing is feeling that you have not been invited into the text, I intentionally refrain from providing much context. The uncomfortable position reminds us of the expectations we have of most texts and how Annie intentionally leaves those expectations unfulfilled.

The Extraordinary Work of Ordinary Writing

RAY. and it dried me very much. how...
ing my head began to ache. We stayed t...
fire works which were very good. By th...
ready to come home & was very sick. ...
to hold me up in the wagon. And whe...
home I could not even undress mys...
had sick head ache.

The celebration B was pretty good.

5: Thursday. rdy. and showery. I have scarcely don...
try today. But put away our clothes. ...
me and Baby were over to see me ...
feel better today than I expected to of ...
so sick

day 6 quite cool. We have had frequent sh...
rms Strictly Cash today. I have done ve...
today read a little. do not feel very we...
as a matter of course if quite abundant...

urday 7. Very pleasant. I dressed and e...
ckenpox. made Buiscuit. Packed Butter...
floor &c. and am quite tired f...
onger than I have any time since the...
cow had a calf this morning. It is a...
ce one.

nday 8 July. very pleasant. C has ...
to the Place. R & P have gone to ...
feel rather down-hearted. C thinks he...
to give up working in the Shop on ac...
his eyes. I don't know what we can do.

nday 9. Hot. a slight Breeze, I moo...
ad today. Have felt very weak and tire...
y. Have done very little today took a...
m. and rummaged among old papers...

ly #0.10. Tuesday. very warm. I done ...
shing. and churned today. Had Beef a...
d Beet Greens for dinner. I am 2...
to day. 21 seems pretty old for all...

We are a people. A people do not throw their geniuses away.
And if they are thrown away, it is our duty as witnesses for the future,
to collect them again for the sake of our children. If necessary, bone by bone.
ALICE WALKER, *Zora Neale Hurston: A Literary Biography*

Stories That Matter, the Matter of Stories

The world of my childhood was a recycled one, spent in close familiarity with the discarded. To this day, members of my family can hardly pass by a dumpster let alone a garage sale. As a child, I did not find it unusual that when the family Volkswagen van needed a new part, we journeyed to the junkyard and not the auto parts store. Very little arrived in our house in its original packaging; rather the "new" came from the Sunday swap meet at the local drive-in theater. Needless to say, my family was a bit of a neighborhood oddity, and my friends delighted in driving around with us as we mined for treasures left on the curb. Can you believe what people will throw out, my dad would say, shaking his head, the stomach of the van slowly filling.

Lumber was a particularly good find. On our first tour of duty in Hawai'i, we reclaimed old boards and beams to burn in our fireplace on those "cold" Hawaiian evenings. While our military quarters had a fireplace, we quickly discovered that there was little market for firewood in Hawai'i. I would not learn about cords of wood until college, and then I would be outraged by the cost of what before had been free. Instead, we would make do with what we would find lying about. What the military had discarded or the neighbors rendered useless burned brightly in our living room. On our second tour in Hawai'i, scavenged lumber was not burned but saved. My brothers and I built tree forts with the two-by-fours that we collected and then argued over who was allowed to sit where. My parents, though, were even more resourceful. They used "found" wood to make improvements upon our somewhat cramped military quarters. Nailing together large planks of plywood and narrow beams, they built a wall that divided the family room into two smaller rooms, creating a needed third bedroom for my brother. When we moved at the end of that tour, we took the wall with us. Later, the pieces were reassembled into bookshelves or a work table in the garage.

Such resourcefulness was, I think, largely economic. My father grew up in the postdepression cornfields of Nebraska. There was never any money. As a young child, he once begged his mother for new leather boots he had seen in a catalog. When they arrived, they were too small for him, but he insisted on wearing them rather than admit they were the wrong size. He knew that he had to make do. In an act he would later regret, he followed his uncle's advice and cut the beautiful new leather to create an opening in the toe box through which his blistered toes could spring. I have imagined my father, a ten-year-old boy walking to and from the one-room schoolhouse, wearing his airy boots every day of an entire Midwest winter. My father's inner sense of there never being enough, combined with his position in the military service and needing to feed and clothe his family, meant that we always drove through neighborhoods with an eye trained on the curb.

Reclamation is not a practice I left behind in childhood. Even in graduate school, my apartment was full of furniture I had collected from the giant, brown dumpsters dotting my apartment complex: a wooden dresser with several bottomless drawers that I spent an entire Sunday morning "walking" back to my apartment and then repainted white; a halogen lamp in need of a bulb; a coat tree whose missing leg kept it forever bowing to me from the corner of my living room. When I finally left graduate school, I made sure that these items had a prominent place on the curb in case anyone else might like to use them. All were gone by morning.

Today my investment in what gets tossed is largely political rather than economic. It began with the realization that as a family we had consumed almost everything ever created by my mother. The imprint of my father's hand remains publicly held in the treaties and negotiations found in military law books. Look into any military document on matters of international ocean law in the Persian Gulf in the 1980s and my father appears. However, we have eaten all that my mother has made, worn through the couches she has recovered, outgrown all the clothes she has sewn. To measure her worth by her record, by what remains recorded, renders her almost invisible.

In determining the values of a society, you need only investigate what gets discarded. Our literal and cultural detritus tell us as much about who we are as do our museums and libraries. Dumpster loads from our past would indicate that, in general, we value the new, the aesthetic, the whole, the extraordinary, the masculine, the Anglo, and the fast — not because our dumpsters are filled with these but rather because our textbooks are. On the historical curb rest the domestic, the broken, the consumable, the useful, the female, and the ordinary. I do not need to travel very far back in my own past — let alone the historical past — for evidence to support this point. In fact I only need return to an interview I conducted with my great-aunt, Billie Schuneman, on August 28, 1998.

"Great Billie," as we called her, was in the hospital, her heart and her head both tired, a tape recorder on the white sheets between us. In less than a year, she would be dead. But not knowing this at the time, I was only willing her out of the hospital, not willing her to remain in this world. I had driven to Chicago from Ann Arbor to visit with her and to hear her recall the past. We had spent part of our visit outdoors laughing together about my inability to steer her and her IV in a wheelchair. The summer—her last summer—still hanging in the trees.

Back in the hospital room, so sunless and shallow in comparison to our drink of the natural world, I asked her questions about the early years of her marriage. As we talked about the writing she had done then, her diaries and her creative work, she said,

> Oh I wrote. . . . I kept diaries when I was going to write the great American novel. I was going to be the author of the century. And then, after I got married . . . I looked for my box with all my stuff in it . . . and I was looking for [my diaries] one day and I asked [my husband] where they were — where was the box of my things — and he said, Oh, I took them out and burned them — said, you don't want any of that stuff — I burned it. My heart. Take your writings and it's like killing your child — I just — I looked at him and I thought who is this person. I don't know him. I've known him since he was thirteen. I didn't know he was a murderer . . . I mourned.

If her diary had not been burned, had it escaped the flames, it would rest between my own diary and the diary that forms the center of this study of ordinary writing, the diary of Annie Ray, Billie's great-aunt and my great-great-great-aunt. However, Billie's diary did not make it into the hands of another generation. Not even valued enough to throw into an unmarked box at the historical society, like most things ordinary, it is long gone. The holes in the fabric of the past left by the burned and the discarded — in my own family as well as in the larger communities in which I claim membership — urge me to recover and revalue what others have been so quick to toss. Already steeped in the literal practice of recovery, feminist theory has given me the theoretical framework for the kind of scholarly salvage work necessary to tend to these holes.

It is the work of feminists and those in the field of cultural studies that has most forcefully drawn our attention to texts and contexts, subjects and objects created by, for, and about those who are politically, socially, and economically marginalized — those on the curb. Scholars in these fields have questioned the arbitrary line separating the high from the low, the public from the private, and the personal from the political. In their hands, my mother's recipe collection and her sewing patterns become valued. In their hands, the formerly discarded is reclaimed. What results when the garbage is taken back for reconsideration is the knowledge and understanding that the tossed is a site of complex cultural formation, a site of both resistance and power — that the dumpster is as compelling a place for the investigation of cultural work as is the art museum. To say that my mother's work is as important as the more publicly minded work of my father is no longer revolutionary. I can now rummage through our cultural dumpsters with pride.

And yet, it is not that easy. I hesitate. Recently, Great Billie's son, the only offspring of the man who burned his wife's heart and the one who had inherited the family papers and heirlooms after my great-aunt died, informed me that he had been going through what his mother had saved and stored for years: the furniture, the documents, the uniforms, the tools, the letters, the photos, the handwritten attempts at memoir. In doing so, he said proudly, he had "separated out the chaff" and saved the rest. What or whom, do you wonder, was his chaff? What writings do you suppose, in this day and age, were relegated to the flames? Whose heart was lost in *this* dumping?

I also hesitate because the recovery work in which I have been engaged for the last seven years, the recovery of an ordinary diary kept by my great-great-great-aunt Annie in the late nineteenth century, has shown me how very few frames exist for valuing that which is useful, ordinary, and plain. Have we really learned to treasure what in the past we might have tossed? And if, indeed, we do *value* the used, the useful, the ordinary, and the everyday, do we know how to *evaluate* it? I question just how far we have come in reading the many ordinary things that surround us. For while I would agree that we have learned to honor that which is typically ignored — one need only look, for example, at the ways a phenomenon like Oprah's Book Club has become an object of critical study — all too often we continue to read these texts through very conventional lenses. So even though we have begun to look along the curbs as well as at what occupies our museums and fills our textbooks, we often insist on asking of the discarded the same questions we want to ask of the saved. And the discarded will never answer these questions well.

* * *

Ordinary writing, writing that is typically unseen or ignored, is primarily defined by its status as discardable. It is made up and makes up, as Laurie Langbauer suggests, "the very things we cannot read because they are so commonplace as to be boring, to refuse our regard or interpretation."[1] Ordinary writing is everywhere, though largely unreadable and unread. Determining what qualifies, in the abstract, as ordinary writing is an exercise in the impossible. Notes, calendars, canceled checks, telephone messages, ordinary diaries, letters, grocery lists, and memos can all be ordinary writing. But they may just as easily be something else. To categorize would ignore the complexity of ordinary writing as a form of writing governed by its own rhetorics. It would equally reduce the role we have in determining the writing that matters. For example, my mother has saved some of the first drawings I did as a child: wobbly shapes and crooked lines neatly titled underneath, by the teacher, "Mountains" or "My Family." My mother, however, does not save the doodling I leave behind on the notepad by the telephone after I have been home to visit for a week. Both are kinds of writing: one is ordinary; the other is not. Ordinariness is not a quality intrinsic to a text but rather one afforded to it. In large part, my mother's reception of my writing — to save one and to throw the other out — produces the category of ordinary writing. What she chooses to toss or save, how she makes the decision, replicates larger assertions and cultural scripts dictating what matters. Further, I would suggest that what makes it into my scrapbook, that I even have a scrapbook marking the occasion of a trip or a birthday party, reveals our cultural preference for writing that can or does tell a story about "the time when."

More than simply its status as the discarded, I want to suggest that what separates ordinary writing from other (more valued) writing is largely the fact that it does not story, meaning it does not tell a story. Because it is unremarkable — does not mark an event or narrate an idea — it also remains unmarked, unnoticed. The fact that when we talk about writing that matters we value writing that stories is a result of the literary lens we have traditionally applied to written texts. This lens effectively creates a limiting binary that divides writing into that which is storied or crafted and that which is not — the ordinary. Amy Shuman pursues the boundary between the storied and the ordinary in her book *Storytelling Rights: The Uses of Oral and Written Texts by Urban Adolescents*. She draws the distinction between that which passes unmarked, the ordinary, and that which is frozen into a moment or occasion as soon as it is surrounded by narrative and given remarkability. She cites John Robinson in saying that it is "the presentation of the commonplace as remarkable" that makes writing "storyable" and hence valuable.[2] In her work, what marks the ordinary as ordinary is the very fact that it does not story. The common must be pulled into the extraordinary, dressed in story, to be read or valued. Put another way, in her essay "Absolute Commonplaces," Laurie Langbauer writes, "The absolute commonplaces of our private and public histories make those histories — and history itself — ultimately unreadable" (127). Her emphasis on the unreadability of ordinary texts highlights the failure of favored reading lenses to adequately adjust to the contours of the unremarkable.

Such neat distinctions between texts that story and texts that do not are, like all binaries, ultimately reductive. But in pitting the literary against the nonliterary or the common, these writers reify such categories to demonstrate absence and privilege rather than perpetuate a binary that historically relegated the nonliterary to the trash. These categories become useful in illuminating the ways in which the privileged category of the literary, the storied, fails as a critical approach to other, less literary writing. While I, too, for purposes of contrast, will often use the categories of literary and ordinary writing, I hope to demonstrate in my own writing — in the ways I work to question the integrity of any text — that it is these very boundaries, artificially erected to police the province of genre, that limit both the production (what the writer can do) and the consumption (how the reader can respond) of texts. To reduce our writing and our world to either/or fails both writers and texts. In particular, such categories fail writers like Annie who write in less readily readable ways.

* * *

Like stones across a river, we mark our days — in fact we make our days — by the stories we tell, the events we name as special, the moments we raise from the unmarked flow of "time in" to the privileged status of "time when." In the meantime, slowly, quietly, urgently, the rush of the ordinary surges past these mossy-edged tales. It is into this river that I wade.

* * *

This project is a defense of ordinary writing and takes as its center the ordinary diary kept by an ordinary woman, Annie Ray, who lived on the Dakota plains in the late nineteenth century. A text that is typically tossed because it lacks matter, her diary is one example of ordinary writing. By finding the tools necessary to value and, more importantly, evaluate her diary, we can learn to read and value other examples of ordinary writing as well as other examples of ordinary texts (and here I am including nonwritten texts like landscapes and bodies). Annie's diary will also allow us to reread literary texts. But learning to read her writing requires asking questions a text like hers can answer well, questions that matter for her as an ordinary writer. As we will see, they are not the questions we typically ask of more storied and literary texts. To do so turns our attention away from what the writing does (whether it is coherent, valuable, literary, readable) and toward what the writer is doing. Investing in matters other than the flash of a well-turned tale ultimately reveals the complexities of ordinary writing as well as the skill of the ordinary writer.

* * *

And I see Annie's as a skillful hand, conducting vigorous and complicated work. My reading stands in contrast to more conventional understandings of ordinary writers or ordinary writing, readings that see — if and when they see at all — less skill and sophistication on the part of the writer. By focusing on the particular work that Annie undertakes — rather than taking a broad overview of ordinary writing — my goal is to make visible the typically indiscernible action and agency on the part of the writer. Enough, perhaps, to make some readers uncomfortable.

At times I veer markedly close to authorial intention, and I certainly claim a good bit of authorial control. It is not that I am ignoring the fact that Annie is a product of her culture or that I want to resurrect the singular, originary, and essentialist conception of the Author. Both theoretical stances, historically, have been damaging to women. Rather, I feel more urgency in naming what she as an individual at a particular moment in time makes (her text) rather than in broadly describing the cultural scripts that disempower and confine her and women like her. She is a woman living in the late nineteenth century, trapped in a claim shanty surrounded by miles of Dakota grass. She is — and will always be — childless. She has little formal education, few nearby friends or relatives, and a husband who is often absent. Clearly she has little power to shape her world — either culturally, historically, or theoretically. I can write pages about how she is conscribed. In paying heed to how she also inscribes, makes her text, I am not suggesting a unitary notion of self but rather, following the work of other feminists, focusing on the particular to articulate the acts and actions necessary for both identity and text formation. I readily assume the risks of assigning Annie too much authorial control over her text or context. I would rather err on that side than create another uncomplicated, flat readng of a writer and text we would conventionally name as flat and uncomplicated. Language is not a pipeline; texts are never free of their contexts; and speakers always utter someone else's words. Given this, I am interested in defining and naming the outer limits of the ordinary writer.

*   *   *

The challenge in reading ordinary writing is in learning to read differently by refusing to ask the same questions or assume the same readerly position we do when we read literary texts. The entries in Annie's diary are not readable in the same way that a story I can tell about Annie is. Rather, we face the following:

June 7 [1881]
Tuesday
Have not cleaned up the house yet. Will try to straighten things up soon if I keep well. Worked a little on the garden, sowed a few cucumber seeds. Robbie brought down one of their cows for us to keep all summer. It will be a great help to us. We will soon have all the milk and butter we can use. It has been rainy all P.M. I made bread and it is good.

June 8 [1881]
Wednesday
Worked considerable in the garden for me. Am pretty tired.
Mrs. Babcock spent part of the PM with me.

June 9 [1881]
Thursday
Got up quite late. Done a little house cleaning. Scrubbed the floor. I
put a paper holder together. Charley came home at noon. He made
the cellar stairs and done some other carpenter work. He and Babcock measured some land. A.M. windy and cloudy. P.M. warm and
clear. I sowed some melons.

* * *

What questions would we ask of this writing? What would we say of
this writer? How will we value this work?

In the end, I think, what makes such a study ultimately so rewarding
is that ordinary writing, by definition, is writing that should not have
survived. It should have been discarded. In fact, most of Annie's diary
has been discarded — that is how precious this remaining text is. I
know that more of her writing existed at one point because of a letter
written by Annie's niece — Fannie — the future aunt of my great-aunt
Billie.

Annie writes on December 7, 1882

Very cold and clear. The wind has gone down. C[harley] has gone
to town and to father's and I forgot to send up the work I had done.
Last night was the coldest we have had this season. I knitted a good
deal and ironed and done some other little things. It seems foolish
for me to keep a memorandum of my uneventful days but I have
little to do and might about as well do that as any thing and then it
will be nice to read after a long time.

Though she has no idea at the time, few will have the opportunity to
read her writing. Fannie burns most of it. What she does not burn, she
censors. Once again, the ordinary writing by the women in my family
is relegated to the flames. One match. I envision Fannie hunched in
front of a black woodburning stove, holding the square metal door
open, watching as the pages curl and writhe in the orange flames. More
and more pages are stuffed into the belly of the stove; their sheer thick-
ness protecting her hand from the heat. At one point the fire is almost

smothered by the weight of Annie's ordinary words. Still, Fannie begins her confessional letter with the word "unfortunately" — as if it were akin to being caught in the rain without an umbrella. A piece of bad luck, rather than erasure. She writes to Great Billie years later, "Unfortunately, I burned the whole box of Uncle Charley's and Aunt Annie's love letters, written in the Seventies — which, incidentally, contained the family history at that time, in detail." She also mentions burning the diaries, only to conclude, "I have wished many times since that I had kept both the letters and the diaries."

· · ·

That ordinary writing ever survives is extraordinary. Its very transience gives us the incredible opportunity to read what is so often so ordinary as to remain unread, unrecorded, and unsaved. Therefore, ordinary writing becomes a highly productive site for investigating how both writing and culture get made *every day*. What makes the project even more compelling to me is its inherent failure. One of the ironies found in studying ordinary writing is the fact that as soon as you mark it as ordinary writing, lift it from the stream of the everyday, you make it remarkable and, therefore, no longer ordinary. I fail before I even begin.

· · ·

Dear Annie,

What I have learned from reading your diary is the failure inherent in both our texts — the one you made and the one I am making. The inability of any writing to capture it all. The deception found in wholes. Intellectually, I know that failure might be the best that I can do, in fact that failure is best. Though given the way you endlessly remade batches of bread until the dough would finally rise, what would you possibly say to that? To begin with failure as the goal must seem self-defeating to you, a woman who ran a homestead virtually on her own.

What perhaps worries me even more is that I am failing you, that I will make your diary speak and act in ways that you neither intended nor would welcome and, barring that, that I will not be able to explain to others how learning to read your diary makes a difference. Recently I heard James Dapogny, a musician and scholar, describe the recovery of a one-act opera by Langston Hughes and James P. Johnson called "Da Organizer," an opera long thought to be lost, thrown out, only mourned. Dapogny, wandering the shelves of a departmental library one day, had stumbled upon bits and pieces of the original score — tiny jewels collected in a three-ring binder and clearly marked "Da Organizer." What he had, with that discovery, were all the sung notes in the opera. What he lacked was everything else — the music, the orchestration, the mood, the original vision. Two years later, he had filled in most of the in-between. Through sketches and research, his knowledge of musical composition, his love for Johnson's music, and a lifetime of playing the piano, he was able to say with confidence that the long lost opera would have sounded like so.

What struck me the most about his lecture was the certainty of his recovery. I asked him if it made him nervous to occupy so much space in the opera, to have filled in so many of the gaps. How did he know he had done well by the artist? How could he claim success?

He answered that he was the best person for the job, the only person who could even come close.

Is that enough?

Here are the bits that I know. You kept a diary almost every day for four years while you homesteaded in the Dakotas, a territory that I can only imagine and never touch. Whenever I think the word "Dakotas" I feel the emptiness of the plains in the long "o." Waist high grass whips around the word. There is no path to follow through the long grass when walking to your distant neighbor. There is no phone. When you fall sick, someone must go and fetch the doctor, who is sometimes too drunk to come. In 1881 when you begin keeping your diary there is only one Dakota. The plains stretch ever farther between the letters of that word. Beginning, middle, and end, this is all I know.

The diary you kept is most ordinary and this is what I love. You write about baking bread, washing clothes, and mopping floors. The wonder of the ordinary diary as a form is the way it measures these moments. Marking your experiences as you move through time and space in an immediate rather than reflective way. As a reader, I am forced to be fully present with you. No foreshadowing. No climax. No closure. You grant me a tiny space, a ledge it feels like, really, at the edge of your ordinary.

Monday 19
[June 1882]
Cloudy and sometimes drizzling. I washed, made bread, sewed and done some little jobs also read some. Charley hoed A.M. and worked on the kitchen P.M. I set a hen today.

Tuesday 20

[June 1882]

Pretty cool and very windy. I ironed etc., made a pair of pants. Charley worked on the kitchen and hoed some. Evening I set out a lot of tomatoes. The little chickens are hatching.

Here is what I have learned from books (not the lovely books you read like *Anne of Green Gables*, the yellow-covered book with your name in it that has been handed down to me now — but rather books that live in graduate libraries, books that do not tell stories as much as they work to ascribe a value to story). In general your diary is not the kind of diary that receives any attention. Not enough story matter to be of any use. It is too ordinary and too bare to really do much for feminist theory or cultural studies. Too private. Too boring. Your diary is too spare even to serve as a repository for historical information. An empty mine.

Instead, the kinds of diaries that receive critical or aesthetic attention (those that get published, read, referenced, pillaged, or those that simply escape being discarded) are those that qualify as "diary literature." The diaries of Mary Boykin Chestnut, May Sarton, Virginia Woolf, Anaïs Nin, and Charlotte Forten Grimké. They tend toward the literary — exhibiting plot, action, suspense, length, allusion, metaphor, linearity, sparkle, self-reflection, extraordinary events, deep introspection, and/or some kind of authorial presence (usually a rather strong and witty one). Your diary contains none of these things.

Yet, they have changed the way I think. And this is what I am at pains to convey. At pains because you have not asked that your diary be read by others; there is so great a chance for my misstep. Assuming the risk because I believe I am the one who can come the closest to reading it well. Is it enough for me to acknowledge that as writers we both will fail? In a recent essay, Cynthia Huff, one of the leading scholars on the diary, said that diaries like yours, manuscript diaries, must be approached with care by a "loving" reader. An emotional commitment seems necessary when reading unreadable texts. Is it enough for me to claim the authority to read based on love? Some might suggest that the blood bonds we share only confuse the work, raise the stakes, rather than facilitate the reading.

And what would you say? Love, Jennifer.

* * *

For so long, I thought the question we needed to ask in reading Annie's diary, in reading any piece of writing that appeared fragile, fractured, halted, or holed, was a question of ourselves. How can we be accountable for someone else's story, especially when that someone cannot tell the story on her own? I have read writers like Patti Lather, Shoshana Felman, Linda Alcoff, and Ruth Behar who, whether working with testimony, field notes, student writing, or transcripts of an interview, consider how to remain accountable to and for the lives these texts represent.[3] It is a concern that comes partly from knowing that interpretation is not a choice. Alcoff writes that "feminist scholarship has a liberatory agenda that almost requires that women scholars speak on behalf of other women."[4] But such speaking comes with a price, the inevitable betrayal of the subject that Kamela Visweswaran writes so urgently about, the failure to get the story "right."

Only after learning to read Annie's diary and thinking about ordinary writing as a "thing itself" have I realized that, while the question of my own accountability for another's story is clearly important, the question rests on two unexamined assumptions that can work to remand as much as to recover. I have learned that it is often not the best question to ask of texts that, for whatever reason, appear — as Laurel Thatcher Ulrich writes of manuscript diaries, unable to "stand alone" — in need of bearing. The first assumption is that the text I am reading, the one I am being accountable to and for, is a story and not something else. This is an assumption that predetermines a reading lens honed in expectation of a narrated moment or collection of moments, the reading of a time when. And the second assumption is that it is my accountability that deserves the closest attention and not another's, which is an assumption that may allow me to leave the text too early, to bear the text too readily. My foray into the tossed has caused me to revise my questions and examine these assumptions. I have had to learn to heed more carefully what is already there.

Ordinary writing asks us to pause and consider the matter of stories simply by refusing to give us story matter. Rather than the fullness found in character, motivation, dramatic tension, selective detail, and metaphoric language, the matter of ordinary writing is almost non-existent, intentionally less crafted, and much closer in form to something like testimony — which also arrives in fits and starts and is never closed, narrated, and whole.[5] Like testimony, ordinary writing is a text not made with the reception of others in mind, not aesthetically crafted.

Rather, the ordinary writer is writing for use. As writing that is firstly put to use, ordinary writing lacks the context and the embellishment we find (and value) in other texts. A grocery list, a scribbled note found in the wallet of a loved one who has died, the messages left on an answering machine while you are on vacation. There is no preface, no arrival scene, no birth moment, no once upon a time. Like Annie's diary, ordinary writing always rests in the middle of things.

> January 15 [1881]
> [Saturday]
> Snowed a little. Very pleasant this eve. I am very tired. I hope to have only one more Saturday here. R[obbie] helps me a great deal. It seems as though I am wasting time in living this way — without society — comfort or pleasure of any kind — and most of all without my husband. How I wish time would stop — I dislike to grow old so fast and see all the pleasures of youth slipping away from me before I can enjoy them. A drunk man insulted me this eve by professing great admiration and love for me — and Granger was too much of a coward to order him out of the room. But Robbie was there to stand by me. I do not know that men are really accountable for what they say or do when they are under the influence of liquor.

Even in this, her first entry, Annie's writing glimmers with the hint of story matter — a pleasant eve, a lonely woman, a confrontation. Already I feel the tug. But as a reader I must be content to read this entry and all her entries as another moment "in" rather than a moment "when." It is an unfamiliar position for most of us. We are taught to locate beginnings and ends. Questions of story — motivation, setting, plot, and pacing — like questions about the identities of Granger and the drunk man, prove inadequate tools for the task of reading a diary. Unlike more familiar forms of writing such as memoir or short story, Annie's diary never "adds up" to even a fleeting whole but rather accumulates in a measured wealth of days. Writing as she lives, always in the middle, she never knows when her last entry will be her final one.

> Jan[uary] 16 [1881]
> Sunday
> Very pleasant. All the strangers have gone and there are only the six of us here now. I am always thankful when the family is small. Preaching here this A.M.

Jan[uary] 17 [1881]
Monday
Worked hard of course. Washed a little and mopped the floor. R wrung the mop for me. The mail has come and there is no letter from Charley. I had been trying to think there would be none so that I would not feel so disappointed if there was none. But my heart sank for all that. O! What can be the trouble, is my experience of last winter to be repeated? I wish I was home so I would not have to work with my heart aching so.

When first reading Annie's diary, I strained to see behind the lightly penned words on the page, the words that seemed to name loss at a slant. With a great sense of urgency and duty I found the matter necessary to fill the holes. The result of my efforts was an ordered, tidy, and dramatic story about a woman who homesteaded in the Dakotas in the late nineteenth century and whose husband, Charley, was absent and unavailable. By distilling her daily tally of days into five or six remarkable entries, I furnished the stuff of story without thought. To find the interesting and the dramatic, I read past the repetitious, the daily, the chores, and the tedium. I read past the very qualities that mark the diary as a distinct kind of writing, rather than simply distant kin of the literary. And, most importantly, I read past the strategies Annie utilizes that assure her diary the status of an ordinary text. What I have come to realize is that being accountable for Annie's story begins first with the recognition that she is not telling one.

So what is she doing instead? The second assumption my initial question rests upon is that it is *my* accountability that deserves the most attention. The making of ordinary writing, the fact that it is made by a writer who must negotiate the same desires and constraints all writers negotiate, reveals the danger in assuming such a writer is not largely in charge of, not accountable for, the writing she produces. Often writing like Annie's diary is considered simple, disjointed, bare, and one-dimensional. Because it lacks detail and does not present a linear, whole text, it is overlooked or deemed unimportant. Writers of ordinary writing are afforded the same uncomplicated position as their texts — ironically affirming Thomas Mallon's decree that a diary is the flesh made word. The uneasy conflation of writer and text has two results: that conceptions of the writing subject are as reductive as conceptions of the text and that the presumed unreadability of the text requires a translator.

The decision that a text cannot stand on its own, that it lacks context, or that it is unreadable spurs the need for a mediator, the presence of one who can bear the story. Because neither the text nor the writer can speak, someone must speak for them, story for them. The ethical recovery of the marginalized text. But what happens if instead of deciding a text was unreadable, you approached the text through a different reading lens? What if, instead of considering the gaps as something in need of bridging, as moments the story fails, you questioned how the writer is strategically using or producing these gaps, willfully writing against story. Turning our attention away from our accountability in making sense out of a text that seems limited or empty and toward the writer's agency in producing the text in the first place not only complicates the site of ordinary writing but also the subject position of the ordinary writer. The more agency we ascribe to the writer, the less work we have to do ourselves in framing the text for others. Our work, instead, becomes generating the kinds of questions that allow us to meet the writing and the writer on their terms. A harder task by far.

Of course, I am not suggesting that I do not need to be self-reflexive in my work with Annie's diary. Annie kept a diary that, as far as I can tell, was never meant for other readers, let alone the inclusion in my text. Her diaries were initially kept in a bank safe. They sought protection. I am putting them at risk and must claim responsibility for my representation. Furthermore, Annie is a blood relative. I personally care how her life and her writing are viewed. The objectivity conventionally valued in research is impossible for me to obtain. But it is also a stance that is unobtainable by any researcher, and it is this kind of backyard ethnographic work that serves as the best vehicle for naming just how little objectivity there is in the creation of subjects and texts. To that end, I work to destabilize my own authority and call attention to my position as maker of this text largely by refusing to recognize the line between academic writing and, for lack of a better phrase, more creative writing. My own stories, extended metaphors of reading the world, argue alongside more academic analysis of texts and criticism. I make no attempt to persuade readers that this is a more effective or "authentic" approach to critical work. I see no choice. Ironically, these stories worry the category of academic writing in the same ways that ordinary writing worries the category of story. Both acts, mine of telling stories in a space that most often refuses them and Annie's of refusing to story in a space where most readers welcome them, call attention to the matter of stories and the stories that matter.

My own reflexivity in research and writing, while extremely important, only accounts for part of the necessary work in recovery. The decision that renders a text unreadable is one that equally renders the writing subject a nonwriter — or maybe I should say more carefully, a decision made about the ability of a text is one equally made about the ability of the writer. Being accountable for your own presence in the recovery of a text is important, but not as important as making sure that the writer is afforded agency in the production of the text in the first place.

Annie is a writer.

Her diary is a piece of ordinary writing.

How will we read it?

*   *   *

My reading of Annie's diary begins, in chapter 1, with an examination of diary scholarship. I suggest that the historical and theoretical work on diaries has privileged those diaries that exhibit literary features — those that tell a story of a famous life or a famous moment and tell that story well. When read through a literary lens, diaries like Annie's, ordinary diaries, are dismissed as being "bare boned." They are hard to read and fail to answer well the literary and textual questions that scholars want to ask of them. The very features that define the diary as a distinct form of writing — that it is measured, daily, and open — are the features many scholars have actively read against in their quest for texts that story well. I suggest that reading an ordinary diary as a piece of ordinary writing requires a different reading lens — one that takes its shape from the object it studies rather than one ground with story in mind. It is a reading lens that demonstrates the limitations of story and story matter while capitalizing on the capacity of diurnal form.

Such a lens, I suggest, must take its shape from dailiness, the single most defining characteristic of the diurnal form and the central quality that sets diary writing apart from other forms of writing like memoir, autobiography, or literature. Out of dailiness — the act of writing in the days rather than of the days — flow other aspects or features of the diurnal form that will also prove important in reading an ordinary diary.[6] Writing in the days produces the immediacy, the *middleness*, we attribute to diaries, the fact that the writer writes in the moment and is unable to create the kind of critical distance we associate with reflection.

Writing in the days determines the *openness* of the diary as a form of writing, the fact that the diarist never knows when her diary (or often even her "day") will end and therefore never gears up for an ending.[7] Writing in the days means the diarist cannot shape events or stories because she will never know when an event or story has begun or ended—or even that it is an event in the first place. Instead she traces the *measuredness* of "time in" rather than the occasion of "time when." Writing every day also means the diarist documents the dailiness of the everyday and can make decisions about how those typically undocumented moments will be put to *use*. Middleness, openness, measuredness, usefulness. These qualities — those that mark the diary as a distinct kind of writing and that equally mark the diurnal form's distance from story — are rooted in dailiness. Reading an ordinary diary, then, necessitates a diurnal lens.

In chapter 2 I start to read Annie's diary through such a lens by examining theoretical and historical roots of dailiness. In tracing the rise of the diurnal form, Stuart Sherman suggests that a change in seventeenth-century horology — the creation of the pendulum — necessitated a new form of writing that could capture most effectively the new experience of time. The invention of minutes and seconds was simultaneously an invention of in-between time. No longer did clocks run tick-tock (a beginning and an end) but ran tick, tick, tick (endless measured moments). The diary arose as the form of writing that could best seize temporal middleness. The empty daily spaces in the diary replicated the empty open spaces of time produced by the minute hand, allowing the diarist to recognize, document, and put to use her experience of "time in." Chapter 2 examines the physical and material terrain of Annie's diary and considers these features as extensions or products of dailiness. Specifically, I consider the strategies Annie employs in choosing the book that will be her diary, how her entries will assume space on the page, the role of the margins, and how she represents, through form, the multiple forces pulling on her. These are strategies that Annie, as a writer, uses to extend the capacity of the diurnal form to measure the dailiness of "time in." I argue that the recognition of the mutually defining relationship between temporality and form allows us to name more clearly her agency as a writer at the same time that it points to the constraints of her form.

Turning the focus of the diurnal lens onto the rhetorical choices Annie makes, in chapter 3 I consider what Annie gains and loses by capitalizing on the diurnal form's ability to document the measuredness of days. Sherman's work helps us think about the ways in which the diary, as a tool, allows the diarist to seize these in-between moments of time but considers less closely how these moments are not simply empty but are tightly regulated spaces, spaces regulated by a multitude of discourses. The work of ethnographer Ralph Cintron illuminates the tension between the seemingly empty, open, measured spaces of the diary and the discourses of measurement that bind them. I suggest that while Annie is, indeed, constrained by these discourses, she also extends their ability to make order and keep the unstable at bay. Specifically, she employs parataxis, reduces possibility in her entries, limits language and syntax, and uses repetition in an effort to order out what she cannot or does not want to contain in her day. At the same time, that which has been ordered out still threatens to disrupt. To fully understand the rhetorical work of the diurnal form, I argue, we need to highlight Annie's skill at perpetuating these discourses, even as we acknowledge that her skillfulness leads to the continuation of a damaging fiction, a fiction that conceals the messy reality of living in a time and place that erases rather than sustains women.

Having identified the strategies Annie employs as writer as well as the questions we might ask of a piece of ordinary writing such as her diary, the final chapter returns our attention to ordinary writing broadly conceived. Informed by a reading of Annie's diary, in this chapter I outline the attributes of ordinary writing, including the form's connection to the repetition and the measure of the everyday. I suggest that reading ordinary writing results in at least three outcomes: (1) it illuminates more clearly the making of both subject and text and in so doing reveals the partiality of all texts, (2) it complicates the site of ordinary writing beyond simple considerations of the ordinary that work to either idealize or demonize that site, and (3) it ushers ordinary writing into conversation with lifewriting and in so doing demands a broader definition of what counts within the field of lifewriting.

In chapter 4 I consider how reading Annie's diary as a piece of ordinary writing results in a clearer vision of Annie as a maker of text. In chapters 2 and 3, I detail the choices Annie makes in her writing as she works to keep the unstable at bay. Because Annie's diary is not a highly wrought text, because she is not working toward a neat whole, and because she strategically reduces possibility and eliminates detail, her writing puts into greater relief the choices all writers make. While no text can account for everything, some texts — professional, literary texts — cover their seams more craftily. The seamless appearance of these texts can infer stability and believability. Yet texts are always only the sediment of choices. Unlike those in most nonordinary texts, the choices made by the ordinary writer are more apparent and allow us to see the partiality of all texts. Ordinary writing becomes a space for critically examining the making of more crafted texts, for naming the choices that all authors make as they reduce the complexity of the world to a tenuous order.

In the final chapter I also consider how current conceptions of the ordinary work to see the site as either one of resistance or of disempowerment. The ordinary either traps individuals — historically women — to the rote and the mundane, never allowing them to transcend to a more reflective space, or it provides the particularity, the local context, necessary for individuals to recast larger cultural scripts and exhibit agency. Neither view fully complicates everyday life. Annie perpetuates the opportunities found in her writing to create an order. Rather than resistance or rote reproduction, I suggest that part of her work involves creating safety and familiarity through her ordinary writing. She uses the repetition of the ordinary to create necessary stability. Seeing the ordinary in less dichotomous terms opens the space for more complicated understandings of how individuals make themselves and their texts.

Likewise many of the discussions that are currently happening in the field of lifewriting seem too often to avoid rather than seek complication. The texts privileged as lifewriting — those that are anthologized or critically considered — illuminate the power story has over us and suggest that the writing that comes out of a life is largely narrative. Examples of lifewriting are often whole, crafted, and coherent. I suggest that ordinary writing, writing produced *in* the moment rather than *of* the moment, captures the in-betweenness of lived experience. These are the only texts that can account for that which is so ordinary that it passes unaccounted for. Ordinary writing makes visible the unremarkable moments that make up the majority of our days, adding necessary depth to our conception of lifewriting.

In addition to these chapters, I have included two intertextual chapters: lengthy excerpts from Annie's diary for the years 1881 and 1882. I have placed Annie's text alongside my own for a number of reasons, most of which are readily apparent. Annie's diary is not the kind that would be published or saved. Even though I would argue it is a paragon of the diurnal form, students of diaries would typically not have the opportunity to read even short excerpts of an ordinary diary, let alone lengthy sections. These texts only exist in the holdings of historical libraries or in trunks tucked away in attics. In addition, I also wanted to ensure that readers had the experience of reading a large amount of ordinary writing, rather than only selected excerpts framed by my own text. It is one thing to read a few entries and quite another to read pages and pages of an ordinary diary. The only way to truly get a sense of the diurnal rhythm, the measuredness of things, is to read an untold number of daily entries in a row. Also, including long excerpts from Annie's diary keeps me, as maker of this text, more accountable to Annie's words. You read them with me. You can decide if the strategies I attribute to Annie as a writer and the sophistication I attribute to ordinary writing is evident. Finally, there would not be this book without her diary. Of this fact I have tried never to lose sight.

*   *   *

A final note about the making of this text. Part of the work I have undertaken as writer is to foreground the fact that my writing, like all writing, is an illusion of order. To that end, as I have suggested above, I destabilize both my authority and your reading by including stories alongside critical texts. Such disruption, I hope, calls attention to the act of reading, of making meaning, and, in effect, reproduces the readerly position required when approaching ordinary writing, one not based on expectation of what you think you have. There is another way, though, that my hand as maker can be seen in my text and that is in what I have chosen to leave in and what to take out. The reduction you hold in your hands represents absence more than presence. All that was lost, disregarded, and forgotten remains unmarked. As the writer, I privilege the ideas of some scholars — in particular the work of Stuart Sherman and Ralph Cintron — because their ideas resonated with me at the time I was reading and writing. Our paths crossed. They are not the only possible paths, the only intersections. Their work is no more stable, their authority no more intact, than my own. Every time another enters my text, whether that other is Annie, my brother, or Elizabeth Hampsten, it is my decision. Which means, if we follow the lessons Annie's ordinary writing teaches us, as readers we should question these choices, remaining attuned to what has been left out, left behind, left over. In many ways the unsaid, the unmarked, weighs heaviest. No text accounts for all.

This project lies close to my heart. I think the fact that I share blood bonds with the ordinary writer at the center of my text has made all the difference. From the start, I was unwilling to see Annie as anything other than a complicated, accountable, and strategic writer. I was unwilling to see her diary as boring and unsophisticated. If nothing else, my hope is that you will see the power and complexity of ordinary writing as well as the vigor of the writer who makes the ordinary text. Annie's words are, indeed, bare bones, yet they are the only bones that remain.

BONE
—for Georgia O'Keefe

I am a saguaro, ribs thrust gray
against blue hot sky.
                              I am
a polished jawbone, teeth white
against the grass.
I have become all that I see:
an elegant bone gnawed clean,
leaving only bone the end,
bone the beginning,
bone the skyline mountain.
                    — Linda Hasselstrom, *Windbreak*

1 : A Story of the Diary

Once, when I was eleven, I returned home from playing one afternoon to meet my mother rushing out of the house carrying a glass of milk. Handing me the milk, she said, Your brother has lost his tooth. It's somewhere in the park. Find it and put it in here.

In the milk?

Like you would a finger.

His tooth?

The front one.

So I headed for the park, milk in hand. I wasn't particularly distraught. This seemed like just another link in a chain of bloody scenarios produced by having two younger brothers. Broken bones. Black eyes. Missing teeth. My mother's request was no more unusual than other requests made of me during my childhood: get a book from your bookshelf that will serve as a splint for your brother's broken arm; find some cream of tartar for your brother's man-o'-war bite. A glass of milk for a tooth seemed a familiar enough request so as not to rattle me.

The neighborhood park consisted of a glorified patch of red dirt, a pitted slide, and a giant iron swingset. When I arrived I found Scott's friend, Michael Brown, already on his hands and knees grazing the red dirt, presumably looking for Scott's tooth. Wooden planks forming a highly suspicious bike ramp lurked to one side. I asked what had happened.

It seems my brother and Michael had built the ramp together. Michael, being older, wiser, and pretty much trouble at the time, had persuaded Scott (a gullible eight) to jump the bike ramp first. Scott, eager to impress, agreed and pedaled to the top of a nearby hill. It wasn't until Scott hit the ramp, having hurtled down the hill, that both realized that the ramp was pointed directly into the iron poles of the swingset. Scott's face collided with a pole and his permanent tooth broke free.

Michael and I spent what seemed like hours looking for Scott's tooth. Tossing rocks and bits of twig over our backs, we searched and searched. That's not it. That's not it. That's not it.

The milk grew warm.

We worked our way toward the very edges of the park, the amount of red dirt left to cover growing thin. I was just about to give up the search when all of a sudden, having tossed a long white rock over my shoulder, I realized: tooth. I scrambled to find it again. And sure enough, it was Scott's tooth. Only it was longer and uglier than any tooth I had ever seen before. I had been looking for a neat white box of a tooth, something a bit larger because it was a front tooth, but something small, something like what I put under the pillow for the tooth fairy to find.

What I learned then, however, is that uprooted teeth bear little resemblance to what we think we see when we look in the mirror every morning to brush.

*   *   *

I am also eleven when I receive my first diary. Christmas of 1980. It comes unexpectedly amidst the rest of the gifts that my brothers and I receive that year: skateboards, helmets, new sleeping bags. Of the three of us, I am the only one to get a diary.

What I remember most clearly about my diary is the girl dressed in blue on the cover. She is a quiet kind of girl in a big floppy hat, sitting on a fence with her cat. A tiny branch of a tree drops in from above. But it is clear that this girl, wearing her blue flowered dress, would not climb a tree. Her back is to me and she is watching the sun go up or down, probably up because this girl would be an early riser. Her cat is patchwork blue like her dress. It does not look like a real cat. Upon closer inspection, I realize the cat and the girl are edged with stitching, as if quilted. They are sewn down. Not only will she not climb a tree, this girl will never move. She will always be quietly contemplating the sun with her back to me. She is a certain kind of girl. I wonder if she is a diary girl.

What I also remember is my fear of losing the diary's key. Fear that I will be locked out of my own thoughts. To be safe, often I choose to leave it unlocked, though hidden deep in my desk as a diary should be. The small key hung on my keychain full of found and useless keys.

Long after I have ceased writing in my first diary, it continues to hold a place of inexplicable power in my memory. As an adult, I retrospectively fill those skinny-lined pages with the traumas I remember of being that age. I confess to my diary the fact that I hid *Playgirl* pictures in my bottom dresser drawer; that I lied to my parents about what my brothers did or did not do; that I wanted desperately to wear a bra. When I think about being eleven, twelve, and thirteen, it is these casualties of adolescence that I want inscribed in my first diary. Evidence. What I find when I rediscover my first diary in a box in the attic almost twenty years later are none of these stories. Instead I find recorded ever so briefly where I had been, what I had seen, and how much I wanted my friends to like me. While there are moments of trauma (when will I get my period?), mostly I record ordinary moments in ordinary ways.

> Friday, December 26
> I went to Erin's house tonight and she's so nice we went shopping down to the shopping center agian Mrs kaup doesn't allow Stacy to do much she won't allow her to go with us but were going camping the 9–11 of Jan. I hope Karen can go

* * *

Where is the war?

At first I am disappointed. The "real" diary is so much less interesting than the imagined one. Why did I not write about these deep, dark things? Where was the evidence that thirteen was the worst year of my life? Why didn't I mention not wanting to move to Virginia? Why don't I tell the story about stealing from the Brach's Pick-o-Mix display at Safeway? These significant occasions are replaced by seemingly unremarkable daily entries. My childhood looks so much less vivid, less eventful, less traumatic when viewed in the pages of my first diary. My memory is so much more storied.[1]

> I've never really had a diary so I don't know how to start. I will get into personal things tomaro I will try to write in it every night. We went to Mrs G house it was fun.

My first diary entry. Completely impelled by the cultural and textual messages that surround me, messages encoded in the material diary:

that it has a lock, that eleven lines are allotted for thought per day, that a sweet girl is on the cover of *My Diary*. Cultural messages I have absorbed about what it means to keep a diary: by reading *The Diary of Anne Frank*, by watching movies in which young girls hide their diaries under their pillows when mothers are heard climbing the stairs. I begin by saying that I am unsure about what is expected from me, indicating that I am fully aware that diary space calls for a different kind of writing than the writing called for by my homework, letters, or the secret notes I fold at school. However, I admit by the second line that I know exactly what fills diary space: "personal things." Personal things that get guarded by the lock. And I vow, like millions of diary keepers before and after me, that I will write every day. The diurnal contract. I hardly have time to write that I don't know how to start before I immediately fashion myself into the diarist I think I need to be in order to join those already standing in the long line of the diary tradition.

Private. Gendered. Autobiographical. Daily. Elements that I glean from cultural and textual messages constellate into the diary model I aspire to. These elements also form the basis for four of the most pivotal questions that have occupied and continue to occupy diary scholarship today. What does it mean to say the diary is public or private? Is the diary a particularly female form of lifewriting? What does dailiness ultimately mean for literary value? Can the culmination of daily, personal writing "add up" to autobiography? These questions pose more than just possible entryways into diary discourse, ways to join the diary conversation. How scholars take up these questions and work to answer them is all about the kind of space they want to claim for the diary. And how scholars ask and answer these questions (even the fact that it is *this* set of questions they want to ask) ultimately determines how we think about diaries, how we value diaries and those who keep them, and how we decide what the limits and conditions of the diary as diurnal form are.[2]

It is a tricky line that I am going to try and travel. I want to value the work that has been done on diaries while, at the same time, suggest some important losses. As I begin, I recall Gayatri Spivak's essay, "Three Women's Texts and a Critique of Imperialism," in which she demonstrates that the recovery of one text, character, or idea, can and often does mean the silencing of others. No recovery is complete. These are the unavoidable risks of research. I, too, am equally complicit in such silencing. My recovery of the ordinary diary will certainly be accompanied by equally dramatic silencing. Given this, I make every attempt in what follows to celebrate the recovery work that has already been done. At the same time, to read the ordinary diary requires pointing out work still in need of undertaking, to illuminate the gaps left by previous salvaging operations.

The diary, as a form of writing, has so long been delegitimated, unseen, feminized, and privatized that the fact that there are any women's diaries left from the past to read is astonishing in and of itself — let alone the fact that a scholarly field has risen up around the diary. And I want to consider some of the goals and outcomes of the recovery process — which means questioning a process that has led to the validation and publication of the words and voices of so many forgotten women. It also means questioning a relatively young recovery, one that has been going on for just over twenty years. In fact, the year I received my first diary is the year initiating the decade when the diary finally comes into its own — a decade when, for the first time in its history, the diary as a form of writing is finally being authorized as autobiography, as art, as literary, as worthy. Yet, it is exactly this hard-won legitimization that I am going to suggest has brought some accompanying losses for the diurnal form. Losses that, while perhaps once necessary, no longer seem so.

There are things at stake, things that compel me to ask different questions, seek different answers. One of those things rests beside me — the diary of my great-great-great-aunt Annie Ray, a very ordinary diary, the kind one could easily miss or dismiss. Another of them no longer exists — the diary of my great-aunt Billie Schuneman; all that physically remains of her days is what I have captured on tape. Another of them runs the length of the bottom shelf of my bookcase — my own diary, volumes and volumes, also very ordinary, an ordinary that I know. And quietly, rhythmically in the background are the words of Stuart Sherman and the memory of looking for my brother's tooth.

All remind me in their lapping that often (and to great detriment) you only find what you are looking for.

* * *

I first read Annie Ray's diary in April of 1995. My great-aunt Billie, the family member bound most by duty to the past, has sent the diary to me in care of Federal Express. Her hope is that I will publish Annie's diary through my newly established "university connections." It is a dream she has harbored for years. Perhaps because she does not trust my intentions or convictions, perhaps because she does not trust the mail, what she actually sends me initially are the transcripts she has made of Annie's diary, rather than the thin, frail book I will later hold in my hands. These transcripts, pages and pages lovingly pounded out at the typewriter, are populated by enough x's and dried puddles of correction fluid that I am unable tell which are Annie's "errors" and which are Billie's. What I hold are two generations joined together by their mis-scriptions, both literally and figuratively. What has not yet occurred to me, what slips past me the very first time I read Annie's entries as re-inscribed by Billie, is how my own meeting with Annie's words brings with it the weighty possibility of even further "error."

The only responsibility I initially feel is toward my great-aunt rather than the great-great-great-aunt whom I have never met. In return for sending Annie's diary to me, Billie asks for half the royalties. Annie's words arrive as a commodity.

No one really seems to know for sure what to do with diaries — crit-ically, practically, or aesthetically. Read them? Save them? Mine them? Enshrine them? What makes the diary more difficult to read and cate-gorize than other genres or kinds of texts are the same qualities that mark the diary a distinct kind of writing: the fact that a diary is immedi-ate rather than reflective, open rather than closed, and that the diary is daily. These qualities mean that the diary resists traditional approaches to reading and defies a typical reader's expectations. It can appear as if nothing is happening in a diary, at least nothing of any interest. The dif-ficulties in reading diaries, compounded by the fact that, especially since the nineteenth century, diary keeping has largely been associated with female, domestic space, have meant that the diary has historically been seen as generally lacking (if and when it was seen at all).[3] The form and content of diaries and the social positions and gender of most diarists guaranteed the diary a position as a not genre.[4] Donald Stauf-fer's sentiments, from his 1930 book *English Biography before 1700,* are representative of how the academy has, until recently, viewed the diary:

> The diary makes no attempt to see life steadily and see it whole. It is focused on the immediate present, and finds that the happenings of twenty-four hours are sufficient unto the day. It becomes, there-fore, not the record of a life but the journal of an existence made up of a monotonous series of short and similar entries . . . in a study

of biography as literary form the diary has scant claim to consideration, for it makes no pretense to artistic structure. The diary should . . . be considered . . . as raw material.[5]

Even as raw material, the diary has generally accrued little capital. Suzanne Bunkers and Cynthia Huff write, "within the academy, the diary historically has been considered primarily as a document to be mined for information about the writer's life and times or as a means of fleshing out historical accounts."[6] Of course, those diaries that were thought worthy enough to mine were those by already famous people, not those kept by ordinary women. Mostly men. Mostly public men of letters or politics like Boswell, Pepys, Emerson, and Thoreau. Not all, but definitely most. The few diaries by women that were published were also the diaries of the already famous — like Fanny Burney — or the scandalous — like Marie Bashkirtseff. These diaries were most often used by scholars to "pad" biographical scholarship or were held up by readers as exemplars of how one should (or perhaps should not, as in the case of Bashkirtseff) live. The Staufferian attitude toward diaries as a lesser form of writing continued until somewhat recently.

In this chapter I will be considering two efforts at recovering the diary from such a legacy. The first began in the 1970s and has continued into the present. The second is a more recent turn in approaching the diary, a much less traveled route. These routes represent two approaches scholars have taken when working to reclaim the delegitimated category of the diary. The harm does not result from taking them both, rather from taking only one (to the exclusion of the other). The first route, the one I will suggest has been chosen by most diary scholars, is to try to expand the definition of what is valued, in this case what counts as literary, to broaden that definition, opening the literary canon. To do so requires finding ways that the diary is similar to already privileged literary texts. In other words, to find teeth that look like what you think you see in the mirror in the morning when you brush.

The second direction, and the one I will explore in the rest of this study, is to consider how the diary is a distinct form of writing, a "thing itself," with its own rhythm, its own style, its own timing, its own value. It is a path only recently taken, but equally, if not more, necessary. When Cythnia Huff writes that manuscript diaries "require us to engage them as friendly explorers, as students who leave behind as much as possible of our former preconceptions and prejudices about the value and design of a text in favor of tentative, genuine inquiry," I see her calling for a new approach to diaries, one steeped less in the aesthetics of writing and more in what is actually on the page.[7] To approach a diary this way requires reading the diary for difference, or reading the diary differently. Such a decision entails waiting to see what the dirt offers before deciding what you will find in it.[8]

.　.　.

In the mid-1970s, partially due to the waning influence of New Criticism and its reverence for the poetic, partially due to the rising influence of feminist theory and its reverence for the personal, attention in the academy shifted toward alternative texts.[9] The diary, like many kinds of personal writing, benefited. While a few books that compiled diary excerpts had been published in the earlier part of the twentieth century, 1974 marked the publication of the first full-length diary studies, studies that began to theorize the diurnal form.[10] What is significant to me about this moment in time is less the fact that the diary was finally being given credit as a "thing itself" and more the ways in which these scholars claimed space for the diary. For when the diary made its academic debut in 1974 it entered, stage left, draped in the robes of the literary.

In 1974 Robert Fothergill published *Private Chronicles: A Study of English Diaries* — a thematically arranged study of previously published English diaries in excerpt. In chapter 2 of *Chronicles,* Fothergill traces the historical progression of the diary as a form, beginning with four protodiary forms. Fothergill's protodiary categories include seventeenth-century journals of conscience — those diaries kept by the religious, mostly Puritans and Quakers, to record moments requiring repentance or marking spiritual progress. The second are what he terms travel journals found throughout the sixteenth, seventeenth, and eighteenth centuries, diaries that document a journey. Public journals, like ship logs and those documenting military campaigns, were also kept in the same years. And finally, the journal of personal memoranda, journals containing lists of expenditures and visitors.

Each of these four protodiary forms, though inferior in some way for Fothergill, set the stage for the appearance of the "real" diary. Their influence is found in some combination in the "final" and much improved form the diary took in the early nineteenth century, the personal diary — the form most of us think of when we think of a diary, a daily record of the personal.[11] Fothergill sees the personal diary as the exciting culmination of a historical process. By outlining where the diary has been, Fothergill, for the first time, gives the diurnal form a tellable story as well as the legitimacy we tend to ascribe to any long-standing tradition.

But he does something else as well. Fothergill's intentions extend well beyond merely the establishment of a diurnal tradition. Rather, he sees his goal as patiently tracing "the growing consciousness in the mind of the diarist of diary-writing as *literary* composition." [12] To support this growth he excerpts diaries written mostly by famous and literary men: Lord Byron, Samuel Pepys, James Boswell, Sir Walter Scott. These are men who, for Fothergill, wrote "great diaries," those "that lean toward acknowledged literary forms" (52). The diaries that he wants to see as great, as worthy of attention, are a certain kind of diary. The diaries not included by Fothergill are the same kind of diaries Stauffer identifies and reacts against: "a monotonous series of short and similar entries," the kind of diaries I call ordinary. Fothergill says: "The great mass of diary writing is poor stuff, interesting only to the antiquarian or social historian" (2). Fothergill's diaries, the literary gems that they are, are decidedly different.

In the same year, Mary Jane Moffat and Charlotte Painter published *Revelations: Diaries of Women,* the first book-length diary study that focuses on women as diarists and the one that will establish the diary as a form of particular importance for women: both for women who wrote diaries when they could write nothing else and for women today who work to recover the voices and history of past women. *Revelations* is based on thirty-three published diaries by remarkable women from the nineteenth and early twentieth centuries; the excerpts are arranged thematically along the lines of love, work, and power. Included are Anne Frank, Dorothy Wordsworth, Virginia Woolf, and Anaïs Nin as well as the somewhat less (but still) famous like Mary Boykin Chestnut, Frances Anne Kemble, and Florida Scott-Maxwell.

Like Fothergill, Moffat and Painter select their diarists based on whether a diarist exhibits "gifts for language and observation." Moffat remarks in the foreword that "the form, with its repetitions and — in some hands — relentless concentration on the minimal, can be boring, an excellent sedative." She hastily assures her readers that they have "put aside the uninteresting" in their efforts to see "if it is possible to define the diary . . . as a valid *literary* form." [13] Again, it is not ordinary diaries being studied. Those remain outside. Rather Moffat and Painter include the more interesting, the literary, the diaries by those like meta-diarist Nin who raise the diary "to the realm of art"(6).

My point is not that the work of Fothergill and Moffat and Painter is not valuable; their work literally jumpstarts the conversation about the limits and reaches of the diurnal form. They bring the diary into being as a text worthy of study. In particular, the work of Moffat and Painter introduces the diary to a growing conversation within women's auto-biography about the value and significance of writing that historically was overlooked. These early books form the leading edge of the ensuing wave of diary scholarship. Foundational texts by Elizabeth Hampsten, Margo Culley, Thomas Mallon, Steven Kagle, and Harriet Blodgett are barely a few years away. My point is more about *how* the diary entered into discourse. Until 1974 the diary basically occupies no space within the purview of academic scholarship. When it does enter, it enters un-der "literary" auspices. The goal: to show how the diary is a literary text, meaning a text that is *consciously shaped for aesthetic reception* and, therefore, marked by stylistic conventions and matter lofty enough to have historically qualified as "all that is great in what is thought or said" (with all the white Western male privilege Matthew Arnold's comment accords).[14] For the next thirty years, the diary will continue to be read mostly within such a literary framework. What I examine below is how that framework, a reading lens ground in the literary, works to remand a text like Annie's diary to the attic.

*   *   *

A few weeks after receiving Annie's diary in the mail I turn to it. In fact, I turn to her diary the same week I recommit to my own diary after sev-eral years of neglect. It makes sense that way — women with blood bonds writing down the daily. Looking back at my first experiences with Annie's words, I remember little of what I actually read of her life, but I remember all of what I felt. Deep, rain-drenched sadness. In her first entry, an entry begun in the middle of the month, she writes, "I wish time would stop — I dislike to grow old so fast and see all the pleasures of youth slipping away from me before I can enjoy them." What moves me then is the sense of loss and sadness she generates in her initial en-try. I am hooked by the promise of story, the apparent drama shimmer-ing in the scant words of a young woman who feels she is wasting away. What will eventually move me, what will cause me to take pen in hand and write about Annie two years later, is the return to my own diary, a hardbound book with a quilt on the cover, a diary I begin in the middle of the month, in the middle of the Pacific Ocean, a hundred years after Annie. In my first entry I write, "I chose this book because of the quilt on the cover. I think a quilt symbolizes so much. The way women could create entire family histories out of rags and scraps. A way of writing without words. I am 25. A quarter of a century. In many ways it seems old but I feel so young."

While I am lured by the story in Annie's diary, I am overwhelmed by the connections found in laying these two diaries side by side. Both begin in the middle of the month, both women in their mid-twenties, both writing of mortality and loss. When I begin to write, it is these parallels I pursue.

• • •

The move by Fothergill, Moffat and Painter, and others is not very surprising given the location of the scholarship as well as the scholars. Prior to the 1970s, literary scholars had been invested in upholding a split between the ordinary and the literary. New Criticism's belief in the superiority, autonomy, and artistry of the poetic left no room for ordinary, nonliterary writing like diaries. Efforts to demonstrate that the diary was poetic enough to pass through the gates guarding the literary tradition make sense given the advantages being enjoyed by literary texts. It was this very boundary the diary had to push against — as, perhaps, most clearly evidenced by Earl Miner's essay, "Literary Diaries and the Boundaries of Literature," in which Miner takes great pains to examine the diary for enough "literary symptoms" that might cause a reader to exclaim: "This is literature." [15] In addition, though, Fothergill, Moffat and Painter, and most of the other initial diary scholars share literary backgrounds. They were trained to appreciate the poetic. The literary is something they know well and love. To find the literary in a deliberately unliterary place is like finding a jewel in a dust heap.

But to see the diary as literary is to see only in one way. The literary lens is indeed a powerful one, one that is perhaps becoming more and more inclusive — as Miner writes of literature, "the boundaries . . . are as wide as we believe but wider than we pretend" (48). Still it is a lens that has been shaped historically by certain assumptions and expectations about what is waiting to be seen at the other end of the lens. It asks questions that only certain kinds of texts answer well. When you sit down to read a poem or a short story or a memoir, the reading lens you assume is largely shaped by what you think it is that you are reading, the values of that particular reading site, as well as your entire reading past. It is not the same lens that you apply to the note left on the kitchen counter or the old datebook that you came across while cleaning out your desk. The questions you ask of the text and the expectations you have of the answers depend on what you think you are looking at — or looking for (a neat, white, box of a tooth). And it is largely for the same reasons that you would not think to apply a literary lens to your recently discovered datebook that I am questioning its application to diaries.

*　*　*

While it may not be surprising that the initial recovery of the diary was through a literary lens (given the place of, and values in, the scholarship in the 1970s), it is troubling that such expectations continue to haunt much of diary scholarship. Before thinking about alternative, nonliterary approaches to reading a diary, I want to demonstrate the ways these conversations have evolved and how they rarely fail to land in the literary. The goal of claiming a literary space for the diary permeates much of even the most recent scholarship. Few alternative strategies for reading a diary exist. (That is not to suggest that *all* scholars are interested in the relationship between the dairy and the literary. In particular, those working with manuscript diaries or particularly fragmented diaries — Cynthia Huff, Molly McCarthy, and Judy Nolte Temple — are calling for and practicing alternative, nonliterary approaches to diaries. In turn, they, as I do, explicitly or implicitly reference the work of Laurel Thatcher Ulrich, whose reading of Martha Ballard's diary first demonstrated that bare-boned diaries are anything but bare. Nor is it to suggest that some diaries do not benefit from being allied with the literary. Some surely do.) Even recent scholars continue to consider the diary only in terms of its literary potential. And it is the "only" that is troubling. For example, Elizabeth Podneiks's *Daily Modernism: The Literary Diaries of Virginia Woolf, Antonia White, Elizabeth Smart, and Anaïs Nin* centers on the argument that "diaries deserve a place on the literary map."[16] And Alexandra Johnson's *The Hidden Writer: Diaries and the Creative Life* considers several of the same diarists in demonstrating how their diaries serve as "creative blueprints" for their more public, literary work. While both Podneiks and Johnson have compelling reasons for demonstrating how diaries blur the boundaries of literature, my point is that very little has been done to consider alternatives to a literary approach. And we need alternatives.

*　*　*

Two examples of how the literary lens has dominated diary scholarship will demonstrate the need for alternatives. The first example explores how the scholarly debate over whether the diary is public or private is ultimately derived from concerns about its literariness. The second example shows how efforts to include the diary within the genre of autobiography are equally impelled by the literary. With both examples, I want to demonstrate why such a move by diary scholars may have been necessary initially but also why it is ultimately troubling in terms of the kind of diaries that get valued within such frameworks.

I fully recognize the limitations in my examples. Both examples represent entire conversations within diary scholarship. Furthermore, like all scholarship, diary scholarship is not static, unified, or easily summarized. I am brushstroking trends that are significant not for what they say (the ideas are compelling and important) but for what gets missed. In outlining the general form of the conversation, you will see that these conversations do not stay within the bounds my categories suggest. It is impossible to talk about public and private without also talking about gender. And questions about literariness and dailiness intersect with conversations about what "adds up" to autobiography. My goal, again, is only to describe the areas enough to demonstrate how a desire for the "literary" operates beneath them. And how such literary underpinnings work to disregard ordinary diaries, the very diaries that mark the form as a distinct kind of text, diaries like Annie's.

      *   *   *

The first time I write about Annie's diary publicly is in April of 1997, exactly two years to the month after receiving it. The resulting essay, ultimately entitled "Waiting for the Words of Annie Ray," moves between Annie's diary and my own. An essay of process, the recovery of Annie's story, it includes only a few entries from Annie's diary. Not insignificantly, the chosen entries are unusually long and pulsing with undisclosed pain:

Aug[ust] 23 [1881]
Tuesday
It did not rain much last night. There are indications of rain this morning it is thundering both in the north and South. Walter dropped a few words last night which brought to my mind some olden memories which were it in my power ~~I would blot out of my mind forever, I can not put it away from me. My heart aches with~~

~~bitterness and indignation and a sense of the wrong done me~~ ~~which can never be~~ [crossed out and illegible] ~~The ones having~~ [crossed out and illegible] ~~can never in anyway atone for such a~~ ~~wrong.~~ [crossed out and illegible] ~~They have lost my faith and~~ ~~confidence in mankind. I had too much confidence. How blind I~~ ~~was not to see through it all. Especially~~ [crossed out and illegible for remaining twenty lines].

Because I am steeped in the values and practices of the literary, because the pull of story is so strong, I determine that underneath all the repetition, the dailiness, the chores, and the restraint live the "real" moments in Annie's diary. To carve ordinary writing into a narrative, though, requires jettisoning so much: the blizzards, the warm weather, the shelling of peas, the making of pies, the airing of mattresses, the darning of socks, the ironing, and the mopping of the floors. Annie's husband, Charley, an itinerant blacksmith, comes and goes, comes and goes, comes and goes. I only pay attention — only stop to read, to excerpt, to consider — when his appearance in her text is accompanied by censored lines or loneliness. Annie suffers from rheumatism, neuralgia, and cancer. There are drugs, doctor's visits, and treatments. Her closest neighbor has a baby whom she sees from time to time. She writes letters, bakes countless loaves of bread, washes untold pieces of clothing, burnishes, blackens, mends, pieces, bakes, and waits, and I only stop at the remarkable.

*   *   *

The question of whether the diary is a public or private document is a question that has occupied diary scholars for the past twenty years. Although most recent scholarship works from the assumption that diaries are both public and private, delighting in the ways such spaces are negotiated (see, for example, Carter, McCarthy, Wink, and Huff), this has not always been the case. In tracing the outlines of the conversation, I am interested less in the answer to the question and more in what asking the question in the first place gets for us.

Initially, the question of the public vs. private nature of the personal diary may appear on the surface a relatively simple one — the general belief being that diaries are private documents. After all, don't they come with locks and keys? Yet, the question is actually much more fraught, largely due to the differing values historically ascribed to these spaces. Many scholars have wanted to retain the importance of recognizing the diary as a "private" space for women, one that is all their own — especially in historic terms. As Judy Nolte Temple and Suzanne Bunkers note: because women in the nineteenth century were "culturally muted" in the public, they found connection, validation, and empowerment in the private.[17] The diary was one of the only places for self-inscription available to women historically. As such, it is a space we need to remember, preserve, and value. At the same time, given the willingness (and historically, the determination) to see the diary as private and domestic (and, hence, with little cultural, social, or intellectual value), most diary scholars have contended that the diary is actually a public document.[18] What is worth consideration, it seems, in these conversations is not the space in which the diary is better served, but rather the impulses behind claiming "public" status for the diary in the first place. What is being gained when scholars suggest that even the most private of diaries is very much a public one?

Part of this impulse, as I suggest above, stems from the fact that the private has historically been seen as a space of deprivation, a space apart from the democratic ideal realized only in the public.[19] Something written "in private" is not written with intention of being made public, of publication. As a space of lack, it is, not unsurprisingly, also the space historically inhabited by women. In the female domestic space all things bloody and bodily occur. It is dark and unknown. It is a deeply interior space, one that must be kept constantly in check.

And diaries have long been equated with the private. After all, the personal diary is kept "in private." It is kept alone. It is a place where one records "inner" thoughts. And it is not (usually) intended for publication. A published diary, is, as Kathryn Carter points out, somewhat of an oxymoron and, for the Victorians who witnessed an increasing number of published diaries, a paradox worthy of much anxiety and public conversation. The much too easy alliance between what is private and what is unimportant, not valuable, or not political initially compelled diary scholars to demonstrate how diaries — both historically and theoretically — are, while personal, not necessarily private. Rather diaries have been privatized.[20]

One way to reveal the diary's public propensities is by showing that the sentimentality for the secret diary is strictly a twentieth-century preoccupation, a point Bunkers makes strongly in her work. The lock on the diary is a turn-of-the-century addition. Women writing in the nineteenth century neither had the privilege nor expectation of "true" privacy. Rather than a woman recording confidences in a diary kept under a pillow, many nineteenth-century diarists worked collaboratively or with an intended audience in mind.

For example, families often chose to keep diaries together. Bunkers writes about the Holton family from Milwaukee who kept a journal together for close to sixty years in the mid-1800s.[21] When Lucinda Holton is sick or in bed giving birth to one of their children, Edward Holton writes. These diaries served as family documents and could be read aloud in the evening for entertainment. The very title (taken from a nineteenth-century letter) of Elizabeth Hampsten's book *Read This Only to Yourself: The Private Writing of Midwestern Women, 1880–1910* captures the collaborative and complicated nature of private writing in the nineteenth-century. Lillian Schlissel, a scholar who has examined diaries kept on the frontier, adds that "[a]s a general category, the nineteenth-century diary is something like a family history, a souvenir, meant to be shared like a Bible, handed down through generations to be viewed not as an individual story but as the history of a family's growth and course through time."[22] For these reasons, women often kept diaries to pass on to their children. [23]

In her recent examination of pocket diaries kept by nineteenth-century women in New England, McCarthy explores how the publishing houses encouraged women to negotiate public and private lines by including in their diaries space to track public information like household accounts and weather as well as space for more open, perhaps personal, thoughts. In these ways, sparse, pocket diaries were a "curious mix of personal and public, family and business information."[24] Publishing houses marketed their pocket diaries to women who had to negotiate both public and private matters. Ultimately these diaries "exerted a discipline that dictated more than brevity" (278).

Finally, women in the nineteenth century did not have the privilege of privacy. Husbands and fathers could demand to read or burn diaries at any time. Jane Hunter writes that "the unviolated diary was rare."[25] Parents, siblings, friends, and husbands all had potential access to a woman's diary. So women often resorted to writing in code, in omission, at slant, or in euphemism. These are the very gaps and omissions that, as Huff points out in her recent essay, "Reading as Re-Vision," make alternative reading strategies so important when considering these texts. Women shaped and censored their writing with the knowledge that their diaries were never truly their own.[26]

There are more theoretical (rather than historical) points diary scholars make in rescuing the diary from the deprived private. As Judy Simons points out, "as written documents all diaries imply reader-ship."[27] In other words, writing is always a social act.[28] The myth of the solitary author producing original work *ex nihilo* has given way to the understanding that the writing subject always writes within a social context — even when writing only for herself. What she writes is produced at the intersection of all her past experiences, her specific location. Her writing anticipates reception by an equally socially constructed audience. As Karen Burke LeFevre writes in *Invention as Social Act*, writing is always a dialectic process between the individual (even when the individual is in solitude) and the social. She suggests that "writers, readers, and texts are inextricably connected."[29]

Such inextricability between writer, reader, and text is especially (rather than less) true for diaries, for the "private" writings of women not only imply an audience but demand an especially active one. Because the form of diaries is less immediately accessible to readers and because reading diaries requires piecing together information, the reader of diaries must make more choices, become more involved than she would if reading a more accessible text. This collaborative relationship between diarist and reader is captured nicely by Bunkers in her essay, "What Do Women Really Mean? Thoughts on Women's Diaries and Lives," in which she describes how reading diaries is a reproduction of the process of writing diaries. Like the diarist, the reader must interpret bits and pieces of information to create some kind of pattern or design. It is the same collaborative and interpretive process the diarist must go through in selecting bits and pieces from the larger context of her day. The ways in which both readers and writers of diaries must work in collaboration with the other testifies to the social nature of writing itself, the ways in which, as Anne Ruggles Gere writes, "becoming literate means joining a community."[30]

Given this, it is clear why, for diary scholars like Culley, the influence of a larger audience, one either explicitly intended by the diarist or one implied by the social act of writing, is the very "vehicle for preserving the life-record."[31] Diarists decide what to leave in, what to take out, and what to encode. And these decisions ensure that the writers are engaging in a conscious act of self construction. Culley writes, "the pages of the diary might be thought of as a kind of mirror before which the diarist stands assuming this position or that"(12). The point is not a little one. For Culley, Temple and Bunkers, Simons, and others, audience is the single most important aspect of diaries. A sense of audience determines the self the diarist constructs: it gives agency to women who, at least in the nineteenth century, had little agency in other aspects of their lives. It also allows us to ask questions about intention, purpose, and style.

What results from these arguments is the undeniable recognition that diaries are not completely private. And the public aspects of diaries accumulate in a notion of audience — either intended or implied. Having said that, what interests me is really not whether or how diaries are public or private documents. Simple reductions pale against the complexities of the diurnal form. Clearly, the act of writing is always social. Clearly, intended or implied audiences always exist for the diarist. Clearly, choices made by the writer contribute to the construction of a diaristic self, shaped within the pages of the diary. What interests me is what the recognition of a public, an audience, gets for scholars. What can you do once you demonstrate that women did not write in secret or in solitude that you couldn't do when the diary was only seen as private, individual, and secret?

One answer to the question, and the one many scholars select, is that you can draw connections to other texts in which audience is never questioned but only assumed — that is, to literary texts. Those that were intended for audiences from the start and that want to stand in the public as art. The distance to the literary is not far. After all, it is a very narrow gap that exists between the recognition that a diarist is constructing a diaristic self (by encoding, omitting, adding, shaping in recognition of an audience) and the argument that diarists consciously craft this self in literary, productive, and artistic ways. So narrow. Yet into that narrow gap fall the ordinary diaries that make no claim to the literary. While some diaries can and do respond to the requirements a public audience places on texts, many cannot make the leap that is often required.

For example, when Culley maintains that audience is the single most important aspect of diaries, the very vehicle needed for self-inscription, she also makes the following statement:

[calling diaries literature] identifies the many examples of fine writing contained in diaries and journals and also acknowledges that *this periodic life writing springs from the same source of art created for a public audience*: the urge to give shape and meaning to life with words, and to endow this meaning-making with a permanence that transcends time. (xi, emphasis mine)

In her words, literary qualities accompany the recognition of a "public audience": fine writing is equated with periodic lifewriting. And diarists write with the "urge" to create a work of art that transcends the ordinary, the ephemeral. Later in her book, Culley suggests that the fact that the diary is a verbal construct, a social text requiring an audience, means that we can ask "literary questions" of it (17). That we have to ask these questions. So in this study the diarist becomes a "protagonist," someone we should study to learn about how a woman constructs a self "and its literary representation" (18).

Such arguments made by scholars are not limited to research published more than a decade ago either. Although working from a position informed by postmodernism's desire to blur boundaries and subvert hierarchies, Podneiks also wants to read diaries, here the diaries of literary women, to see "how the boundaries between supposedly private jottings and more finished pieces of art could be blurred." She adds later that "If a diarist is conscious of an audience, then she or he will necessarily be concerned with the aesthetic make-up of the diary."[32] In order to blur the lines between the diary and the novel, she, like Culley, suggests that diarists see themselves as the protagonists of their own stories.[33]

●   ●   ●

I am not suggesting that diarists do not engage in crafting and shaping their words and their selves — sometimes even in ways that decidedly blur the boundaries of diary, autobiography, and/or fiction. Nor am I critiquing the work done by scholars like Johnson and Podneiks who focus on women who intentionally craft their work for aesthetic reception. Rather I am wondering how questions about craft and the shaping of a diaristic self slide so quickly into questions about art, about permanence, about being in the public, that the literary seems the only place to land.

An essay that many scholars, including Podneiks, cite as they make the argument that the diary is public, audience directed, and, hence, literary is an essay by Lynn Z. Bloom, "'I Write for Myself and Strangers': Private Diaries as Public Documents." In that essay, Bloom is working to draw a line between diaries that are "truly private" and diaries that, while they may begin as private documents, eventually become, through the diarist's recognition of an external audience, public documents. Here again I just want to point out how quickly the recognition of a public audience becomes a discussion of literary quality.

Bloom is interested in diarists who are professional writers, like Nin and Woolf, as well as diarists who recognize the value of their diaries to a larger audience, like Anne Frank and Mary Boykin Chestnut. What these writers have in common is that they craft their diaries with a public in mind and see themselves as part of a "literary legacy."[34] Each of these diarists foreshadows, paces, and shapes her diary because she is consciously writing for, as Bloom quotes Gertrude Stein in her title, "myself and strangers." Bloom maintains that "the presence of audience, whether near or remote, requires accommodations through the same textual features that in all cases transform private diaries into public documents" (24). Such features include foreshadowing, depth, purpose, character, as well as "telling a good story, getting the sound and rhythm right, supplying sufficient details for another's understanding" (25). For Bloom, diaries are either public and, therefore, literary, or "truly private" and, therefore, lacking.

If we ask literary questions of diaries, questions that for Culley include "questions of audience (real or implied), narrative, shape and structure, persona, voice, imagistic and thematic repetition," we will only give certain kinds of diaries space — the kind that answer such questions well.[35] Our gaze becomes focused in only one direction, finding diaries that demonstrate their public propensity by exhibiting literary features. And in that gaze much is overlooked. For example, while not all the female diarists Culley chooses in her examination of the diary literature of American women are famous, all write at length and in interesting ways. The one diary Culley includes that most closely resembles what I call an ordinary diary and, hence, the one furthest from the literary is the diary of Mary Vial Holyoke. Holyoke kept her diary every day from 1737 to 1802. Over that time Holyoke gave birth twelve times but only three of her children lived to adulthood. Her diary entries are indeed "a monotonous series of short and similar entries." That is what gives her diary a diurnal rhythm. To create a dramatic effect from these entries, Culley chooses only those entries written when a child dies. Excerpts from five or six different periods of Holyoke's life — but always excerpts describing the drama of death. Death was an enormous reality of eighteenth-century New England. But not an isolated reality. And to only include sections of a diary that might stand up to literary questions of plot and purpose works to conceal one of the foremost qualities of the diurnal form — the leveling of days, the paratactic refusal to foreground one event over another because all events are experienced within the circadian rhythm.

* * *

I am not alone in my desire to render the remarkable from the ordinary. When I take Annie's diary to share with a group from the community and show them entries like the one from August 23, they encourage me to send her diary to the art school to see if the technology exists that would allow me to read what lives underneath what has been crossed out. They suggest applying for a grant to cover the expenses. Someone else mentions the CIA. My work becomes determining what lives under these censored moments, filling in the gaps, and shaping a story from the fragments, the bare bones, that Annie leaves.

In service to such an effort, one day I call my great-aunt. What I learn from her is that Fannie, Annie's niece, got religion late in life. Toward the end of her life, she took to calling my great-aunt from her home in Florida. "Will God ever forgive me," she asked Billie, "will I ever be forgiven?" Fannie called Billie with the same question so many times and at such early hours in the morning that Billie's husband, Dean, simply started handing the phone to Billie whenever it rang before 6 A.M. "Will God forgive me?"

Then, right before Fannie died, Billie got another call. Fannie was bequeathing Billie her grave plot in the family cemetery in Bridgewater, South Dakota (home to Annie and Charley among other Pringles). Fannie was willing away her grave plot next to her uncle, her uncle Charley.

It seems Fannie no longer wanted to be buried next to her one and only lover. It seems Fannie feared the wrath of God. And rightly so. Even in the world today, an affair between an uncle and his niece is not taken lightly, related by marriage alone or not. The fact that Fannie was so much younger than Charley or the fact that Fannie never married because of her love for Charley seems only to heighten the sting.

I think of Annie writing in her diary, late at night, alone in the claim shanty, absent from her husband for months at a time: "Dear patient, generous Charley. For your sake I wish I was better. I will be better. To become worthy of you will be the main purpose of my life," while

Charley is occupying himself by having affairs. How many remains unclear. At the time the August entry is written, Fannie is not even born. The pain is long in roots.

Armed with this new knowledge, I am able to shape a powerful story. My essay has new direction and energy. The drama is heightened by Annie's pain. In my haste, I pull a single story of loss, like a stray thread, from the complicated fabric woven by a Dakota woman's accumulated days. And I run with it.

* * *

In turning to my second example, I will suggest that similar conflation with the literary occurs when scholars have argued that the diary is a form of autobiography.[36] In tracing this conversation within the history of diary scholarship, as in the case of the public/private debate, I want to demonstrate how the question has led to the exclusion of ordinary diaries like Annie's and the concurrent privileging of diaries that exhibit literary features. While feminists and those in cultural studies have clearly called into question the patriarchal structure of autobiography in particular and genre in general, I want to suggest that the vestiges of autobiography remain strong enough to preclude ordinary diaries from most scholars' attention. The question of the diary's place within autobiography has been asked, answered, and repeatedly complicated for close to thirty years. The conversation within the field of diary studies has followed the contours of the conversation within autobiography more generally.[37]

Whether the diary "adds up" to autobiography is a question often asked in tandem with whether it is a specifically female form of writing — that is, are diaries a form of women's autobiography? Other than the broader question of whether the diary is literature, it is often the only question of genre ever asked of the diary. The answer has never been a unified yes. Many scholars point to two books written by Estelle Jelinek in the 1980s to demonstrate how, even within feminist circles, the halting and fragmented diurnal form was not exactly welcomed with open arms by scholars of autobiography.

Jelinek is often credited with editing the first full-length critical study of women's autobiography. In 1980 she published *Women's Autobiography: Essays in Criticism*. Her introduction, "Women's Autobiography and the Male Tradition," carefully traces the ways in which "autobiography proper" as a masculine form explicitly excludes the life stories of women that fail to meet set standards for both form and content. In her introduction Jelinek does say there is a difference between diaries and autobiography, but she does not specifically exclude diaries from a study in autobiography. However, by the time she publishes her second book on autobiography in 1986, *The Tradition of Women's Autobiography: From Antiquity to Present*, diaries are being specifically excluded. She writes, "though I occasionally refer to diaries, letters, and journals (to place them in historical context), I rarely discuss them because I do not consider them autobiographies."[38] Even as she describes the ways in which the male autobiographical tradition (as outlined below) has worked to exclude women's autobiographies, Jelinek excludes the diary, a form that, for her, fails to qualify as autobiography because it is typically not intended by the author as her life story.

Harriet Blodgett, in both her early and later work on diaries, agrees with the kinds of distinctions Jelinek draws. She, too, wants to see diaries standing outside the realm of autobiography. For her, the issue is also one of construction. The diary is simply not written in the same reflective manner that an autobiography is written. It lacks the kind of perspective autobiographers traditionally have provided — a reflective look back on a long (and typically interesting) life.[39] Similarly, Moffat and Painter, in their introduction, argue that diaries do not demonstrate "the assessive voice of autobiography" and therefore should not be considered part of the autobiographical tradition (10). What diaries fail to do, in the eyes of Blodgett, Moffat and Painter, and even Jelinek to some extent, is gel into a coherent, whole, and reflective product traditionally expected of autobiographies.

These arguments make historical sense, especially when viewed against the backdrop of autobiography proper. Roy Pascal's 1960 work, *Design and Truth in Autobiography,* is useful to illustrate this backdrop in that it speaks specifically about the place of diaries in relation to autobiography. Pascal begins with an assertion that autobiographies serve to satisfy our curiosity "about the ways of men," particularly — actually, for Pascal, only — the ways of Western men.[40] Given the fact that only white Western men can even write autobiographies it should come as no surprise that the "correct form" of autobiography excludes women generally and the diary specifically.

Pascal suggests that autobiography proper must be "systematically retrospective," a quality not found in diaries that are trapped forever in the moment (4). Because a diarist can never assess events on a daily basis for their relative importance, she can never foreground certain important events while dispensing with others. As there is no way in a diary to gain the perspective necessary for systemic reflection, it fails to add up to autobiography. This does not preclude autobiographers from using the diary as fodder for their autobiography. However, for Pascal, even getting this close to the diary is questionable. His illustrative example of how the diary can really only work to sully autobiography proper is (again no surprise) the autobiography of a woman — Beatrix Webb Potter — which Pascal finds confusing and disjointed.

Pascal suggests that besides having a systematic reflective quality, autobiographies must also create a "coherent shaping of the past." Webb Potter's fails because it contains "uncertainties, false starts, and momentariness," qualities that characterize the diary but fail in autobiography (5). One coherent story must be told — a story of a great man or woman — one "of outstanding achievement in life" (10). If the personality of the autobiographer is trivial or uninteresting the resulting work will fail. If the writer does not select important events, does not weave them into a coherent product, the work will fail. Add to this Wayne Shumaker's belief that autobiography — if it is to be a meaningful art form — "has the responsibility of . . . discovering within the life something greater than the sum total of incidents and observations," and the diary with its tally of days can never "add up" in this way.[41]

Autobiography proper, then, as a life story that is retrospective, coherent, important, interesting, and greater than the sum of its parts, by definition is a genre the diurnal form can never reach.

*   *   *

Of course — as so many diary scholars either insist or imply — the enormous danger is that if personal writing like letters and diaries is not counted as the stuff of autobiography — as a kind of life story — then there simply are few autobiographies written by ordinary women in the nineteenth century. A woman was not authorized to construct autobiography proper, but she was allowed (even encouraged) to keep a diary. As Bunkers so emphatically writes, "these diaries and journals *are* their autobiographies."[42] To suggest otherwise continues in the silencing of centuries of women.

Even though Jelinek, in the face of the Pascalian tradition, hesitates to name diaries and letters as autobiography, she does call into question the assumptions surrounding autobiography and she ties those assumptions to gender. Such a growing recognition, largely on the part of feminist scholars, of the ways in which master narratives master both form and content (Pascal writes that the most valuable autobiographies are those that convey a "man's master form" [19]) culminates in the eruption of women's autobiography as a distinct genre by 1980.[43] And diary scholars, for the most part, move quickly to claim that the diary is indeed autobiography *under revised definitions*.

In 1978, Suzanne Juhasz is one of the first scholars to make direct connections between the diary, autobiography, and the female experience. Her essay, "'Some Deep Old Desk or Capacious Hold-All:' Forms and Women's Autobiography," begins by describing the ways in which traditional definitions of autobiography exclude the lifewriting of women. She contrasts the qualities of coherence, wholeness, and publicness to the daily experience of women — an experience largely marked by conflicted roles, fragmentation, interruption, and domestic work. Juhasz suggests that the diary, as a form of writing, is akin to the contextual shape of women's lives. And that "deeper relationships" exist between women's lives and the diary form.[44]

What Juhasz means by "deeper relationships" is not altogether clear. There is a sense that she, like several other diary scholars writing then, believes that the diary is essentially/inherently a female form. Meaning that because women are biologically female they would choose to keep a diary — that the diary is a logical extension of their femaleness. Arguments to support such a point include the relationship between the daily, yearly cycle of diaries and the cyclical lives women lead: the cycles of "maidenhood," marriage, and motherhood; the cycle of domestic chores; and the menstrual cycle. Moffat writes that "The form has been an important outlet for women partly because it is an *analogue* to their lives: emotional, fragmented, interrupted, modest, not to be taken seriously, trivial, formless, concerned with self, and as endless as their tasks."[45]

Others, like Culley, are quicker to dismiss such art/life connections and show how these linkages rely on dangerous assumptions. She points to the fact that while access to publication and encouragement to write supported men's attempts at lifewriting, it hindered women's. Women were encouraged to keep diaries by Victorian culture while discouraged from exploring other, more public forms of writing. That women kept diaries had little to do with whether the diurnal form was analogous to their lives. Others warn that arguments suggesting that diaries are simply extensions of female lives rely upon a certain, late-twentieth-century feminist consciousness. By simply aligning diaries with either the resistance to, or reproduction of, being female, one misses the fact that women historically used their diaries "as a means of self-discovery and self-justification."[46] Blodgett is able to find non-essentializing reasons that women sought the diurnal form when she concludes that "keeping a diary is not a peculiarly female habit. But it has been especially useful to female being" (97). As a form of women's autobiography, the diary comes to discursively represent the restrictions, limitations, and options operating in women's contextualized lives, as well as the dedication and need women had to matter personally and physically each and every day.

More recently, diary scholars have moved to embrace the diary as the paragon of the autobiographical form. It is well established that the diurnal form reflects the physical limitations imposed on women's lives. For example, diary entries are short and unadorned because for many women there is simply not enough time in the day to write at length (or at all). Diarists work to make it appear as if nothing is happening because being a "good" woman historically meant ensuring domestic tranquility.[47] And most diarists write within the space allocated by the physical page, replicating their social and political confinement (see, in particular, Huff's "Textual Boundaries: Space in Nineteenth-Century Women's Manuscript Diaries" and McCarthy's "A Pocketful of Days"). These qualities cohere into what Temple calls the "female design" of the diurnal form. By looking more closely at how these textual qualities work to discursively document a life in process, the representation of multiple selves, and the experience of conflicted roles, more recent diary scholarship has shown that not only is the diary not simply a failed version of autobiography because it is neither coherent nor reflective but actually that it is "the most authentic form of autobiography."[48]

The argument follows that if at its etymological roots autobiography is a representation of a life, then the diary in its daily accumulation traces the process of that life in ways that surpass traditional autobiographical attempts. Temple writes, "lack of closure, of denouement, gives the diary a form similar to life itself and renders autobiography the more lifeless form."[49] Because the diary documents a life in process it is more accurately a representation of the ways in which life is experienced. In addition, as Felicity Nussbaum suggests, the diurnal form allows the contradictions of selves to exist on the page. By recording the daily, by simply showing up to the page, the diarist creates both a continuous sense of self (what Nussbaum calls "an enabling fiction of a coherent or continuous identity") and a discontinuous, changing self (I am not the same as I was yesterday).[50] Such a contestory space is a much more accurate "metaphor of self" than any traditional autobiography provides. Attention to these performative elements found in diaries, the ways in which the writing subject undertakes and negotiates multiple selves often within single entries, replicates larger trends within autobiography studies toward performance. As such, the diary has increasingly become an important site for considering how life-writing is always partial and never whole.[51] It is no longer a question of whether the diary is a female form of autobiography but whether autobiography can look any different than the diary and still be categorized as autobiography.

*　*　*

My point, for now, is that there is very little question in the scholarship that the diary falls under the umbrella of autobiography — as expanded by feminists, cultural historians, and diary scholars. And while I do not necessarily disagree with this categorization, again I wonder what is being gained. What happens in practice when scholars work to blur the lines between diaries and autobiography? What kinds of diaries then get read? How do scholars negotiate the fact that the fragmented qualities of the diary are not a result of a whole broken into pieces but rather bits and pieces that will never fit together as a whole, never add up, never equal a story?[52] As Temple asks, have we really developed "the critical tools that will make the unwieldy form of the diary accessible [?]" (40). Or does reading the diary through an autobiographical lens once again reassert literary privilege?

Autobiography is an example of a genre whose limits and conditions have broadened in scholarly effort to be more inclusive. Metaphorically, the church has been redesigned from the inside, relying on preexisting and preestablished frameworks. I wonder in such remodeling about the vestiges of the Pascalian tradition, traces of autobiography proper. In particular, I wonder if such a reconstruction of masculine autobiography has completely subverted the desire for a story of "outstanding achievement in life," the literary zeal for a well-told tale, and the privileging of texts that give a "coherent shaping of the past." Or if these qualities, instead, remain the rule.

In her 1996 essay, "When Meanings Meet: *The Journals of Charlotte Forten Grimké*," Geneva Cobb-Moore examines Charlotte Forten's journals, five volumes written before, during, and after the Civil War. She suggests that Forten's journals are a "hybrid" of diary discourse, autobiography proper, and racial biography. Unlike the "random discursiveness" of most diaries, Forten's journals exhibit the "symbolic core" found in autobiography proper. Eloquently written, with style and shape, they illuminate the drama of the Civil War, fashioning Forten into the "chronicler of *Zeitgeist.*"[53] They tell a dramatic story.

The majority of Cobb-Moore's article is devoted to "reading" Forten's journals as a record of a black woman's experience in the Civil War South. And she does so by reading the diaries as a story with a beginning, middle, and end: at one point suggesting that Forten's third journal serves as the climax while the fourth and fifth can be read as the anticlimax. Continuing to make literary connections, Cobb-Moore finds symbolism in the "white stone" that appears several times in Forten's journals. She traces Forten's love of literature and poetry — moving back and forth between poems and Forten's literary critique. She argues that a "masculine shaping of events" naturally came out of Forten's Civil War experiences. And she suggests that Forten did more than engage in fantasies in her diary, rather she "crafted an ideal blueprint of how life should be" (149).

Cobb-Moore is clear that she wants to think of Forten's journals as autobiography proper (rather than women's autobiography), so in some sense I should not be concerned by the structured ways in which she wants to read them. However, even given that she is willing to follow Pascal's lead, it is still troubling to see what happens to the diurnal qualities of the journals. In highlighting the drama, coherence, and storyability of Forten's words, Cobb-Moore suggests that such autobiographical qualities mean Forten's journals are "more than 'mere' diaries" (141). Because Forten is able to transcend, Cobb-Moore says, the "momentariness of diary discourse," she creates a lasting work "where generations can experience one woman's private and public worlds" (155). She creates a masculine and master form. Even though what Forten kept is a diary, it is the drama and eloquence of autobiography that interests Cobb-Moore. Diurnal qualities remain an impediment that Forten skillfully avoids — or at least qualities her interpreter ignores.

◦   ◦   ◦

Cobb-Moore's essay presents one example of how the autobiographical framework can deprivilege the very aspects of diary writing that mark the diurnal form as distinct. In particular, the ways in which a coherent story is privileged. Such moves are not unusual when diary scholars are working to highlight autobiographical elements of the diary; even within women's autobiography wholeness is too often valued. Cobb-Moore appreciates Forten's eloquence, sense of drama, careful analysis of self, and literary aplomb. She reads Forten's journals as if they comprised a story with a plot: a book of the self.[54] Autobiography becomes conflated with the literary characteristics that make a "good story."

Only diaries do not tell stories, at least not in the ways these scholars want them to. A point made initially and powerfully by Laurel Thatcher Ulrich in *A Midwife's Tale*. As Temple cautions in her essay "Fragments as Diary: Theoretical Implications of the *Dreams and Visions* of 'Baby Doe' Tabor," the diaries that enter the budding diary canon are those that tell good stories. They are storied wholes. To extend her argument suggests that seeing diaries as a book of the self, as an autobiography, builds a theoretical cage that does not allow us to read or consider diaries that fail to be so engrossing. The diary that interests her is even less of a whole than a diary like Annie's; it literally remains in undated fragments.

Temple makes her point about the privileging of literary diaries that tell coherent stories by looking at the diary of Elizabeth "Baby Doe" Tabor. While Tabor may have thought that the scraps of paper that she kept would be her legacy, the literary limits and conditions currently placed on the diurnal form have meant that Tabor's diary has been ignored. Temple suggests that the diaries that get noticed are those that tell extraordinary stories about extraordinary lives. So that, for example, the diary of Emily Gillespie enters the canon *not* because she is an ordinary woman but more because she records "a Midwestern gothic tale of a dysfunctional family."[55] Just as Forten's journals are canonized because they overcome the pitfalls of diary discourse.

Temple argues that the theoretical limitations of diary scholarship work "to exclude more diaries than they include" (77). While she does not name the autobiographical framework as being particularly limiting, her critique of the current definitions and approaches gather around criteria that turn the diary into a story of the self. Temple writes that such moves by diary scholars have meant that the diaries that I call ordinary diaries receive no attention and only work to "delay the inevitable face-to-face meeting between readers and actual diaries." The three criteria that she sees limiting the entrance of actual diaries include:

1) a central organizing event, that is, "plot" that occurs within an intelligible framework;
2) a clearly drawn geographic and human universe, that is "setting";
3) a core consciousness and voice, that is, "character" that gives the text its internal rationality (77).

Compare these to the autobiographical qualities that Cobb-Moore privileges in Forten's journals:

1) "events naturally unfold for her in a decisive moment as she records the war" (141);
2) "the characters mentioned in her journal form a Who's Who in nineteenth-century America" (155);
3) her journals cohere around a "symbolic core" (140).

Another more recent approach to the blurring of the line between autobiography and the diary can be found in Podneiks's study, *Daily Modernism*. As I write above, she is interested in the ways in which questions of genre fail us all around and feels that "genre distinctions no longer carry the authority they once had" (68). She works to demonstrate how diaries, like all autobiographies, contain elements of fiction and that by blurring the lines between genres we can see the more complicated work being done by many writers, in particular female writers. We see the ways in which these writers succeed as artists by their ability to cross genres rather than maintain distinctions.

What is compelling about Podneiks's study is the way in which her blurring of genres — specifically diary, novel, and autobiography — empowers the diarists in her study. She, too, wants to dissolve distinctions that keep diaries from being considered as works rather than raw material. In recovering the writing of such diarists, she simultaneously reconfigures the diary genre to parallel more closely the very requirements of autobiography proper that first held the diary outside the genre of autobiography. In response to early scholars like Jelinek who excluded the diary from the genre of autobiography based on the lack of coherence and reflection found in diaries, Podneiks contends that diarists are able to achieve a measure of retrospectivity. She says that, like autobiographers, diarists are "equally charged with inventing their past at the precise moment they seek to record it — or step into it — whether twelve hours or twelve years later" (34). Her point, and it is a compelling one, is that even if a diarist sits down to inscribe an event minutes after the event, she is still shaping her past. She still has an eye on history. Further, Podneiks argues that diarists, like autobiographers, work toward closure, create thematically bound and unified volumes, and revise with an eye toward publication. By blurring the lines between diary, novel, and autobiography — rather than simply upholding distinctions bred by patriarchy — Podneiks posits the diarist as a much more radical writer.

As someone who wants to see the diarist as a much more sophisticated writer, I am drawn to Podneiks's study. But, again, I worry about the ordinary diarist, one not shaping a narrative. Rather than reconfigure the genre of autobiography to include the rhetorical realities of diary writing, Podneiks revisions diaries to be more in line with autobiography proper. And while these diarists become subversive, agentive subjects, her ultimate goal is to suggest that they should not be relegated to the status of makers of nonliterary texts but who rather, and significantly, should claim the literary space she feels diarists are all too often denied (10). The intersection of autobiography and the diary leads us once again to the literary.

* * *

While people like what I am doing with Annie's diary, they still ask for more, but what they ask puts *me* at risk rather than Annie. They see me filling in the gaps of Annie's story but only hinting at parallel omissions in my own diary. As I do when reading Annie's diary, they, too, reach for the possibility of an untold tale and urge me to make that story known. So, for the sake of story, I do. I fill in the silences, the ellipses, and the holes, vacancies I began creating even in sharing my first entry. Returning to that entry, I now include:

April 12, 1995
I chose this book because of the quilt on the cover. I think a quilt symbolizes so much. The way women could create entire family histories out of rags and scraps. A way of writing without words.
I am 25. A quarter of a century. In many ways it seems old but I feel so young. John left a month ago—five weeks to be exact. That, too, seems like forever and yet nothing. I have never felt so lost with myself as I do now.

Even retracing these words now causes my stomach to tighten. I remember writing this in a small hotel room in Waikiki, a room meant for tourists on extended vacations, in the Illikai hotel where Jack Lorde stands in the opening shots of *Hawaii Five-O*. I am not on vacation, the beach mats will never leave their home in the closet. John, my husband at the time, has moved back to the mainland. Divorce papers stare at me from the coffee table. Unable to pay the rent for what was our apartment, I have moved into this bamboo-papered room. There is a sofa bed, a kitchenette, and my computer. Suntan lotion, like memory, lingers faintly in the air.

Every day I ride the elevator with families on vacation, couples on their honeymoon, college students on break. They stand in the lobby in only their bathing suits, with their beach chairs and towels and coolers covered in sand.

Every day I am reminded that this is the same hotel where John and I stayed only a year and half ago while waiting for our apartment to be remodeled, where we would watch the sun set every night over Ala Moana beach park, where we would call to the flat white jellyfish swimming in the harbor on our way to work each morning. "Jelly, jelly, jelly."

Every day I write in my diary.

The ways in which I fill my own initial omissions in my diary with the story of my ex-husband's affairs and our divorce are like the ways in which I fill Annie's omissions with Charley's affairs and her pain. The well-worn edges of such stories feel familiar. In stark contrast to most of Annie's text and most of my everyday life, these moments of loss tend toward the dramatic. They appear in relief to the daily. Everyone wants order from the ordinary, narrative from the chaos, a handle to hold onto. Everyone wants to know the secrets, the pain, the dramatic tale: one woman alone on the prairie, her great-great-great-niece divorced at twenty-five, husbands who are repeatedly unfaithful, exhaustion at an age when life should have only just begun.

I furnish the story without thought.

* * *

Some diaries may fare well under the revised rubrics of autobiography. May Sarton's. Katherine Mansfield's. Sylvia Plath's. Maybe even Forten's. Certainly, the ways in which Podneiks blurs the boundaries of novel, diary, and autobiography are recuperative for Woolf, White, Smart, and Nin. But even as scholars strive to read diaries in terms of fragments and dailiness, the pull of autobiography to be a whole and interesting story is strong. The remnants of autobiography proper, the historical assumptions about what adds up to autobiography, all too often police the boundaries of the form. As Caren Kaplan writes in her essay "Resisting Autobiography: Out-Law Genres and Transnational Feminist Subjects," texts that fall outside such genre limitations are forced to form "outlaw genres." These modes of writing "resist" established forms and the accompanying privilege and instead seek new ground.

Kaplan documents the ways in which women's autobiography, let alone traditional autobiography, has continued to privilege coherent stories of place, literary constructions of self, and fixed national, cultural, and gendered bodies. Canonical autobiographies by women have failed to include all women. Third World women, women of color, working-class women, and lesbians have been largely absent from the theorizing of women's autobiography. Instead, they have embraced forms of writing that intentionally "resist autobiography." Theirs are "outlaw genres," subverting the law of genre and working to disrupt and reveal "the power dynamics embedded in literary production, distribution, and reception."[56]

The ways in which the ordinary diary resists the wholeness and literariness of autobiography makes it, too, an outlaw.[57] And as Kaplan points out, any "outlaw" genre will require new "strategies of reading" (122) and "radical revisions of notions of individual authorship and authenticity" (127). Resisting autobiography requires learning to read unfamiliar narrative strategies and shapings. Such reading means, for Kaplan, getting beyond literary aesthetics and thinking instead about cultural survival. Feminist ethnography, autoethnography, and testimony are all outlaw genres, and Kaplan proposes a postcolonial, transnational frame for considering these "extraliterary" texts (123). Huff in her work on manuscript diaries calls for a new interpretive strategy that begins by considering the diary as fragmented, extratextual, and historically situated. In working with the diary of "Baby Doe" Tabor, Temple turns to mysticism as a useful lens for considering the particularly nonnarrative and dreamlike qualities of that diary.

I am going to suggest a diurnal lens.

* * *

The argument I make for autobiography is no different than the argument I raise against foregrounding public aspects of diaries, nor is it different from my overall suggestion that literary expectations work to exclude the kinds of diaries that make the diurnal form unique, specific, and different. They all point to the consequence of finding only what you are looking for. Annie's diary is not an autobiography, nor is an autobiographical framework the one that will illuminate most fully her work. Her diary is not simply a public document, nor will questions of audience (intended or implied) plumpen her skeletal writing. Her diary is not literary; expectations of literary form and style have only meant the dismissal of diaries like hers. To read her diary and writing like hers requires an alternative framework that is not based on literary ideals, stories, or aesthetic reception of texts.

How do you read the ordinary diary through a different lens? How is the diurnal form distinct, different from other kinds of texts? How does the fact that diaries are daily and immediate rather than reflective and occasioned change the ways we need to read? What are the rhetorical effects of the diurnal rhythm? Where is the line between mediation and cooptation with a form as inaccessible as many ordinary diaries are? What does reading ordinary writing like diaries teach us about reading other kinds of ordinary writing? And finally, how does the ordinary diary reconfigure the category of lifewriting?

The place to begin to answer these questions is with the single quality that marks the diary as absolutely distinct from nondiurnal forms of writing: dailiness. As I describe in my introduction, the condition of dailiness informs and embodies all other aspects of the diurnal form: measuredness, openness, middleness, and usefulness. Dailiness prevents the diary from being reflective and forces the writer and reader into the immediate present, a place from which the critical distance I have been taught to obtain and value is impossible. Dailiness means that the diary does not cohere around an organizing event or principle but rather, by documenting the everyday, makes these measured (and typically unmarked) moments available for the diarist's use. Dailiness will not allow some events to be privileged over others — but always rests in the middle. Writing in the days refuses occasion, climax, and closure.

It has taken me years to realize the consequences of furnishing story, years to discern my lack of vision, years to resist the literary and reclaim dailiness. Annie's diary is not a tale of loss. It is not a tale at all. By shaping her diary toward the literary, I created a story that readers would respond to, recognize, and call "good." In the wake of such telling, I ignored nearly all of the qualities that make Annie's diary a diary and not something else. The story I tell of first writing about Annie's diary and my own are stories of complete failure. I succumbed to the drive I see in the scholarship to make diaries interesting, to make diaries into stories, to make them literary. I distilled her daily tally of days into five or six remarkable (and unusually long and detailed) entries. I allayed the fears of those of us who do not want to come face-to-face with ordinary diaries but would rather swim in the literary.

This book is about trying again. To delight in dailiness, rhythm, and repetition. To read her text in terms of what she makes as a writer rather than what she lacks. The capacity of dailiness to shape the diurnal form is revealed even at the level of syntax and requires that I pay attention to aspects and qualities of texts I have been trained to ignore, despise, or delete. The next two chapters read Annie's diary through a diurnal lens, paying attention to both the material and rhetorical decisions Annie makes. Before I begin that reading, though, I want to remember, to be reminded again, just how ordinary an ordinary diary is.

The Year 1881

Annie's diary begins when Charley is in Leadville, Colorado, working as an itinerant blacksmith. Annie has been working at the Granger's Boarding House for room and board. She is waiting to return home to her father's house near Bridgewater, but the winter of 1881 is particularly fierce and all travel is halted. Robbie and David are Annie's brothers. Walter is Charley's brother, a man that Annie dislikes, and Sophie is a girl hired to help Annie with chores.

January 15
Saturday
Snowed a little. Very pleasant this eve. I am very tired. I hope to have only one more Saturday here. R- helps me a great deal. It seems as though I am wasting time in living this way — without society — comfort or pleasure of any kind — and most of all without my Husband. How I wish time would stop — I dislike to grow old so fast and see all the pleasures of youth slipping away from me before I can enjoy them.   A drunk man insulted me this eve by professing great admiration and love for me — and Granger was too much of a coward to order him out of the room. But Robbie was there to stand by me. I do not know that men are really accountable for what they say or do when under the influence of Liquor.

Jan[uary] 16
Sunday
Very pleasant. All the strangers have gone and there are only the six of us here now. I am always thankful when the Family is small. Preaching here this A.M.

Jan[uary] 17
Monday
Worked hard of course. Washed a little and mopped the floor. R-
wrung the mop for me. The mail has come and there is no letter from
Charley. I had been trying to think there would be none so that I would
not feel so disapointed if there was none. But my heart sank for all
that. O! What can be the trouble, is my experience of last winter to be
repeated? I wish I was home so I would not have to work with my
heart aching so.

Jan[uary] 18
Tuesday
This is a beautiful warm day.   Oh! that my life was beautiful,
warm, and sunny too. It is such heartaching as this which makes people grow old before their time. It is bad enough to be separated from
my Husband, but not to hear from him for so long makes it ten times
worse. I am so lonesome. But I am unwise to feel like this.

Jan[uary] 19
Wednesday
Has been warm and pleasant. The mail came and I got a most welcome letter from Charley. I feel differently now. Mr Anderson brought
me one of Mrs Holmes's books entitled "Ethelyns mistake." I can not
help feeling sad when I read parts of it. The heart-aching, suffering
and pain are so much like my own life.

Jan[uary] 20
Thursday
Morning Cloudy — P.M. Pleasant. I felt very cross all forenoon. Everything I touched seemed to go wrong. Felt like scolding someone But
did not and am glad of that. I do not think people are always to blame
for their feeling so at times. I wonder if Charley is thinking of me.

Jan[uary] 21
Friday
Has been cold and blustering all day. The stage did not come. We have
been singing Hymns all eve. and now the men are playing cards. Have
not been very busy. Wrote and read considerable. and now must
warm my feet and go to bed.

Jan[uary] 22
Saturday
We did not get up until after 8 oclock this morning and it was 9 when breakfast was ready. So I have been behind with the work and hurried all day. Had very poor Bread. Do not know whether the Flour or I am to blame.

Jan[uary] 23
Sunday
Pleasant. This day has seemed so long. But it is nearly past now. There is one thing I like the people here for. They have respect enough for the Sabbeth to abstain from playing cards.

The stage driver and several others have been discussing Theology this eve.

Jan[uary] 24
Monday
Done quite a large washing. Made cake & c besides doing the other work. and do not feel so very tired. But I am sick of this place and tired of working all the time. I wonder if I will have to work like this all my life and always do without so many things I want which go a long way toward making life pleasant.

Jan[uary] 25
Tuesday
I have nothing particular to note today. Done about the same kind of work I generally do. It is blowing very hard and growing colder. It seems as though we are elected to stay here. This blockade is said to be the worst of the season — no trains in Mitchell since last Wednesday. So the letter I mailed to C- is lying at M- instead of speeding swiftly to him as I would have it. I wonder when he will get it. It is dreadful to be away from *home* so long.

Jan[uary] 26
Wednesday
Went through with the usual porgramme and done some washing got very warm and took some cold my throat is quite sore. The R.R. is blockaded worse than ever. R- is grinding coffee for me. I am tired and dont feel well.

Jan[uary] 27
Thursday
Only *worked all day*. I wonder where Charley is and what he is doing.
I have a bad cold.

I have been thinking, thinking, thinking. Have heard it said that we
never stand still — But either grow better or worse. I wonder if I am
as good as I used to be.

Jan[uary] 28
Friday
A telegram from Mrs Granger says she is on the way home. So I can
go soon. Made Apple Dumplings for dinner and Cinnamon Rolls for
Supper.
Mrs Stiffler done them both justice. My thoughts all day have been
with one who is near and dear to me. Home is where the heart is
hundreds of miles from here.
Have just finished reading "woman our Angel." According to that a
good many women might claim to be angels.

Jan[uary] 29
Saturday
Warm and pleasant. Trains have not got through yet. Granger went to
Mitchell. R- & I washed some and cleaned the floor.

Jan[uary] 30
Sunday
Mrs g- got back today. I have not been well. * Several strangers are in
tonight. One of them a fine violinist. His playing is equal to the best I
ever heard in the Opera. This does not seem like sunday. It is snowing
hard this eve. Picked up an old Minn Paper and among the theatrical
notes saw that Miss McAllister was about to make her debut to the
Minneapolis public in the character of Mercy Merrick. Would like to
see her play again.

Jan[uary] 31st
Monday
Very cold and stormy part of the day. When will this end — I can hardly
bear to stay here any longer and cannot get away. Worked hard.

Feb[ruary] 1st
Tuesday
Mrs G- paid me off today. I have earned just $40 since I came here.
R- & I started to Mitchell this P.M. After we were down about 4 miles,
Granger thought it would be dark long before we got there and that
we had better come back so here we are.

Feb[ruary] 2
Wednesday
Quite warm and pleasant. Trains have not got through to Mitchell
since Sunday. No chance to get home yet. I am so tired of waiting to
get home and for Spring.

Feb[ruary] 3rd
Thursday
Sudden change — very stormy and cold. There are quite a number
here — The prospects for getting home are no better. The blockade is
worse than ever. And coal almost gone. I am tired of the winter. I
wonder what Charley is doing and if he is comfortable — and if he
has heard from me yet.

Feb[ruary] 4th
Friday
Stormy — Had more music on the violin. He played "Home sweet
home". It was beautiful.

Feb[ruary] 5
Saturday
Still storming — quite warm — Trains still at Algona and men tired
out shoveling. No prospects of getting home for some time. Have been
working for my board since the [illegible]. Read of an indian outbreak
in N.M. I hope C- is not in that vicinity. It is so hard to be away here.

Feb[ruary] 6th
Sunday
Snowed hard all day. Some teamsters who put up here pulled out this
morn — But they had to come back. The horses could not pull the
loaded wagons through the drifts. We got up quite early. I made a lot

of splendid bread today. This day has seemed so long and lonesome.
I wish I was home, I can hardly stand it any longer.

Feb[ruary] 7th
Monday
Still storming and warm. went through the usual programme. and
knit a little. Read some. Am tired of everything here.

Feb[ruary] 8
Tuesday
We had indications of pleasant weather this morn. But it is storming
again this eve. It is really discouraging Finished a pair of wristlets for
my Charley. Jan 30 was the last time I had a chance to go home.
Roads have been blocked ever since.

Feb[ruary] 9
Wednesday
Stage got through today. Saw indications of clouds breaking up this
morn. Some of the people laughed at me for watching the sky so ea-
gerly. It grew brighter and brighter untill the clouds all cleared away,
and has been pleasant ever since. I cleaned the Cupboard this P.M.
and over-hauled my Trunk. I sincerely hope this pleasant weather will
last a long time.

Feb[ruary] 10
Thursday
Colder and clear. Pieced some quilt blocks this P.M. Am glad I happened to have them with me. This waiting is almost past human
endurance. And there is no telling when it will end. It may be a few
days a week or a month before we can go.

Feb[ruary] 11
Friday
Clear & cold. Blowing hard. Traveling almost impossible. I wonder if
Mother Shipton's prophesy that the world would come to an end this
year is not coming true. This is terrible weather on poor people in a
new country. Pieced a few quilt blocks. I will be thankful and so will
many others when spring comes.

Feb[ruary] 12
Saturday
Cold. Blowing very hard. Worked a good deal. and sewed some on my quilt. Young Lea May is our only guest.

Feb[ruary] 13
Sunday
Pleasant and I do hope it will continue. Did not sleep well last night. A few words I \over\heard in the eve disturbed me. My dreams were of an unpleasant nature. I hope we will never have such a winter again. [a line crossed out]

Feb[ruary] 14
Monday
Blustering and cold. Pieced some more quilt blocks and done my share of the work.

Feb[ruary] 15
Tuesday
Clear & cold. All the people round here are nearly out of coal and flour. Mr Nye came over to let us know they are all right. Done my work and pieced some more.

Feb[ruary] 16
Wednesday
Clear and cold. 26 below zero last night. I am thoroughly disgusted with the Granger family. They are both deceitful and dirty. Last night they put a filthy, lousy man in bed with Robbie and we let them know we did not like it. I wish we could go home. I shivered about 4 hours after I went to bed last night. Mr. Shiffler and Anderson are the best people in the house.

Feb[ruary] 17
Thursday
Very pleasant and warm. We had concluded to go to Mitchell the first opportunity. Had a houseful last night. A man, nickname of "Red-cloud" who has traveled all over and been in Leadville, stayed here last night. I done a good days work, and all for my board.

Feb[ruary] 18
Friday
This has been a clear pleasant day, though not as warm as yesterday.
A year ago I was very busy getting ready to go to Leadville. What an
eventful year it has been to me. Pieced quite a number of blocks for
my quilt.
Do not feel well. I believe I have rheumatism.

Feb[ruary] 19
Saturday
Very pleasant. Mrs G- has been cleaning up the house. I done the other
work with great difficulty. I feel rather worse than I did yesterday. I
think I have taken cold it has settled all over me and I feel so sore.

Feb[ruary] 20
Sunday
Still warm and pleasant. Slept very little last night — feel better than
I did yesterday. If all goes well we will be in Mitchell tomorrow night.
We have a chance to ride down with Mr. Seville. Heard a very amus-
ing and foolish religious argument this P.M. Mr. G. on one side. Mrs. G.
and the boarders on the other.

Feb[ruary] 21
Monday
Got up early — Started to Mitchell at 10 A.M. We are thankful to leave
Plankington.   Got to Mitchell at sunset. I have a fearful headache.
May not get home for a week. The trains will not be through for some
time. Put up at the Milwaukee house.

Feb[ruary] 22
Tuesday
Got up very late. It was cloudy and stormy a while this A.M. But it has
cleared off. and is now pleasant. There are quite a number here
whom I have met before. Several loads of provisions arrived in town
this eve from Sheldon. They return tomorrow and R. & I can ride
down to Bridgewater with them. That is one streak of good luck.

Feb[ruary] 23
Wednesday
Home.   Pleasant — That is not very cold. Started from Mitchell
this morning without breakfast. Dined at Alexandra. Dinner was good
But I did not eat much, my head-ached. Arrived at Bridgewater at
4 P.M. Robbie went home to get the team and came for me and the
Trunks. Had quite a comfortable ride today, had plenty robes to wrap
up in. and warm bricks at my feet.
It is just one year ago today since I started to Leadville. I remember
what a sad day that was. I did not know when I would see my folks
again. Received two letters. One from Charley and one from Jennie
Child.

Feb[ruary] 24
Thursday
Am not Well. Am decidedly unwell. Only get two meals a day at present. Pruned and done a few other little things. Looked over some of my
things. Charley may be here before long. The house looks pretty well.

Feb[ruary] 25
Friday
Pieced the remainder of my quilt blocks today. and repaired a few gar-
ments. I feel as though Charley will soon be here.

Feb[ruary] 26
Saturday
Not very cold. Snowing and Drifting hard. Patched a lot of pants & c
for the boys. Heard S- recite her lessons. It is hard as ever to get her
to study.

Feb[ruary] 27
Sunday
It has been severely cold today. Wrote a letter to Mrs Ward and one to
Miss Virgile. Some way I feel down-hearted and lonely. The way
seems so hard and dark.

Feb[ruary] 28
Monday
Pleasanter. Done a lot more patching for my self and others. R- and
father went to town. One year ago today, I reached Leadville. [the following is in a different color ink] It was about 7 P.M. when I got into L.
I did not see Charley that night. I could not get anyone to let him
know I was there. I did not arrive at the time he expected me or he
would have met me there.

Mar[ch] 1st
Tuesday
R- went to town. Got some cloth for shirts and I cut them out. Began
to fix over a suit of underwear for myself. and cut out a slipper case
for R-. We unpacked the Sewing Machine, and I will get it in running
order this eve. Read a little.

Mar[ch] 2
Wednesday
Stormy and blustering. Sewed some on Robbie's Shirts. We moved a
bed up stairs and sorted over a lot of clothing.

Mar[ch] 3
Thursday
Blustering. Finished R- shirts and darned a lot some socks. Read
some. It seems as though we are never going to have any more pleasant weather. I am lonesome. The dusk always sends a chill through
my heart. Sophie has the blues and is crying and I feel like doing the
same thing.

Mar[ch] 4
Friday
Very cold and blustering. This winter is dreadful. Sewed a little but it
is so cold we can scarcely do anything.

Mar[ch] 5
Saturday
Warmer and very pleasant-looking. S- got a letter from Leadville informing her of the death of Mrs Haverstroh. It has been so long since
we got mail that I felt sure I would get a letter from Charley but did

not. and was very much disapointed. Sewed some and cut out shirts for Johnnie.

Mar[ch] 6
Sunday
Very warm and pleasant. But cloudy this evening Had to make bread today, as we were out. and only got flour yesterday. I have a head-ache. and my cheeks have burned all day. I wonder when Charley will come. My life seems so strange and lonesome. There are two things I crave above all things, a home and perfect rest, where I will not have to work so hard to earn my daily bread I am so tired.

Mar[ch] 7
Monday
Warm & pleasant. Thawing. Read considerable. Made two shirts for Johnnie and done a few other things. I do hope this pleasant weather will continue. I will be glad when Sophie can go back to L. I have trouble every day with her about her lessons.

Mar[ch] 8
Tuesday
This has been a beautiful day. We melted snow snow [sic]and I washed the clothes, and scrubbed. The house looks nice and clean. I have just been watching the sun set. It was beautiful. I do not feel quite well. I have such strange feelings. it is a kind of shock which flashes all over me in an instant.

Mar[ch] 9
Wednesday
Clear, And colder. Had a hard time with Sophie. gave her a whipping. Have had a head-ache ever since. I do dislike having trouble with any one. She is all over it now. Made two or three collars and a few other things.

Mar[ch] 10
Thursday
Very high winds and snow drifting had a few minutes of rain. Ironed. The clothes are nice and white. S- is in a better temper than she has

been for a week. This winter is so long and lonesome. it seems as though it will never end. The sullen roar of the wind sounds dreary. I feel a little better today.

Mar[ch] 11
Friday
Very stormy all night and today. Snow and rain have fallen together and the wind blew a perfect gale. The east windows are nearly covered with snow which at intervals falls with a crash. Nearly all the animals about the place are in a wretched condition There being water standing in the stables. I have Rheumatism.

Mar[ch] 12
Saturday
It is not storming quite so hard as it did yesterday. My head feels dull. I dont feel well at all. It is a long time since I heard from Charley. Had rheumatism last night.

Mar[ch] 13
Sunday
Clear & cold. Wrote letters to Ida H. and Emma Smith. Mrs & Miss Babcock called on me. Sophie does not look well.

Mar[ch] 14
Monday
Very stormy since noon. The boys went to town this morning and got flour and provisions, and some calico. Also a letter from David. Two men came in who had got a little out of their way in the storm, But they went on again as they were anxious to get home.

Mar[ch] 15
Tuesday
Cloudy and warm. Felt well this A.M. but not P.M. Made two aprons and cut a wraper [sic]. Have $50 in my Pocket-book. I wonder what it will be used for, and when I will have as much again. I wish C- would come or that I could go to him. It seems as though half of my life has been wasted.

Mar[ch] 16
/*/ Wednesday
Pleasant. I have not done much of anything today — My head feels better than it did yesterday. Lay awake a long time last night. Got to thinking about things. It is hard to live here this way.

Mar[ch] 17
Thursday
Foggy and warm. Made bread and had trouble getting it to raise. Began repairing my black Dress. Got along all right with Sophie's lessons today.

Mar[ch] 18
Friday
Clear & warm. Washed a few pieces, and mopped the floor. And felt tired so that I just wanted to lie down every minute. Can scarcely eat a bite of what we have to eat. Lay on the bed an hour or two this P.M. But S- kept up such an incessant talking that I could not rest at all. And she would not stop when requested to.

Mar[ch] 19
Saturday
Clear but drifting pretty hard Finished repairing black dress, and sewed a little on wraper. Do not feel well enough to do much. Time seems so long. It looks just like mid winter yet. "The days are cold and dark and dreary" And so is my life. I wish I was one of the kind who cares for nothing
"Who cares for nothing alone is free."
I feel strangely.

Mar[ch] 20
Sunday
Cold and windy. I do not think the trains will be through for a month. Got two letters from Charley. I am so thankful. He had not heard from me for two months. I do not feel any better. If it is so the boys can go to town tomorrow The Dr will send me medicine and then I hope to improve.

At this point there is a large gap in the diary. Annie is overcome with illness and does not write again until May 6 when she writes

The last time I wrote any It was cold and the ground was covered with snow. Now it is warm and pleasant.

I was taken down sick on the 20 of Mar and have been very ill. I have suffered a great deal. But am so well now that I can sit up part of the day. I have been well cared for and tenderly nursed Jennie came home after I had been sick for about a week. She was my nurse most of the time during the day, and Robbie at night. All have been kind and attentive to me.

Charley came home quite unexpectedly on the 18 of April. And then I had another nurse, better than all the rest. I am likely to be under the Drs care for some time yet. As my convalescence is very slow.

I have lately received a letter informing me of the death of my Dear, true, friend, Emma. She died on the 22 of Feb. *She died*, and I am getting well.

Charley remains home for the planting season. While they look for a claim, they are renting a house. Charley works in the fields for others. He is often away.

August 1
Monday
Hot & windy. I churned this A.M. and lounged round the rest of the day. There is a bank of clouds lying off in the west. It looks as though it might rain.

Aug[ust] 2
Tuesday
Warm and cloudy. It began to rain about 3 A.M. and rained untill 11 oclock. It was the finest rain we have had this season. We are very thankful for it. All our crops and especially the Beans and vines were suffering greatly. Every thing looks fresh and nice today. Watch made us a flying visit this eve.
A shooting affray occurred yesterday west of town. A man named Garner shot his brother the wound is said to be fatal.

[August] 3 [3 is underlined twice]
Wednesday
It has been very pleasant today. Patched a little this forenoon. Charley went up home. He happened to see the Butcher and got some Beef, so

I concluded to Wash, Brown Coffee, and do a few other things while the meat was cooking and improve the fire and so I have been quite busy. C- helped me. I am quite tired. I feel almost as well now as I ever did. and have for about a week. It is so nice to be well.

[August] 4 /*/
Thursday
Very hot. Had just got through with Breakfast when C's Brother came over from town. His uncle & family are there Jimmie came down and informed us that he had a young son up at there [sic] house. I went up this morn and stayed till eve. Then came home and flew round as fast as I could till dark. There was so much to do. C. and W went over to town after supper. Johnnie came down and stayed awhile Waiting for them to come home and went off a few minutes before they came. I am tired, my head aches. It has been a very eventful day to me.

[August] 5
Friday
Very hot. Had a short thunder storm about 1 P.M. I got my work done up early and waited an hour for James to come for me then went to churning and got it done before he came. It was nearly noon when he came. Mrs Babcock came over while I was up there. C. & W. were off to town and the house was locked when I got home. C- has gone to town again this eve. W. has gone up home to Fathers. T.D.s lost. I wish *some* things were different. They will have to be, sometime.

August 6
Saturday
Very pleasant. Charley is binding up at Fathers, Walter went up with him. I done ever so much work today. Made Bread & Cookies, Ironed, Scrubbed &c. Cut out some sewing for next week. Took a bath and then got supper.

[August] 7
Sunday
Pleasant. Charlies Uncle Gus and his family visited us today. and got here before I got my morning work done up. I like his Uncle quite well. The children poor little things are noisy and boistrous. I always

feel so sorry for motherless little ones. I got worn out before night. This is a beautiful moonlight evening.

[August] 8
Monday
Very hot. Charley went up to bind at Jimmies. Walter went over to town then came back for Charley to go and work at Well digging. I do not expect him home to night and I am going to try staying alone. I went up to Jims and helped Jane awhile. The mosquitoes are very bad tonight.   .

[August] 9
Tuesday
Very hot. Indications of rain this P.M. I got along all right last night, Had not one adventure. But I did not sleep much. It was to warm and mosquitoes to numerous /and/ I was a little too watchful to sleep well. Watch came down last eve and I got him to stay all night for company. He came again tonight. I churned today and sewed some. I am tired and I have not done much either. It seems like a long time since Charley went away.

[August] 10
Wednesday
Very warm. It drizzled nearly all night but did not amount to much. Charley came home last night, so I did not have to stay alone. He started off to work again early this morning. But came back after he got to town to get some money, having bought the relinquishment of that claim. so we are sure of a claim at last and I am so glad. It is such a relief not to have that to think about. It seems as though we have a home now. I do not feel well this A.M., sewed a little. Afternoon I washed. Walter carried water for me, and went to town with some Butter and made a few purchases for me. I am very tired. I wonder how the baby is getting along.

[August] 11
Thursday
Very pleasant. Watch came about 5 this morning and I got up and let him in. I do not feel as well as usual today and have not for several days. Charley is going to Mitchell tonight on land business.

[August] 12

Friday

Cool and pleasant. Charley started to Mitchell last night at 12.30. I got up at the same hour and kneeded my bread. and got up at 4.30 to get breakfast for Walter. He went out to work with the well auger. He did not come until 6 so I had my cream in the churn and was all ready to go to churning when he came. did not feel well this morn but felt better later part of the day. I done lots of work, made Bread, browned Coffee, Roasted Beef &c. and Ironed and scrubbed. It seems like Saturday, because I done my Saturday work.

2 years ago I went to Bloomington with Lizzie & L. Larkins & some friends of theirs. I remember it well. I had my wedding dress cut & fitted and done a little shopping. And I remember telling Mother all about what I had done when I got home and how interested she was. Dear, Dear Mother how I miss you.

August 13

Saturday

Cool & pleasant.

C arrived from Mitchell at 12 oclock last night. Have felt lazy all day. C. was at home all day. He and I walked over to town about 5 this eve. Made a few calls and purchases. We have got the homestead at last.

[August] 14

Sunday

Cool & pleasant. Got up at 7 oclock. Before I got the dishes washed we were thunderstruck to see Gus & all the children coming who had started to Neb last Thursday and we did not expect to see them again so soon. I had a little rather he had stayed where he was. Robbie came down a little while this forenoon and helped me pick beans for dinner. It is almost cold enough to freeze.

[August] 15

Monday

It began to rain about 12 last night, and rained untill after day light this morning. It has done a great deal of good, although things were not realy suffering. Walter went up to Bore wells. Charley went up to father's and they agreed to have Robbie do some breaking on our claim. After dinner Charley churned for me, and after we got the work done up Robbie came down with the Breaking plow and we all went down to our claim. We only laid of a landing this P.M. so I saw the first sod turned on our farm. While we were eating supper two of Gus Rays children came over and asked C to go over town and see him as they are going to leave for Nebr. this evening. He acts very strangely. He is the most changeable man I ever knew. am glad he is gone and hope it is for good.

Aug[ust] 16
Tuesday
Extremely hot. I did not feel well all day feel some better this eve. The butcher came along and I got a small roast of beef. C- & I done a little washing while the meat was cooking. It looks like rain again to night.

August 17
Wednesday
Had quite a storm last night. It has been close and sultry today and rained some. Charley picked a watermelon this A.M. and it tasted pretty good although it was not quite ripe enough. It is the first I have tasted this season. I wonder what improvements we will have made and how we will be fixed and, what doing a year from today.

Aug[ust] 18
Thursday
Very pleasant. Mr. Nelson came with his Harvester to cut our Flax but found the machine would not work so went home at noon. Dr. Smith & Lady and Mrs McKinnan called this A.M. Charley went over town and changed some flour this afternoon. I feel better today since the weather turned cooler than I have for several days.
I paid out two dollars today that I had always intended to keep.

Aug[ust] 19
Friday
Cool & pleasant. Nothing of any consequence has been done today. I do get so tired having the work drag so. C & W went over to town this A.M. The cow got loose and I had quite a time to keep her out of the garden. At last she struck out for Father's and I was afraid she would get in mischief so I took the Picket rope and went up there, so the boys could tie her up. I wish I knew of a good place for this winter.

Aug[ust] 20
Saturday
I done my Saturday work as usual. After a great deal of trouble Charley has got a man to cutting his Flax. He began this P.M. I went up to fathers and back again. C. went over town to see Morse. It seems too bad to have so much time wasted it is hard to get work here.

Aug[ust] 21
Sunday
Pleasant. Stitz did not get through cutting the Flax yesterday so he finished it today. C. & W. put up some hay. I don't like sabbeth working, but I suppose it is somewhat excusable under the circumstances. Father was down a little while. Johnnie sent down a nice lot of Beets. Charley has just started off to his place so as to be ready to go to work in the morning on a well he is boring for Mr. Pease. So I will have to stay alone tonight. /❀/

Aug[ust] 22
Monday
Pleasant. Charley did not get to his place last night but waited till this morn as he would then have a chance to ride out. I washed & churned today besides doing considerable other work. It looks very like rain tonight There is a big Thunder storm of to the west of us.

Aug[ust] 23
Tuesday /Some people set out at naught a lifetime of sacrifice and devotion if their "Pride" is wounded nothing but a sickly sentiment declares that *nothing* can atone a wrong.   A minute without love is nothing more than a Legalized Prostitution   Cast out the Beam that is in thine own Eye./ /I forget sometimes but something always brings it back/

It did not rain much last night. There are indications of rain this morning it is thundering both in the north and South. Walter dropped a few words last night which brought to my mind some olden memories which were it in my power ~~I would blot out of my mind forever. I can not put it away from me. My heart aches with bitterness and indignation and a sense of the wrong done me which can never be~~

[crossed out and illegible] ~~The ones having~~ [crossed out and illegible]
~~can never in anyway atone for such a wrong.~~ [crossed out and illegi-
ble] ~~They have lost my faith and confidence in mankind. I had too
much confidence. How blind I was not to see through it all. Especially~~
[crossed out and illegible for remaining twenty lines]

Aug[ust] 24
Wednesday
It has been very warm all day. It is cloudy this eve. Walter finished
putting the Flax together. I patched some for Robbie & Charley and
done up a fine shirt, it looks real nice. I read a good deal today.

Aug[ust] 25
Thursday
Robbie came down with Js team to stack our Flax, afternoon it got so
windy they had to stop. Patched some and ironed and made bread. It
is very warm. /10.30P.M. ❀ ❀/

Aug[ust] 26
Friday
It has been excessively warm all day. Charley came home from Pease's
last night, quite late, the auger having been broken and requiring repairs. We wrote to David. Charley got James's team this P.M. and has
been stacking Flax. I hope it will rain soon it is so warm I can hardly
endure it. Mr. Pease is an Advent. so Charley will not be there at work
tomorrow.

[August] 27
Saturday
Cooler. James worked here all day. They finished stacking the Flax. I
drove the team some. I am glad that job is done. I scrubbed &c today.
/11 oclock P.M. ❀/

[August] 28
Sunday
Very hot. Charley intended to go back to Mr. Pease's this eve to be
ready to go to work tomorrow morning. But Pete had not done his job
he had left at the shop so he could not go. I took a ride out to Curriers

with Father and the boys and enjoyed it very well. All the Farms along the road seem in a prosperous condition. The boys got several shots at Prairie Chickens Ducks &c. The cattle are in fine order. I am glad my little cow is doing so well. Mr. Curriers people are very kind. We had all the Melons we could eat. I was sorry C- was not along. he would have enjoyed it. I am very tired and sleepy. I must have ridden 16 miles.

[August] 29 /*/
Monday
Warm. I am very tired. I rode more than was good for me yesterday. Charley went away to work today but returned during the P.M. the auger having broken again, and then went away again. He brought me a little puppie. It is the strangest looking animal I ever saw. I have not done much today.

[August] 30
Tuesday
I feel a little better today. Made Bread & washed. Charley came home again this eve. The machine is broken again. It is so much trouble. Father came down for yeast. Watch came also, and was surprised to see a Pup here. They did not seem very friendly, indeed they were decidedly unfriendly. Had a good Melon this eve.   /❀/

Aug[ust] 31
Wednesday
Very Warm. Father has been quite ill today. Robbie came down for me so I went up and baked Bread and done the other work. I tried to do my churning after I came home. it was so slow about coming that I had to give it up till morning.

The diary continues daily for the next several months. Charley leaves on October 28 to find winter work. Annie does not return to the Granger's Boarding House but lives instead with her father.

Thursday
Dec[ember] 1
Still pleasant. Though it begins to look as though it would storm soon. Have done very little work today. done my ironing. Browned some Coffee and sewed a little. Father went to town and got a letter for me

from Charley. He has not got the letter mailed nearly two weeks ago. Nor the one I addressed to Aitkin. Looked over a lot of old letters. Both Charlies & mine. Found one written to him years ago by his little sister Which I never saw before. The whole letter is one lonesome pathetic cry of, "Come to me Charley"

Dec[ember] 2
Friday
Warm & cloudy. The sun sometimes shines through a little. P.M. went down to Walters but he has not been there yet. I cleaned up a little. I think he must have gone. I brought up the looking glass & a few other things, and the key. We churned this eve. Am Baking Bread.

Dec[ember] 3
Saturday
Very pleasant. Made Bread, packed Butter, Washed and done up a lot of collars and done lots of other work. Got a letter from Charley dated Nov 30. he has not heard from me yet and is anxious. it is too bad. I know how he feels. Took a bath. Have not felt strong lately. I wish I could get a letter to him.

Sunday
Dec[ember] 4
Very pleasant & warm. We got up late Had Breakfast at nine A.M. P.M. Robbie and I went down to the little house and packed the rest of our things. Walter has not been there for a week, and must have gone so I thought we would not need to leave the things out any longer. It seems like home down there.

Monday
Dec[ember] 5
Very pleasant. Rather windy. Wrote card to Milt. James started to Sioux Falls this morn. R. got a letter from David in which he says that Walter was in Sheldon about the 30 of Nov. Am glad to hear of him for one reason.

Tuesday
Dec[ember] 6
Very pleasant /and thawing/. The wind blew very hard from ten A.M.
till about 4 P.M. Robbie is working at Matsons. We washed & scrubbed
today. Father done the rubbing and I done the rest. Johnnie helped a
little about moping. Received cards from David, Charley, & Jennie
Childs and a dunning letter from Bullards.

Wednesday
Dec[ember] 7
Pleasant. It clouded up about noon rained a few seconds then cleared
off again. It is colder than it has been for some time. Froze hard last
night. Done a lot of patching for Father & the boys and a little for
myself.
Walter is working in Sheldon and I hope he will stay there, or at least
not come back here.
Mailed letter to Charley.

Thursday
Dec[ember] 8
Pleasant, knit some and sewed. Got a good letter from Charley and
$10. The letter was registered. I had to ride down for it and back, a
splendid ride. Answered Charlies letter. Sat up till 10 oclock writing.

Friday
[December] 9
Colder. Clear. Made Bread, Ironed & c. Sewed & knit some. finished
Charleys letter and mailed it.

December 10th /*/
Saturday
Cloudy and chilly all day. Began to snow at 3 P.M. did not snow long.
Wind blowing. Browned coffee, made gingerbread. Knit some
finished a chemise. Do not feel very well.

Sunday 11
[December]
It cleared of last night and is growing colder today. We got up very late did not have Breakfast till 9.30 I wrote to Jennie Child. Do not feel well as a matter of course my back aches & c.

Monday 12
[December]
Very warm and pleasant. Robbie done quite a large washing and I helped some. James paid me the rest of the Bean money. I have $7. on hand now. I knit a good deal. We had 2 straw ticks filled this P.M. We have got every thing pretty well cleaned up.

Tuesday 13
[December]
Colder. Clear. My head ached last eve and all night and is still aching. I feel so badly. If I do not get better soon, I will go and see the Dr. knit a good deal. R- went to town. Johnnie is going to stay at the Drs. We had chicken for dinner.   8 P.M. my head still aches very hard. Ironed this P.M.

Wednesday 14
[December]
This is a beautiful pleasant day. R- cut up and packed some meat we got yesterday. I made Soup for dinner, cooked the scraps of meat for Watch, and rendered the Lard. Also knit some. Johnnie started to School today. I feel better today. Would like to hear from Charley now. It is a week since I had a letter.

Thursday 15
[December]
Pleasant. We got up late. had breakfast at 9 Dinner at four.   I got a letter from Charley. I am so glad, was not expecting it, for a wonder. He has a good place and good board. Patched all day. Knit this evening.

Friday 16
[December]
Very warm and pleasant. We got up and had our meals at the same times as yesterday: knit some, Patched some clothes for my self and done my own washing. Knit all evening.

Saturday 17th
[December]
This has been a remarkably fine day. It was so warm we could have
the door open. I took a bath this P.M. Knit some and ironed a little.
Johnnie was home a few minutes this P.M. Baked some Beans.
The evening is lovely.

Sunday 18
[December]
Very Pleasant. R- & I went down to town this eve and heard Miss
Cleaveland a member of the Womans Christian Temperance associa-
tion deliver a lecture on temperance. She is a very fine powerful
speaker.

Monday 19
[December]
Pleasant. This is Charlies birthday. He is 28 years old. Went to town.
Paid Bullards part of the account — saw the Dr. He gave me something for my arm. Had a good ride. Had an invitation to the Dr.s for
my Christmas dinner. But did not accept. Bullards offered an apology
for "shutting down on us" as Art calls it, and asked me to go and trade
there again.

Tuesday 20 [20 is underlined three times]
[December]
Cloudy and pretty warm. It looks like snowing Patched some, also
knit. Made a lid and finished papering a little box I found here which I
used to keep my Treasures in when I was a little girl. Began to rip an
old dress of my mother's to pieces & intend to fix it so I can wear it my
self. It makes me feel very badly to do any thing like that. It seems almost wrong to change any of mothers things. But I know she would
want me to if she knew and I know If I don't wear them some one else
will after I am dead. Robbie churned this eve.

Wednesday 21
[December]
Warm & cloudy all day. Began to snow at 4.30 P.M. Worked some on
the dress I am making over. Knit some. I dreamed last night that I was
dying. I thought I was drawing my last breath. It was a strange sensa-

tion I was glad when I awoke. Worked over & packed the Butter. Had
vegetable soup for dinner.

Thursday 22
[December]
This is a beautiful day. It only snowed for a few minutes last /night/,
then cleared off. R & I cracked nuts last eve. I am going to make a nut
cake for Christmas. Made Bread today. Knit some and done quite a
few little jobs. Cracked more nuts tonight. Received a letter from
Charley.

Friday 23
[December]
This is a beautiful day. I went down to Smiths. The Dr was absent
most of the time. He had not time to give me what I required. He let
me have a book to read. Had an introduction to Mrs. Pierce she seems
nice.

Saturday 24
[December]
Very pleasant. The year is almost ended. I made some Nut Cakes,
Doughnuts, Pumpkin Pies, Cinnamon Rolls &c. and got a chicken
ready to roast tomorrow. Read some in the work I got from the Dr.

Sunday 25
Christmas
[December]
Pleasant. The wind blew very hard for a few hours today. Johnnie
came home and had dinner with us we dined at 3 P.M. This dont seem
like Christmas. Have not seen anyone today but Father Robbie and
Johnnie. I wrote a letter to Charley and sent it to the Office.
There is a big prairie fire out west tonight. studied some today and
this eve.

Monday 26
[December]
Clear Pleasant. This day has not profited me much. Read some sewed
a little and knit some. Heard that Mrs Foss of Sheldon is dead. She
was a strong, healthy looking woman. We little know how soon our

time will come. It often happens those who are always sickly live longer than the stronger ones.   I am not very well.

Tuesday 27
[December]
/Pleasant. The wind blew pretty hard a while today. / R. went down to the dance a little while last evening. I was quite sick a while in the night. I felt very badly. Slept very little. Felt better today. I went down town saw the Dr. It is chronic inflammation of the Uterus that is troubling me. He says he can soon cure me. I have neuralgia this eve. It is 35 years ago today since Fathers mother died and 19 years since my little Sister Bettie died. If she had lived she would have been 20 years and 7 months old. I am sleepy tonight and am going right to bed. it is only 7.30.

Wednesday 28
[December]
Very pleasant. It is two months today since Charley went away. We washed this A.M. Had quite a large one. I feel better than usual today with the exception of that inflammation. That seems worse. every motion hurts me. I lost my ring and had a two hour hunt for it before I found it. I had begun to think I would never find it and felt very badly about it.

Thursday 29
[December]
Cold. I began to fix a pair of pants for Charley. Ironed the clothes. knit this eve. David came home today. I had Neuralgia this eve. I got a letter from Charley dated Dec 19&20 and I began a letter to Charley.

Friday 30
[December]
Clear & Warm. I cooked some things for New Years and made bread. We churned and dressed chickens this eve. I knit a good deal Sat up until 10 oclock.

Saturday 31
[December]
Quite cold. The windows have been covered with frost all day. I
worked on a pair of Pants I am repairing for Charley.

This is the last day of the year. And I cannot but feel sad as I review
the years that are gone especially the last few years. They have
wrought many changes in my life, and the lives of my friends. They
were fraught with both joy and sorrow. We have so many disapoint-
ments to bear. I hope I will not make any one unhappy next year. And
that I will be happy myself. I wonder where Charley and I will be a
year from now. If we live. I hope we will be on our claim and enjoying
ourselves. This winter seems so long. It is so hard to be away from
Charley so long.

It is 8 oclock P.M. The year is old and in a few hours it will be
ended. There is a strange and lonesome feeling in my heart tonight. I
have wasted so much time, and have been unhappy sometimes, when
I might have been happy and ought to have been. And I had a great
deal of happiness. One cannot expect to have all pleasure and no
pain. Bitter and sweet must evermingle in these lives of ours. /Father
said this eve That he can remember where he has been the last day of
the year for 49 years.
It is 65 days since Charley went away./

2 : Time, Days, and Page

Have you ever been swimming in glacial water — water turned milky blue or deep maroon by minerals and deposits seized by the glacier as it ponderously made its way across a continent? You would have been high atop a mountain, maybe in the Canadian Rockies or in Montana, where glaciers, now in retreat, still press down on the earth's crust. And it would have been in the summer — late August perhaps — the sun warm and still and bright, making you feel as if a dip in this remote glacial tarn is just what your tired body needs at this point in your day. Maybe you would have tested the water with your hand before undertaking the arduous process of unbooting. And your fingers would have said, yes, get in. Off come boots, wool socks, and liners made dank by sweat and three-day-old dirt. Off come your shirt, shorts, underclothes — your body not quite so warm, a tiny breeze lifting over the pass. Still the water waits, still.

Only now, virgin feet wobbling on the hard-rocked edge, you notice for the first time ice caves at the mouth of the tarn creating an underwater maze of holes and caverns. Now for the first time do you notice the lack of fish, of bugs, of life in general, and you look high and back at the sun to make sure it is still there. And when you place your feet in the water, feet still marked by the corrugated folds of your socks, it feels cooler than you had expected, and you think to yourself that you had better jump in all at once or not at all, so you begin counting aloud to three. It is definitely colder. You move quickly, steel yourself for the shock, and, on three, merge into the chest deep water, legs bending so as not to touch the sharp rocks that line the bottom of the tarn.

Only the shock is so much greater than you could have imagined, the cold so much deeper, the water so much stronger, that you cry out in an animal voice. It just happens. And then you realize, quite quickly, that you can no longer breathe. Your chest heaves and puffs, your hands flail and tread and flail again, and your eyes are unable to focus. When the water, unchecked by the lack of oxygen, combusts into flames on your skin, you begin to believe you are going to die here, 13,000 feet above sea level, naked and dirty. Unable to move, unable to breathe, unable to think, you have only enough presence to realize that this water is unlike any water you have ever known. And you wonder how you will ever get back to the hard-rocked shore.

* * *

Annie's diary beckons to me like a tarn, inviting me in, resembling any other water, any other writing. I dangle my feet, draw my fingers along its surface and think I know what it is. But like most things in this world, it defies easy description; its form resists simple, comfortable ways of reading and knowing. The danger lies in assuming otherwise.

* * *

I worry that having read part of Annie's diary, having come face-to-face with an actual diary, you are now relaxed, even comfortable. That the ordered illusion of typeface, the way the entries are centered and spaced on the page, the fact that the marginalia has been gathered in by me, that the entries are crisp and chronological have worked to undo in you any anxiety I may have been able to produce so far. That you may think, now, that this water is no different than any other water you have ever known. My work in this chapter is to show otherwise. A diary — by its form and content — demands that the reader never feel at home. A reader must always recognize her outsiderness, not only feel it but actively cultivate it, worry it like a canker sore. The reader stands outside the action, the people and events that move through the diary, and outside a form of writing that is often illegible, out of order, coded, and crossed out.

We are not being invited in.

* * *

How do we read an entry like this?

Saturday, June 4, 1881
I do not feel as well as usual. We are getting ready to move. It is very warm.

What are the questions we need to ask of the writer, of the text? What does the writing ask of the reader? What do we need to know?

What about those lines written in the margin of the entry dated August 23, 1881? "Some people set out at naught a lifetime of sacrifice and devotion. . . ." When were they written? Before the entries were written? During? After? Years after? Before this blank book was even a diary? How do the two physically distinct texts speak to each other? Or do they? Did the diarist write them? Or was it her niece, having come across the diary in a box of old books, wanting to add her own thoughts?

      *   *   *

There is a danger in feeling too much at home with a diary, with ordinary writing in general. Or maybe I should say more clearly that there is a danger in making a diary feel too much like home. The ordinary diary occupies a tenuous position; it bears the traces of just enough recognizable narrative features in combination with just enough gaps, omissions, and general disarray to make it highly vulnerable to hyperperformative reading. Rona Kaufman makes the distinction between reading as hyperperformance and reading as halted performance in her unpublished essay "Navigating the Limit Points of Reading." According to her, hyperperformance occurs when a reader assumes so much authority in reading that she disregards the text, trammeling right over it. She rearranges, ignores, and makes demands, forcing the text to fit into her predetermined space. A halted performance, on the other hand, happens when the reader garners so little authority that she brings no influence to bear upon her reading. The reader is overwhelmed by the voices of others. While halted performances may be the kind we are more apt to see in a college classroom, when, for example, students are asked to model George Orwell's "Shooting an Elephant," it is hyperperformance on the part of the reader that is most dangerous for the ordinary diary, a form whose sheer openness and historic delegitimation afford a great deal of rambling room.

Kaufman's argument circles around the position of the reader — how a reader's authority intersects different sites of reading. The risks she identifies are mostly for the one who is reading. I am more interested in the damage incurred by the text (and, following the ripples, the risks for the one who is writing). With its empty spaces and apparent disorder, the ordinary diary begs for hyperperformance on the reader's part. It calls out to a reader who is willing and eager to bring closure and order. These diaries are vulnerable to hyperperformative readings, in part because they appear, like the tarn, simple and known. The overwhelming number of gaps, the omissions, codes, distancing strategies, the decontextuality, illegibility, secretness, and messiness produce a text too easily filled in by a reader, too easily edited down, too easily ignored, too easily trammeled. Which makes ordinary diaries vulnerable to readers who see what a diary "could be" and are more than willing and able to put things straight. Readers have been granted a permit for such remodeling by the historic devaluation of the diary.[1]

For example, think of Anne Frank's diary — a diary that, unlike Annie's, was revised by the author with readers in mind and therefore more readily equipped by the diarist for such interaction; yet a diary that bears the scars of hyperreading. Even given the fact that Anne Frank intended (here meaning crafted, revised) her diary for some kind of future readership, diaries, as personal papers rather than "finished" manuscripts, require a more vigorous editor who makes important decisions about the "story" the diary will tell. Otto Frank's editorial hand initially guided a certain kind of reading — one that was sexless, bodiless, and sweet. His decisions resulted in an uncomplicated picture of the diarist because messy, contradictory entries were simply removed.

How we view ordinary writing is, of course, largely a matter of how we view ordinary writers. The tradition of devaluing ordinary writing as being simplistic and flat is equally a devaluation of the writer. Affording the diarist, the ordinary writer, a simple, one-dimensional, and static subject position contributes to the vulnerability of ordinary texts. Susan Miller in her book *Assuming the Positions: Cultural Pedagogy and the Politics of Commonplace Writing* works to describe ordinary writing as a collection of complicated texts inscribed by authors with complex and mobile identities. I mention her work not only because she is concerned with ordinary writing but because she highlights the fact that writing that occurs in spaces outside formal institutions are powerful local sites for tracing how dominant discourses are internalized as well as subverted. She concludes that to overlook these writers and their texts would be to miss important cultural processes whereby subjects assume varied positions and create multifaceted cultural scripts. In her words, such a myopic reading would miss an "invitation to watch how cultures are made, remade, and finally ensconced in 'memory.'"[2]

The recovery of an ordinary text is the recovery of the ordinary writer. Not in terms of her "voice" or her "absent presence" within a tradition that silences and erases these writers but a recovery of her agency as a writer. Such a reading reveals the fact that she is participating in a complex cultural process and producing a text that is equally complicated — even when it appears on the surface to be simple and known. To read differently has as much to say about the writer as it does about the writing.

Ordinary diaries, then, are doubly vulnerable: they are vulnerable to readers who are willing to remodel them and to a tradition of reading that refuses to view diarists as authors. Such willingness and refusal has consequences that extend well beyond continued intellectual narrowness. There are more immediate outcomes. For example, Bruno Bettelheim writes with great anger about the play based on Anne Frank's diary, a hyperperformance that ends not with the murder of Anne Frank but with her "returning" via a voiceover to reassert her belief that in general there is more good in the world than evil. Anne Frank was not able to bring her diary to a close, could not have the final word; it "ends" when she is taken away by the Nazis. The play, a hyperperformative reading of the diary, supplies an ending that, according to Bettelheim, grants permission to forget the Holocaust.

Seeing our way out of a tradition of reading and valuing that can quite literally end in the denial of the Holocaust requires an approach that is as complicated as the writers who produce ordinary texts. Ordinary diaries are not simply preconditioned to hyperperformative readings. Mysterious, cagey, unfamiliar, and triumphantly inscrutable, they require a different line of approach. If at any point I feel at home when reading Annie's diary then chances are I have been seduced by the narrative traces. Do I catch myself skimming Annie's diary? Moving lightly, rapidly over the "unimportant" to find those narrative markers that I have learned signify plot — the longer entries, those moments of disruption rather than order. Do I have a list of characters (Walter is the bad guy), a setting (a tiny town in the Dakotas), a narrative tension (will Annie reveal what has happened in the past), a potential climax (Annie decides whether to leave Charley)? Am I eyeing the censored entries like nuts to be cracked? Do I see ideology operating beneath the repetition without having really thought about the repetition?

I constantly ask these questions of myself because I know the strength of narrative's undertow. How easily the skeletal diary can be fattened. A diary as ordinary writing, almost more than other kinds of writing, allows a great deal of seemingly familiar space for the reader to negotiate.[3]

The water is colder than it looks.

. . .

Keeping the vulnerability of the text in mind and minding the tug of narrative, this chapter sets out to examine how Annie makes her days on the page in line with the opportunities afforded by the diurnal form. Because I seem to approach the world through metaphor, I have worked to find an image that captures the focus of this chapter most effectively. Central to my project is an examination of how Annie "fills" the space of her diary in ways that align with dailiness. For a long time I thought that in this chapter I was looking at the materiality of the text or the physical ways the text assumes space. Conceptually, though, these words did not point to the kind of agency I ascribe to Annie as a writer. Metaphors of terrain or geography can suggest that the textual qualities of her diary are completely predetermined, already there. And while, as we will see, Annie does operate under many constraints (both physical as well as cultural), she makes decisions in the making of her text. To highlight her work as cartographer of her days, I want to suggest that she maps her days within the space of her diary following the contours of the diurnal form, nineteenth-century cultural scripts, and her personal experience of dailiness.

There are a number of interesting connections between maps and diaries that make the metaphor of mapping particularly resonant. Both maps and diaries are repositories of useful information, they both serve as tools, and both chart an individual's passage through time and space. The most important connection for me, however, is that both maps and diaries reduce the complexity of the world to a known and ordered space (a failed facsimile of the real). They represent or appear to represent wholes — a whole region, a whole state, a whole day, a whole year. To achieve the illusion of entirety, though, open spaces of time and place must be brought into order, must be ordered. In the next chapter I will be looking at the tension such reductions produce in Annie's diary. For now, I only want to acknowledge that the diurnal form is always selective even though it aims to be exhaustive. It is always only an outline, an ordered space that Annie, as writer, posits on the "blank" pages of her diary. Here, I am interested in the features the diarist chooses to map (and how those choices align with dailiness) and less with what such a map has failed to measure.

·   ·   ·

In suggesting that writing within the seemingly natural unit of the day is the dominant shaping force of diurnal form and content, my claim moves out from Hampsten's suggestion that the diary "accounts for time" and Bunker's point that "dailiness is central" to the study of diaries. In particular, I am considering how the materiality of Annie's diary — how she physically maps content and space — is related to, even conditioned by, the diurnal form's historical relationship to time. Such an investigation focuses our attention not on how the diary counts time or the passing of time literally, but rather on how the page graphically registers temporality, both the writer's experience of writing every day and the form's connection to successive time. From dailiness flow other features of diurnal form: middleness, measuredness, usefulness, and openness, features that equally inform the work of the writer.

Recognition of the mutually defining relationship between temporality and form will allow us to name more clearly the work Annie undertakes in her diary as she negotiates the potentials and constraints of her form. Such a reading serves eventually to complicate the subject position of the ordinary writer beyond a static or simple position. Before turning our attention to Annie's diary and the deftness with which Annie maps her days, I want to consider more closely the historical connection between diurnal form and dailiness.

·   ·   ·

Stuart Sherman in *Telling Time: Clocks, Diaries, and English Diurnal Form, 1660–1785* theorizes the rise of the diurnal form. Sherman's ideas are invaluable to any discussion of the ordinary diary because of the way he wants to think about connections between temporality and the form of the diary. Since his work is not often cited in connection with women's diaries, I will devote more page space than I might otherwise to recount what I see as his main contribution to the work on diaries. His book canvasses a century of diurnal writing, the century prior to what most would see as the diary's pinnacle. I want to think about Annie's diary in relation to a few concepts that Sherman puts into play — most importantly, the distinction he draws between measure and occasion, a distinction with historical and horological roots.

Sherman begins his book by looking at changes in the late seventeenth century in the ways clocks told time. Prior to the invention of the pendulum, clocks were unreliable. Without a way to measure minutes accurately, they chimed only on the occasion of the quarter, half, or full hour. The discovery of the pendulum meant that clocks became much more accurate; they produced small, equal, countable, and successive intervals of time — all tracked easily by the now-reliable minute hand. Moments in time heretofore completely undocumented—minutes and then seconds — were now available for counting, and for experiencing.

Sherman suggests that the consequences of a new horology are almost unfathomable. The ways people now talked about this new time reflected their new experience of it. In spoken language, clocks no longer went tick, tock. They now went tick, tick, tick. And this successive tick, tick, tick required new written forms for filling previously unmeasured time. Changes in chronometry paralleled (even produced) the rise of the diurnal form (not only diaries but also daily newspapers and epistolary novels) as writers struggled to "write the time new clocks told."[4]

Positing an inherent connection between temporality (how one experiences time) and narrative, Sherman argues that a form of writing will "absorb, manifest, and respond to local temporalities, contemporary shapes of time, without necessarily 'knowing' that it does so" (6). We can look to the form of writing to document temporality, and likewise to temporality to understand form. For example, the new spaces of time created by the pendulum needed to be filled in ways that "privilege successiveness and resist closure" (11). Previously "tick," a beginning, was followed closely by "tock," an ending. What lay between was filled by narrative, by plot. Genres that replicated the occasioned and eventful ticktock were the ones privileged. But tick, tick, tick is all about middles, an endless succession of measured (not occasioned or storied) moments. It was the diary, specifically Samuel Pepys's diary, that rose as the form that could grasp most effectively the new temporality — and could respond, as Sherman suggests, to the new structures of feeling about time. Quite literally, measured blank spaces in the diary replicated the minutes on the clock. For the first time ever a writer could realize through a written form her experience of dailiness — not time *when* but time *in*.

Hence, dailiness is not only a defining characteristic of the diurnal form but a condition for it. Dailiness further shapes other features of the diary, not the least of which is the difference between measure and occasion. Sherman suggests that historically, prior to diaries like Pepys's, diarists would keep diaries that recorded occasioned moments.[5] A person might keep a diary marking moments of religious connection, or keep a diary while ill or dying, or while documenting travel, or marking astrological occurrences. These were occasioned documents. A diarist would make an entry when occasion suggested — storied entries that reproduced the occasioned chiming of the clock.[6]

Such documents could not and did not capture dailiness. Products of occasion, they missed the measured, in-between moments of being and writing in the days. In contrast, the diurnal form privileges the successiveness of measure, the tick, tick, tick of days. It is a form of writing that is marked by being open rather than closed, measured rather than occasioned, and immediate rather than reflective. Sherman again gives the example of Pepys's diary to demonstrate how changes in time paralleled or produced changes in the practice of diary keeping. Pepys's diary is thoroughly informed by dailiness. He reproduces the continuity of days through the continuity of entries, specifically in the way each day begins and ends with the beginning and ending of a page. He relies on connectives (then, after) and on repetition ("And so to bed.") to enact the fullness, the plentitude of "time in." He assures each day a place within the measuredness of days, even if he does not write every day.

In addition, Sherman argues that Pepys actively *uses* his diary to produce new information about himself, about his place in space. Pepys relies on the new minute hand on his pocket watch to track his movement through the city of London (much in the same way sailors would soon learn to track their movement across the ocean) and renders his experience of that movement — this new knowledge of his self — in his diary by documenting the cost of fares for such travel. His "traversals through urban space," the fullness of being in the public, become distilled into daily entries that provide him "a sense of many motions closely mapped" (67). In fact, three aspects of his new pocket watch that Pepys values — its precise calibration, its "privacy," and its capacity to produce new data about himself — are all found in the new form of writing his diary takes: that it is calibrated by the day, that it feels secret, and that it always remains in the middle (91–95). Like his pocket watch, the diary becomes a tool he can use to document the self.

The diurnal form, then, is not only conditioned by dailiness but is further marked by usefulness — the ways in which the diarist makes use of these previously unnoticed (because not occasioned) moments that the diurnal form makes available for filling. Sherman thinks of the diary as a tool — he uses the word technology — that the diarist uses to seize or grasp typically undocumented, daily moments, suggesting that what gets produced through the use of this technology are "diurnal documents of the self."[7] The form of writing captures previously unmeasured moments in time, allowing the diarist to construct a diurnal self, one that experiences and inscribes dailiness.

*   *   *

Without going into further detail, I want to make a couple of observations. First, while Annie is writing two centuries after Pepys, she still writes within the diurnal tradition he helped to establish, a tradition that came into existence as a result of historical changes in the structures of feeling about time. So while Annie would have experienced time differently than Pepys, her diary still bears structural, material, and rhetorical similarities to the initial diurnal forms. Specifically, Annie's diary, like Pepys's diary and like all ordinary diaries, is centrally defined by dailiness: writing in the days rather than of the days.

In addition, though, the form and content of Annie's diary differ in some radical and important ways from Pepys's — specifically, in her personal, female, nineteenth-century experience of dailiness. Pepys moved through a public world, through urban space. His days were marked by meetings, lunches, and being in the public. Owning a pocket watch, traveling alone by carriage, and having enough money to require extensive documentation reflect differences in class and gender.[8] Annie moves through domestic space: more contained, largely cyclical and repetitive, unstructured by public events, though structured by historical beliefs about women and the role of the domestic sphere. Her "time in" will be a very different experience of time.

It is here that we need to slow down. The question becomes, if we accept Sherman's argument that a diary functions as a "technology for laying hold of fugitive phenomena and enclosing them within a fullness of time" (45), how does the diarist put these moments to use? What is the diarist doing with these newly named and collected phenomena?

For Sherman the answer to such questions lies with audience, and such an answer should make readers of ordinary diaries wary. As he continues to trace the diurnal form into the nineteenth century, he focuses on British writers (like Samuel Johnson and James Boswell) who were adept at taking these seized moments and constructing a "diurnal narrative of the self" for public consumption (186). These writers produced diurnal narratives that were critical and selective rather than exhaustive, that were interesting to read, and that skillfully straddled the line between the public and private, spaces in which they felt equally at home. In other words, the diurnal form began to look much more literary and occasioned in the hands of these male writers. By choosing to follow the tradition erected by male diarists, Sherman misses the opportunity to see how women continue to capitalize on the rhetorical opportunities originally afforded by the diurnal form, maintaining the form's initial connection to temporality. Sherman's eventual return to narrative means that he abandons the inscription of dailiness — the registration of measured time on the page — that was continued over the next century by female diary writers.

Annie's diary and ordinary diaries like hers further Sherman's argument much more forcefully than the published diaries of the men he chooses to follow. While the experience of time as being repetitive, monotonous, measured, and successive may have been a new experience to Pepys, one that would manifest itself in his writing in transformative and radical ways, women have historically and primarily experienced time as measured rather than occasioned. Their movement from a "new" horology to the inscription of that horology would hardly have been radical as much as it would have been obvious, almost natural. The repetition found in sewing, baking, cleaning, mending, the repetition found in menstruating, birthing, dying, the repetition of letter writing and letter reading, the repetition in waiting, waiting, waiting — in fact the general measuredness of women's bodies, tasks, and days assures both their skill and promise at translating the experience of "time in" to the page. They, women diarists of the nineteenth century, become the writers to watch when charting the impact of a new temporality on form. If the rise of diurnal form begins with a change in horology, then we need to examine the writings of those for whom the "change" was no change at all but rather an opportunity to translate experience into written form. We need to consider how the "new" form simply gave women the space to inscribe what they had been living for centuries.

*   *   *

An ordinary writer, a strategic writer, an experienced writer, Annie is aware of the limits and potentials of the diurnal form. I suggest that she capitalizes on the features afforded by the dailiness of her form to conduct work that is useful to her and that complicates her position as a maker of texts. Sometimes this use means, simply, that her diary serves as a repository for lists or notes to herself. Other times, the use is more complicated and has to do with managing multiple roles, conveying the fullness of "time in," or documenting an unnamable reality. The map she makes, the reduction of her days to the space on the page, are always in line with the opportunities afforded by dailiness.

Annie is not merely writing within a diurnal tradition — she is furthering that tradition by extending the ability of the diurnal form to remain open, measured, and ongoing. And she uses the diary's tool-like ability to capture unmarked moments for her own purposes. Already living dailiness, she will use the diurnal form to replicate the fullness of "time in" rather than encapsulate "time when." Already ticking through her chores accompanied by the tick, tick, tick of the clock, she will capitalize on the repetitive and successive possibilities promised by the diurnal form, remaining in the middle of things and eschewing an end either to her mending or to her writing. Well-versed in her own absence, her own lack of importance to the larger world, she will utilize the possibility of tending to the in-between moments of the daily to name that which typically passes undocumented. What she does with what she seizes is testament not only to her skill as an ordinary writer but also to the power of ordinary writing.

* * *

My dad has always loved tools. He collects them — or maybe accumulates is a better word — like one might accumulate lint or used twist ties. Growing up, tools were what we gave my father for his birthday, for Christmas, and for Father's Day. Drill bits, socket sets, radial arm saws, welding equipment, measuring tapes, levels, even an engine hoist. I think I knew the difference between a flathead screwdriver and a Phillips before I could talk. And I knew that every job required certain, specific tools. A flathead screwdriver would no more work on certain screws than a half-inch drill bit would make an eighth-inch hole. This was because, working with my dad, you needed to know tools by name, produce them when asked, and put them in their proper place when the job was done. Tools were serious business.

They were also a source of tension. Dreaded words heard as a child were, "Your father needs help in the garage." Whenever my dad was working on the car, building a deck, or remodeling the bathroom, I would make myself scarce, climb into the television, a tree fort, even into my homework. It rarely worked. Typically my mom would track me down. Take this flashlight and putty knife up to the bathroom where your father is installing the new shower liner. Put on a coat and help your father in the garage with the van. Flashlights, pliers, plumb lines, chain saws, wood saws, bow saws, harp saws. In the garage, under a car, atop the roof. I have helped him build decks, rebuild engines, lay foundation, replace plumbing, rewire, install, tear down, and reroof. All the while holding, lugging, and using his tools.

I sit on the concrete floor of the garage, my knees up against the tire of the car, reading the rubber letters — G O O D Y E A R — as my dad works away. His voice comes to me from somewhere under the engine, his bent knees shooting out below the bumper. Medium crescent wrench. I hand my dad, surgeonlike, the tools as he calls for them. Locating them in the toolbox, the workroom, on hooks attached to a pegboard wall. Often he does not even name the tool he needs but trusts that I will anticipate the one that comes next, that I will know: stubby Phillips. His grease-covered hand emerges from the axle, open and waiting. "Anticipate," he urges. I scurry for the socket or the flashlight — being careful not to shine it in his eyes but rather where I think his eyes want to be looking.

My dad's tools were also dangerous. They could kill. Or so he would say. Power tools and electric saws, soldering irons and welding tanks. He would tell me, at the age of eight, that if I didn't hold this board just right, didn't pull the cord in this direction, failed to keep these two wires from touching, that he would die. And (he didn't need to say this) it would be my fault. All because I wasn't paying attention, wasn't anticipating. Then the saw would whirl or the ice-blue light of the welder glow, and I would try my very hardest not to let that board move, not to let the ends touch, not to kill my father. Whether it was or not, when working with my dad's tools, I often felt like his life was in my hands.

My mom's tools were never a site of conflict or death; in particular I am thinking of her sewing tools. Unlike my dad's, her tools didn't have names or if they did I didn't know them. They didn't line up like soldiers along the wall but piled around her workspace. My dad had a workroom but my mom would sew in whatever room contained the most people at the moment, most often the family room. Unlike my dad's giant workbench that was bolted to the wall, my mom set up her sewing machine on a folding table or maybe the desk if it wasn't too cluttered. She would sit with us at night, near the fireplace, her Elna humming fast along the straight seams and slower around the curves. Pins in her mouth, laying patterns out, a yellow measuring tape around her neck like a lei.

I loved being with my mom as she sewed. To witness the transformation of flat, squared cloth into fabulous jumpsuits and dresses. How fast she urged the sewing machine, fingers never in the way, how quickly she could thread its needle, conjure the bobbin thread up from its home, crank the wheel by hand to pop free a stuck needle. It was always a mystery, like the rising of bread. Yet neither she nor I ever doubted that it would happen. Her tools were never simply tools. The cams for her sewing machine, black and round the size of Oreos, could be stacked in towers or rolled along the floor. The different stitches each cam produced could make buttonholes or hold seams doubly tight. Buttons from the tin button box made the knobby eyes of our sock puppets or could be strung together for bracelets or sorted and resorted into piles of shiny, round, square, and flat. The empty wooden spools, the gangly sewing machine feet, and the bobbins layered in different colors of thread — winding a short history of her most recent sewing projects — all available and waiting for her, for me.

In her own work it never mattered which tool she used. She could rip a seam just as easily with a pair of scissors or her teeth as she could with a seam ripper. She could face a collar, line a suit, or add length to my pants with just scraps of material she kept in the bottom drawer of my little brother's dresser. Without a pattern, with only paper and a tape measure: a shirt for my dad. She made do with what was there, what was in easy reach, what would hold a pattern in place long enough for her to cut it out and be on to the next thing, not what was supposed to hold the pattern. A shoe, a brick, the thick edge of a book.

My mom used tools as a way to keep going. She made them work for her. Her tools had multiple lives, multiple uses. And she was economical in their use; she didn't have enough of them for them to only perform one function. The brick that had fallen out of the fireplace wall, now holding the door open, became a pattern weight and then my Barbie bed. When my dad used his tools it was an end in itself — a specific, purposeful end. The tool he chose was the right tool, the only tool for the job — a tool that could be anticipated by an eight-year-old, a tool that lived one life. There was no flexibility, no room for error, no way to make the ballpeen hammer stand in for the saw. And then there was always death.[9]

What makes a tool a tool is that it is put to use, not that it comes from a toolbox or off the workroom wall. The brick was a pattern holder because my mom needed it to be, just as Annie's diary becomes an accounting book when she needs it to be, or a scrapbook, or a place to record the fact that her third wedding anniversary went unmarked by her own husband. The diary is not an end in itself; in fact it is not even a diary until she uses it as one. Like my mother, she is economic as well in her use, always conserving. That Annie is in charge of making the diary useful to her stands in stark relief to her own use, one that is perpetually being threatened by the weather, the plains, hard work, hungry stomachs, infidelity, and a cultural engine that works to erase women rather than sustain them. What she makes is an artifact, a material text, that gives evidence, among other things, to the tool-user's existence. In that way, it is as haunted as it is useful.[10]

• • •

Annie's diary is old, over a hundred years old. The ink is faded, the pages bent and thinning to the point of translucence. The edges of the cover are torn, the binding broken and loose; small pieces of the book hang by strands and strips. Only one copy exists and it is threatening disintegration. It is a trace — both of its former self and of the woman who kept it.

In actuality, Annie's diary is not a diary — or at least not specifically meant to be a diary. During the nineteenth century, the apogee of diary writing, books were produced specifically for the purposes of keeping a diary. Small, usually small enough to fit in a pocket for travel, these books were published each calendar year. The first few pages frequently contained an almanac for the year, astrological forecasts, the prices for postage, tax information, and other odd and seemingly useful bits and pieces. The pages that followed were already marked with the date and empty, lined space. In general there would be two dated entries per page. At the end of the book there would typically be a small pocket between the cover and the pages for cuttings, notes, and keepsakes.

In reading commercially produced diaries like these I have wondered what such a book would tell a nineteenth-century woman about what it means to keep a diary.[11] On some level the diary would serve as a dual reference — a reference for the public world of postage and taxes and likewise a reference for the personal world. There is the implication that one will be returning to the diary again and again for information, that it is a document of use. The fact that the yearly almanac shares space with daily entries indicates that weather intersects in meaningful ways with the daily, or should. The same is true for astrology. At the very least, the inclusion of information on postage and taxes speaks to the practicality and readiness of the diary. That you might, perchance, have your diary with you when you went to town or mailed a letter. Just as the allotted space for each entry suggests the amount of appropriate information a day should yield.

Even though Annie does not write in such a diary, her diary does demonstrate in many ways that she is fully aware of diary discourse, a discourse that was shaped by and gives shape to the production of these mass-produced books. For example, each entry of Annie's documents the weather even though her diary is not framed by an almanac. And Annie uses the space in her diary for the useful tracking of visits, letters sent and received, and anniversaries. Broadly, the content of the entries largely duplicates historical expectations of a diary's content.[12] The weather is most often followed by the chores she has done that day in the order that they were done, and then she typically mentions what Charley has done that day. Sometimes the final line of the entry is separated from the text and given to more reflective comments. She might recall an anniversary: "Three years ago Dear Mother was very ill little did I think then that her trouble would end fatally. What a trying time it was." She might use the space, if Charley is absent, to wonder how or where he is. She might record how she feels physically or make a wish for the future. At rare moments, she ends her entry by referring to a public event like the shooting of President Garfield or a local hanging. Generally, what Annie writes about in her diary are topics not vastly different from what other nineteenth-century diarists were writing about — even though she is not writing in a commercially produced volume. Such an observation reveals some of the ways in which Annie's diary writing is determined or constrained by such cultural factors. But how she chooses physically to map or represent the content is more in her charge and where the work of the diarist is most clearly seen.

Rather than writing in a commercially produced diary, Annie initially chooses to write in a ledger book that is seventeen inches long and six inches wide. Originally meant for accounting, each page is lined vertically and horizontally, creating numbers of thin columns for recording financial transactions. Because so many pages have been torn from the beginning, middle, and end of the book it is difficult to tell the original number of pages — at least 134. Annie uses this book for the first two and a half years of her diary keeping.[13] While the reason that Annie initially chooses a blank book as a diary is a point of conjecture, it is not a point of inconsequence or happenstance. When Charley chooses a diary to keep during his travels out west in the winter of 1881, he selects a commercially produced volume. It is a book specifically meant to serve as a diary. While it lacks the framing materials of a lady's diary, it does afford lined entries for the events of each day. Annie's choice of the ledger book, then, is not necessarily an economic one (i.e., there is enough money to buy at least one commercially produced volume); it must also speak to how she wants to use her diary.

On the most basic level, of course, Charley will be traveling; Annie will not. He needs a diary that can fit easily into his pocket. Annie rarely leaves the yard. Even that point is too conciliatory, though, because on the occasions that Annie does travel (to see the dentist or take care of her father), she often takes her diary with her. This indicates that Annie chooses to write in a ledger book rather than a diary for more than simply geographical reasons. The fact that Charley can and does travel means that his days are structured in event-full ways — he writes about what it is like to be on the trail, to witness "Indian outbreaks," to roam the West. The space he occupies is larger than even Pepys's London. It is the whole frontier. At night, he fills the prelined entries of his diary with the occasion of his days, noting the distances traveled, the towns passed through, the people, the number of horses shod, the sight of the Rio Grande.

Annie's days are not structured by occasion, by larger public events; rather they are marked by repetition and measure. Any structure to her measured days is one she must impose. Confined to a claim shanty three miles from town, her dailiness is less event-full than that found by rambling the frontier, even, I would propose, less occasioned than the minutelike blocks a commercial diary affords to the day. Both her day and her page sprawl before her, bounded only by daylight and margins. In many ways she has to bring order to her time and represent that order on the page. She makes a savvy choice in a blank book for a diary, a book with capacity enough in its pages to map the complexities of her time and space. More important still, as we will see, it is a book that can serve multiple purposes at one time. Because her pages are not confined, not predetermined, she graphically and rhetorically registers the fullness, the sheer accumulation of her days. Seeing her choice of the blank book as deliberate rather than given, opens up to us the possibility of seeing how other material choices equally reveal a strategic writer.

* * *

To demonstrate how Annie replicates dailiness in her diary, I want to look closely at a single page from her diary. A hybrid set of entries, the example testifies to the literal and textual tensions Annie negotiates in her day and on her page.

What perhaps strikes us initially in looking at this example is the list of expenditures that accompanies the daily entries, a list documenting the purchase of tools for Charley's blacksmith shop in Bridgewater. Though the majority of the diary is dedicated to daily entries, Annie does use her book at times to track financial transactions. On one of the initial pages (initial in that it is one of the first remaining pages) there are references to other pages that no longer exist, for example "Jackson p. 39," and "Little Chief Mill p. 32." These references hint at business dealings that appeared at one point on these pages. In addition, there are financial records contained within the actual diary. For example, on a page containing entries for October 1882 there is a short record made of the purchase of a single cow. McCarthy suggests in her essay "A Pocketful of Days" that it was not unusual for women in the nineteenth century to use their diaries to track financial matters as well as chores or letters. She suggests that such tracking was encouraged by the publishers in the layout of the preprinted diaries and "answered the needs of a society bent on keeping accurate records of their families as well as household and business accounts."[14] Publishers met this need by marketing diaries that were part almanac, part cost record, and part daily entry, in effect determining through layout what should happen in a diary. While, as McCarthy demonstrates, diarists often extended their work beyond the suggestions made by publishers, what makes Annie's diary significant is that, as a blank book rather than a preprinted diary, it becomes her decision as to when it will serve what purpose. Because she does not record financial matters often, let alone daily, when she does we have to consider her intention, purpose, and approach.

What is interesting about these accounts are the ways in which they help graphically depict the fullness of writing in the days. The above list of tools appears in the top margin of page 95 in the diary and continues well into, intersects with, the space typically given to daily entries. Where we would normally expect to see daily entries, then, we find a list of expenditures. One way in which the inclusion of such a list in her diary is useful to her is that it documents initial investment and financial status. They will need to recoup that money in the business to

Cost of Tools &c

Blower	25 00
Screw Plate	32 00
Anvil Vise & Figure	27 00
2 Wrenches	1 75
1 Hammer	1 75
Lot Second Hand Tools	5 50
Rasp	1 50

Ray Rasp &c Rasp Bridgewater
Bismark

Annie
Annie
Annie

(some text Home)

1881

August — about. It seems as though we have a home
now, & did not feel well this A M. sewed
a little. Afternoon & washed. Walter carried
water for me, and went to him with some
Butter, and made a few purchases for me.
I am very tired. I wonder how the baby
is getting along.

"   11

Thursday — Very pleasant. Watch came about 5
this morning and I got up and let him
in. I do not feel as well as usual today and have not for several days.
Charley is going to Mitchell tonight on
land business.

12

A hybrid set of entries from Annie's diary.

pay their loans. Charley and Annie can return to the list if necessary — either to recall the kinds of tools purchased or amount spent. Yet, more is happening on this page than simply record keeping.

The space is further embellished by — in fact is overlapped by — Annie's sketch of their claim shanty, the only drawing in the ledger book. We also see her daily entry butting up against the sketch. Annie's daily entries, her sketch, the list of tools — these three documents of daili-ness — overlap on the page and allow Annie to map multiple moments within the same physical space. Almost like hypertext, the page is lay-ered in dailiness: she records, in detail, the number and cost of Charley's tools, she documents the days for August 1881, and she draws their first home together. While such economy of page space speaks to their own financial status, it also works to graphically depict the kinds of con-straints pulling on them — the financial imbedded in, even in conversa-tion with, the intimate or ordinary thrumming the day. These realities — the daily weather and the financial strain of a new business — are neither experienced separately by the writer nor inscribed separately on the page.

Neither does the list of expenditures replace her passage through space — does not replace her day — as Pepys's carriage fares stand in for his movement or even in the same way that Charley tracks his move-ment through the West largely by how much money he makes each day shoeing horses or how far he travels during the day. The list is not placed in a separate section of the ledger book. Neither is the drawing a doodle in the margins. Rather both accompany physically the other work of her day, a day that cannot be tracked solely by expenditures or by the weather but must account for all. Her day is not defined by a sin-gle event, a single occasion, and it should not, therefore, be surprising to find that her diary is not dedicated to a singular purpose (i.e., a record of the days), but rather each document of dailiness bleeds into the next, signaling, replicating the connection, the tick, tick, tick of her days. The way she uses her diary — to capture the complexity of her life — reflects the multiple roles she must negotiate as well as the pos-sibilties found in writing in the days rather than of them.

And "use" is the precise verb to describe the approach Annie takes to this blank book. Annie does not begin her diary on page 1 of the ledger book, rather she places the entry for January 15, 1881, on page 68, gen-erally the middle of the book. Even though (as we will see below) the pages immediately preceding Annie's initial entry are empty, she does not begin where the blue numbers indicate one should begin: page 1. Significantly, she derails the only ordering directive given by her chosen book. In doing so, Annie replicates the middleness of the diurnal form, literally refusing to give her diary a beginning. She begins in the middle of the week, in the middle of her life, in the middle of the book.

For the next many diary pages the year 1881 unfolds diurnally, each page bearing the year in the top margin in Annie's hand. On page 122 the year 1882 begins, right on the heels of 1881. However, Annie runs out of space on page 134 — or seems to. The entry for Saturday, June 24, 1882, is the final entry on the bottom of page 134. The binding indicates the existence of more pages originally, but these are now cut away in neatly razored cuts right at the binding. Whatever documents followed, they must have preexisted because at this point Annie returns to an earlier page in the book and continues writing her diary. Pages are removed in the middle of entries as well: in August and December of 1881 and August, September, and December of 1882. But the diary continues as if these interstitial pages never existed, the diarist moving in and out of other, now lost, writing without ever halting the continuity of days. Either these pages were already full with other documents and therefore in need of negotiation by Annie and then later (by her or someone else) cut out, or she wrote something else on these pages at the same time that she was keeping a diary and then removed them at a later date (either due to irrelevance or embarrassment).

The majority of the above documents no longer remain, leaving the daily entries as the only writing in the ledger book. You can tell that Annie made her diary fit into the leftover spaces not by knowing what occupies the other spaces but by seeing how Annie fills out the remaining ones. A few months into 1883, Annie bumps up against the entry for January 15, 1881. The ledger book, now full. Appearing random, even crazed, with days and years running in and out of other texts (at the same time hardly losing a day), what she has when she fills the blank book is the closest possible representation of the multiple moments of the day as well as the multiple positions she occupies within the day, that of wife, accountant, poet, writer, cook, painter, reader, boarding house maid. How different the effect would be had she written in any other way.

In addition to reproducing the accumulation of her days, though, the fact that Annie negotiates these other documents, these other products of dailiness, rather than produces a chronological and seamless account of days, is significant for another reason. The point speaks to

Annie's choice to write a diary rather than something else. While business dealings probably inhabited some of these other pages, there is evidence that Annie may have used some of this space as a place for other kinds of writing. For example, on page 58 (ten pages before she actually begins her diary on January 15, 1881) she has written some verses about the New Year (dated January 1, 1881). These lines of verse are not in the margin but begin on the first lines of the page. At the bottom of the verse, Annie has written "1882" followed by entries for November of that year. The verses, then, occupied page space long before the daily entries made a year later. It was not unusual in the nineteenth century for women to fill their diaries with verse (both their own and the verse of published poets), a residual of commonplace books. And Annie's diary is dotted with examples — none however as long or privileged enough to occupy their own space. As far as I can tell, the poem is hers and as such it indicates that Annie used at least some parts of her ledger book for creative writing, quite possibly the writing that she refers to now and then in the diary.

What makes such a realization so significant is that it indicates Annie saw discursive options. She did not see her diary writing as the only kind of writing she was capable of or allowed to produce. In her book *Mormon Healer and Folk Poet: Mary Susannah Fowler's Life of "Unselfish Usefulness,"* Margaret Brady demonstrates how Fowler, a healer, poet, and diarist in the nineteenth century, used the diary discourse when it seemed most useful to her and relied on other kinds of writing for other kinds of work. In other words, the choice in diary writing was a conscious choice made on the part of the writer in recognition of what that form of writing could do. Brady suggests that the diurnal form, for Fowler, was appropriate for "particular discursive goals." [15]

While Annie does not publish these other kinds of writing, unlike Fowler, and while these moments are rare and largely conjecture on my part based on hints in her entries, missing pages, and the very, very few examples of verse, they do indicate that Annie was aware of other forms of writing and chose the diurnal form. Perhaps, like Fowler, she liked the restrictions of the diaristic form. As we will see in the next chapter, the order called for by the diurnal form allowed Annie to conduct work imperative to her own self-preservation.

We continue to see Annie replicate her experience of dailiness when she switches to loose pages once the blank book is filled. A haphazard collection of random pieces of paper, these pages have been folded or cut to approximately the same size — seven inches by four. While this is a significantly smaller page size than the ledger book, there are even fewer textual directives about how Annie should use the pages. For instance, there are no page numbers or other ordering devices. She dates each loose page carefully with month, day, and year. There is also nothing that binds the pages or holds them together. They simply sit in a bundle, folded in half like tiny books. In addition, when she switches diaries from the ledger book to the blank pages she leaves behind the ordering directives of both lines and margins.

Most of these pages are large ledger pages that bear the heading "Bought of Ray and Bennett: Wagon Makers and Horse Shoeing. Miners Tools a Specialty." These sheets were apparently taken from the accounting books of Charley's blacksmith business in Leadville (a business that would have been defunct a few years prior to 1883). Annie also relies on forms from the railroad, a document for filing an accident report. It includes such questions as: "How did the animal get on the track, and through whose negligence?" and "Who disposed of the carcass and hide?" As they do with the headings from Charley's business account, her entries ignore these questions, maneuvering in, out, and around them. In these pages we see a writer even more in charge of dividing and filling her space, a writer who is even more willing to engage with the remaining preprinted obstacles on the page (a point discussed more fully in the next section).

In addition to the ways these pages demonstrate her agency as a writer, we also see her economy. Not her economy of language, which is certainly there, but her economy of page space. In addition to the above pages, Annie also uses a sheet of lined paper dated in pencil September 30, 1882, and containing the start of a letter Charley wrote to a business client. The letter ends in midsentence where Annie's entries, documenting days in September 1883, begin. This small piece of paper, hardly more than a scrap and the only one of its kind in the bundle, was saved for more than a year before being put to use as a diary page. In this way, we see both how she makes do with what is within reach and how everything in her day, in her days, must serve multiple purposes. From her ledger book to the loose pages, almost no page is put to singular use. Pages, like her days, are cycled and recycled.

Because both the ledger book and the loose pages are basically blank, in addition to the order of her entries Annie is also in charge of determining their length and their placement on the page. She writes with little textual indication as to how much space her days are worth and, as a result, Annie's entries assume different amounts of space at different times, depending on where and when she is writing. A quick survey indicates that over the course of four years the average number of lines per entry is seven. But she does not hesitate to vary the length: the shortest entry is one line (June 19, 1881: "Washed & made Bread. Pleasant") and the longest is fifty-four lines (March 2, 1883: recounting the dream she has). Generally speaking, her entries are longer in 1882 than in the other three years and often her entries are longer toward the end of the year (October, November, and December) than in the beginning or middle of the year, possibly because she has more time to write in the winter. While she may be limited by how much time she has to write (versus how much work she has to do), she is not being limited by the page or an apparent belief in how much space her days are worth.

She also makes decisions based on the conservation of space. When Annie begins keeping a diary in the ledger book she writes one line of text per printed line. Each page of the ledger book has forty-five lines so each of the initial pages also contains forty-five written lines. This begins changing in August of 1881 when she presses two written lines into one printed line (apparently to get all of the August 5 entry onto the same page). She compresses her writing again in the August 22 entry (this time apparently to make it difficult to read as most of the entry is also inked out). By October of 1881 she is alternating (sometimes within the same entry) between using one printed line per written line and compressing two lines into one. This occurs seemingly at random until all of a sudden in the middle of the October 27 entry she moves back into compressed lines and never returns to one written line per printed line. Her writing becomes much smaller and tighter at this point. The lines are only about one-fourth of an inch wide to begin with and now two lines of prose fill this small space. So instead of four or five entries per page there are thirteen or so. The entries themselves do not get shorter, just more cramped. By the time she is writing on blank pages, both the size of her writing and the shape of her entries changes. Such decisions on Annie's part — in concert with those mentioned above — continue to reveal how she is in charge of her text, choosing the discourse, the form, the content, the shape, and the purpose of her days.

*　*　*

My point here is that Annie is not tentative in her approach to her diary. She does not start on the first page of the ledger book and work until the end. She does not keep her writing to one written line per pre-printed line. Nor does she wait for outside instructions as to the form her diary should assume. She takes charge of her diary and of her writing. While, as we will see, the content of many entries reproduces her powerlessness and lack of control, the ways she uses her diary reveal it as a space where she can also set boundaries. In particular, she decides where to begin, where to end, and what purposes the ledger book will serve. The facility with which she moves in, out, and around other information demonstrates her agility as a writer to realize the openness of her form and to capitalize on its ability to document her experience of dailiness, the experience of being a woman living on the plains in the late nineteenth century writing in the days.

In reading ordinary diaries the risk is in limiting our understanding of what the ordinary writer is making. Annie puts her diary to use in complicated and layered ways. Some uses are obvious, for example the list of tools she makes and how much they cost. The money spent on Charley's tools is an enormous sum — over a hundred dollars. In contrast, at one point Annie bakes biscuits for an entire group of transient workers and is paid twenty-five cents for the job. By remaining with this example, though, we can see her using her page space in a more complex way, in a way more congruent with Sherman's understanding of the diary as a "document of the self," a tool for self-knowledge. In March of 1883 Annie is going through a particularly difficult time. On March 2, she records at great length a dream she has about Charley and his affair with M. H. Entries during this time are marked by her anxiety — often she is "thinking, thinking, thinking." Additionally, the decision to move to town is seemingly made without her input. She is angry. On March 28, 1883, she ends her entry with the number 95. On the following day she writes, "I made out an account today, a very novel one." It is the only time in four years that she explicitly refers to accounting of any kind within the diary entries. And one of the few times that she qualifies her work with any adjectives (see the next chapter). The number 95 continues to appear at the ends of entries — particularly when she is upset.

Page 95 of her diary contains the account of Charley's tools (see p. 104). At first glance it hardly seems "novel" in any way. That is until you look more closely. At the end of the account, following the final entry for a rasp and mixed in with a sketch Annie has done of their claim as well as the beginning of the entry for August of 1881, she has written "Ray Rasp Rasp." By her hand, the tool morphs into her husband and back again — and the two become physically linked in the ways they are both harsh and grating. It is possible that Annie was just doodling, that "95" refers to something else, that this account is not novel. But it is also possible that Annie is using her page space to carve a place where she can document the specifics of her sadness in a time and place where women were not allowed to talk about themselves.[16] We certainly see her literally inscribing her identity, her presence, in the way that she writes her own name over and over on the same page. She uses her diary to assert her identity and concretize the hierarchy of tools and privilege, seizing an unmarked moment and naming an unnamable reality. If nothing else, the possibilities presented by this complicated entry should make us hesitant to limit the agency we ascribe to Annie as a writer.

In the final section of this chapter, I want to look closer at the map Annie makes, the outcomes of dailiness. Keeping in mind that dailiness is the defining feature of the diurnal form and that the form of diary writing will register dailiness, I want to suggest that Annie strategically extends the capacity of the diurnal form to remain open and measured by creating ongoing interactions or conversations within her text. We begin to see evidence of these layered interactions in the way financial accounts communicate with the weather as well as with her anger at her husband — all within the same space — or the way in which the entries engage with other, now missing, writing. Rather than presenting a single, linear story of a day, she works to replicate the experience of being in days. These interactions between her entries and other writing or between the weather and the bills are part of a larger conversational strategy Annie employs in the structure of her diary. It creates a conversational experience that she quite literally can have in no other way.

Annie is alone much of the time. Often physically isolated. By herself in a claim shanty or working for others at a boarding house, in a historical period in which female friendships were not only important but requisite for female well-being, Annie is without any close female friends. Such isolation makes the occasional visitor she does have an enormous event; the letters she sends and receives are lifeblood. Charley, in particular, is gone much of the time — sometimes for an entire winter, often for the day. She cannot walk to the neighbor's, to her father's, or to town but must wait for others to visit her or must borrow a horse so that she can ride. Her loneliness and her lack of daily communication appear at times in her daily entries.

Jan[uary] 18
[1881]
Tuesday
This is a beautiful warm day. Oh! that my life was beautiful, warm, and sunny too. It is such heartaching as this which makes people grow old before their time. It is bad enough to be separated from my Husband, but not to hear from him for so long makes it ten times worse. I am so lonesome. But I am unwise to feel like this.

Mar[ch] 7
[1881]
Sunday
Very warm and pleasant. But cloudy this evening Had to make bread today, as we were out. and only got flour yesterday. I have a head-ache. and my cheeks have burned all day. I wonder when Charley will come. My life seems so strange and lonesome. There are two things I crave above all things, a home and perfect rest, where I will not have to work so hard to earn my daily bread I am so tired.

[January] 14
[1882]
Saturday
It was very frosty last night. Today is very pleasant. We got up late. I made a Bed Tick for David this P.M. knit a little. How nice it would be to see Charley this evening.

Less explicitly, her desire for ongoing interaction is found in the way that she maps her days. In thinking about conversational strategies, I am not suggesting that she develops a substitute friendship with her diary or that her diary is her confidant. Many diary scholars have pointed to the ways in which, historically, women would name their diaries — for example, Hester Thrale named her diary Thralina and Anne Frank had Kitty — or would confide in their diaries as they would a friend — Dear Diary — in order to reproduce or extend the network of female friendships.[17] These scholars suggest that through the act of writing the diarist is able to both create and sustain a sense of self that is otherwise being socially and politically discounted, because the diary plays the role of listener in the absence of close female friends.

While I would not suggest that such a relationship is not the case for some diary writing, I do think such arguments can be potentially limiting in terms of how we think about the capacity of the diurnal form and also in terms of which diaries we decide to read. Seeing the diary as simply a partner in a conversation focuses the discussion on the content of the diary and requires that the diarist tell *of* her day in occasioned, narrated ways. So, for example, when Hampsten contends that women's private writing is conversational writing, she looks to letters rather than diaries and to content rather than form in order to demonstrate conversational qualities. The emphasis on content, however, and the occasion of a specific conversation necessitate narrative qualities that discount or fail to include more ordinary diaries.

Seeing the diary as an extension of a network of female friendship or the reproduction of women's culture puts the focus and the value on the quality of the conversation (wit, stories, flair, ability). Annie's diary would fail to measure up. Instead, I am looking at how her choices as a writer reproduce conversation. She is not having a conversation *with* her diary but *within* her diary. It may seem a minor point, but thinking about the interactions within her diary allows us to move away from what Annie says of a day (the sparse content of her diary and the values we might place on that content) and toward how she replicates, through writing, the experience of being in the days.

. . .

I have already mentioned the fact that financial matters and other documents of dailiness interact with the weather and the crops in ways that graphically register the reality that none of these moments are experienced in isolation by the writer but are always in conversation with each other. I have also briefly noted how Annie's entries converse on the page with her own verse as well as that of other writers. Often these verses are in the margins, but at other times they appear quite suddenly in the text. An entry might look like this:

Saturday, March 19 [1881]
Clear but drifting pretty hard Finished repairing black dress, and sewed a little on Wrapper. Do not feel well enough to do much. Time seems so long. It looks just like mid winter yet. "The days are

cold and dark and dreary" And so is my life. I wish I was one of the kind who cares for nothing "Who cares for nothing alone is free."
I feel strangely.

In the above example, Annie imbeds the words of others within her entry and, in doing so, intertextually converses with the work of that writer, or more accurately with the sentiments of that writer. She is not drawing the writer into conversation with her. The lines are decontextualized. They appear unauthored — quotation marks being the only evidence that another text has entered her days. Untethered within the entry, they refer to nothing in particular and to the entire day at the same time. Like a stone tossed into a pond, this disembodied reference ripples outward, increasing the space of the entry and extending her days beyond the page. The conversation keeps going.

She creates other conversations when she writes about the books, both fiction and nonfiction, that she has been reading. In her diary, she sometimes notes that she has begun a novel or has finished one. Every now and then she will make a qualifying remark as to whether she enjoyed her reading. The practice of documenting the books she reads is not atypical of nineteenth-century diary keeping in any way. I only make note of the way in which these books, like the verses she quotes, participate in the openness of her days and the openness of her chosen form of writing. In the example below, Annie's reference to *Woman Our Angel* physically continues her day beyond what appears to be an initial boundary. Her day overflows. In this particular example, the final line also reverberates with impossible conversations. While the untethered verse in the above example refers to no one and everyone at the same time, rippling outward, she cannot afford this comment to have even a general reference.

Jan[uary] 28
[1881]
Friday
A telegram from Mrs Granger says she is on the way home. So I can go soon. Made Apple Dumplings for dinner and Cinnamon Rolls for Supper.
Mrs Stiffler done them both justice. My thoughts all day have been with one who is near and dear to me. Home is where the heart is hundreds of miles from here.

Have just finished reading "woman our Angel." According to that a good many women might claim to be angels.

At a slant, Annie engages in social critique, or at the very least personal critique. Whether Annie is openly questioning the role of woman as angel of the house or only the actions of the women around her — actions she has criticized in earlier times — is unclear. But this conversation between her diary and another text opens a space that contains the possibility of critique. As Kathleen Stewart so convincingly argues in *A Space on the Side of the Road,* simply pushing open a formerly unrealized space — she uses the metaphor of a car breaking down along the side of a road — allows the possibility of new ways of knowing and telling. While Annie cannot write explicitly about personal and social constraints, simply conversing with other texts in her entries opens a space filled with the promise of what cannot be said.

The above examples contemplate the form of Annie's entries and the interactional ways that she maps that space. Turning to the conversations between her text and margins or her written text and preprinted texts complicates that mapped space and the work of the writer. In the ledger book, Annie uses the left margin to write the date. She then keeps her entry, for the most part, in the body of the page. So a typical entry spatially looks like this:

[January] 2nd   Very cold. I put away all our wraps last night so I
[1883]   did not have that to do today. I have had a severe
Tuesday   headache most of the day. did nothing but sit
                around the stove all day to keep warm. I practiced
                the guitar this eve.

However, when she moves to the loose pages she no longer minds either the preprinted lines or margins. Her writing becomes more cramped and less mindful of leaving empty, marginal space. This is partially due to the fact that she is folding pages and what was once the left margin is no longer, but it also points to the ways she makes the materials she has work for her. The lines are also no longer horizontal nor do they run evenly the entire length of the page, so it is less clear where one might begin or end. Additionally, unlike the ledger book, there are now impediments to her writing — the printed heading of the accounting pages and the questions on the railroad form. She must choose to negotiate them or disregard them and determine how important it is to her to keep her writing legible. What this ultimately means for the writer is that her diary is even less constrained physically. She now draws lines to separate entries, naming her own boundaries, and she darts in and out of the printed words, conversing with their Gothic presence. A typical entry could look more like this:

Thursday 8 Pleasant very warm. I am feeling
& Bennett some better
sewed a few carpet rags am almost through. Wrote a letter to Mrs. Flint
BLACKSMITHS went up town this eve. Stopped in Mrs. Hapgood's went to
ing prayer meeting with her **Miners Tools a Specialty.**

Annie insists that her entries interact with the account book heading. She could have easily begun below the preprinted words or written over them completely. Instead she chooses to engage with them. Like financial matters, the weather, and her loneliness, these large black words are part of her day. She could have chosen to structure her diary differently, found another ledger book, purchased a commercial diary, or only written in areas of large white space, but she didn't. That decision speaks not only to her desire for conversation but also to her understanding of her chosen form.

A great deal of interaction also happens in the margins of Annie's diary, in large part because the margins represent the most logical place to extend the day, to continue her conversations.[18] What she writes in the margin might be an extension of her day or, less often, a thought or feeling not "allowed" within the more formal space of the day's entry. It is not readily apparent when Annie chooses to write in the margins rather than the body of the entry — or which position is the more privileged space — the important point is that Annie strategically taps into the ability of the diurnal form to replicate these measured spaces, embedding them within each other.

Sometimes her decision to move to the margins is one based on spatial constraints. For instance, on January 31, 1881 (the last entry of the year), she runs out of page space while writing her entry. Perhaps because of the orderliness found in starting the new year on a new page, she chooses to complete the entry in the margins. She adds two separate comments:

June 15. 1895. Friday

we had a light rain last night. A. S. BENNETT. It has been very warm all day. I have done a good deal of work today. adville, Colorado, this a.m. I made curtains for Fathers Bed.

I done a great deal 16. Saturday Exceedingly warm. of work today made a large batch **BENNETT** of bread. an cleaned things up generally. Business in the shop has BLACKSMITHS, only been moderately lively this week.

Miners Tools a Specialty.

Sunday. 17. Cloudy and warm. C- intended to go down to the farm today but it Jefferson Avenue, near Locust Street. looked so much like rain that he did not go. I have so much to do that it seems I can hardly get a spare moment (untell after noon any- way) on sunday no matter how well I do up the work on Saturday. Read a good deal this P.m.

Monday Very pleasant- I done my washing and done a lot of other work. I got my Photos tonight- they are pretty good. we had to fix the Bedcord tonight-

Tuesday 19 This has been a beautiful day. I churned Ironed and browned coffee this a.m. and P.m. Sewed a good deal. Jane and Baby were here a while this P.m. my head aches and I feel sick.

Wednesday 20 It rained this morning. also thundered & lightened but cleared off about 8.oclock. Has been pleasant since. I have sewed a good deal today. Miss B. Smith and Mrs Laughlin called today to solicite aid for the church.

Thursday 21 very pleasant. I made Bread. Baked Beans. and boiled ham today. Sewed some this P. m. Read a little. Jane & Baby were here this P.m.

Friday 22 very hot. I have not done much work today. Charlys Eyes are very sore he can hardly work at all. Poor fellow I hope they will soon be well.

Annie's entries sometimes interact with the words already printed on the page.

Father said this eve that he can remember where he has been the last day of the year for 49 years.

It is 65 days since Charley went away.

This entry is interesting also in the fact that her marginal remarks do not finish a thought as much as they present new ones — furthering the conversation and not concluding it. It appears that these comments might have been written at a later time than the actual entry. Though they are written in the same ink as the entry, the entry itself ends in the middle of the last line of the page. If Annie was only interested in saving space (thereby using the margins only when page space was gone) she would have filled that final line completely and then continued her sentence in the margins (as she does, for example, on April 26, 1882, when she runs out of room at the bottom of the page and writes the few remaining words in the margin). Entries like the one above suggest that Annie also used the margins to add additional thoughts and comments that occur to her later in the day, after she has already written "the" day's entry.[19] Such a decision on her part highlights how Annie revisited her entries as the day went on and made decisions about what to add and when.[20] The entry she produces at a certain point in the day is not sacred, not the only entry her day is capable of producing. Rather her day is always in process. She can reenter and embellish "the day" further; keep the conversation going.

Annie also places comments in the margins as a result not so much of the chronology of things but the allowability of them. At times marginal remarks are not afterthoughts but not-thoughts, or at least not "allowed" to be thought. For example, several times over the course of the years she writes "I am lonesome" in the margins. While she writes about being lonesome in the body of her entries as well, there is change in the significance of her loneliness when the words are marooned in the margins. The importance of being sensitive to the way these marginal comments, those not chronologically determined, operate is heightened or made more obvious in entries like the one for August 13, 1882, Annie and Charley's third wedding anniversary. The body of the entry reads:

It has been very pleasant all day. This is our wedding day. The third Anniversary. But do not feel well at all. I am weak. I had a most

dreadful head ache while I was sick and could not sit up at all. C-
is digging Potatoes. I can play a few pieces already.

The margin, in smaller, squished letters, reads:

3 anniversary of my marriage and did not celebrate it in any way.

Annie has already documented the fact that the day marks their wedding anniversary. In this example, Annie is putting her margins to use in
an even more transgressive and subversive way than simply claiming
them as her own. By noting her sadness and disappointment it becomes
as real as the potatoes, it counts within the day. She uses the margins,
that space that rests outside the space in which the diary does most of
its daily work, to bring in what she has been taught to leave out. In the
next chapter, I spend a great deal of time looking more extensively at
how Annie orders her text rhetorically. Here I only point to how the
transgression (naming her anger) is allowed to hover in — to extend
into — her margins, speaking with her headache and the weather.

Finally, the margins allow Annie to converse with her body in ways
that the body of the text does not. For example, Annie tracks her menstrual cycle in the margins. She does so to varying lengths and at varying consistencies. This practice is not unusual for nineteenth-century
diarists. In fact it is often the evidence presented when scholars are making the argument that the diary is a female form of writing, an extension of a woman's body — to draw parallels between the repetitive nature of menstruation and daily writing. Scholars also see practical uses
for such documentation. For instance, Lensink writes, in "*A Secret to Be
Buried*," that Gillespie tracked her menstrual cycle in her diary as a
means of birth control.

What is unusual about Annie's menstrual tracking is the added information she provides about the quality of her menstrual flow and the
accompanying pain. The first time Annie marks the beginning of menstruation is on January 30, 1881. She does so by drawing an asterisk in
the entry following the words "I have not been well." The next time is
on March 16 with an asterisk hovering in the margins between the date
and the body of the entry. Then again, in the margins, on June 4, August 4, August 29, and so on. Often the asterisk is echoed within the
body of the entry with words like: "I do not feel well today, as a matter
of course."

Beginning on January 2, 1882, Annie's documentation of her menstrual cycle becomes much more extensive. She still marks the onset with an asterisk but now adds qualifying information. These comments are always in the margins and always written in extra small, tight script. For example, on January 2 she writes in the margins, "* first appearance very faint." Then on the third she writes, "still faint." On the fourth, "a very little more this A.M. more this P.M." On the fifth, "quite natural and abundant — nearly all day." On the sixth, " very scant today. I feel well and had a little pain and soreness a short time — stopped." On the seventh, "have felt pretty sore most of the day — my back aches — especially the left side." On the eighth, "stinging pains. occasionally feel sore." She ends on the ninth with, "had a few stinging pains this A.M. — unusually well this P.M."

Such extensive documentation is particular to this first set of notes. After this, Annie writes in considerably less detail. In fact during the very next menstrual cycle in February she has shortened her marginal comments to "scant," "moderate," "very slight," and "stopped." She reduces her painful monthly experience to a code, one that most often documents the quality of her menstrual flow rather than her physical discomfort (which was severe — "back aches," "head aches," "stomach pains," and "general languor").

Annie also, I believe, tracks the times that she and Charley have sexual intercourse. She does this by drawing a flower in her diary.[21] As with her menstrual cycle, she is meticulous in the documentation of their sexual relations. If they have sex more than once in a day, Annie diligently records this fact with multiple flowers. She also records when in the day they have sexual intercourse by the placement of the flower within the entry. Sometimes a flower will appear in the middle of a day's entry, pinpointing the time with the same exactitude as the temperature.

These conversations she has between her margins and her text are crucial. Annie suffers from uterine difficulties and so her precise tracking of intercourse and menstruation reflect her anxiety over her apparent infertility. Though she never writes about her inability to conceive, the preciseness with which she documents her attempts are as heartbreaking as they are diligent. In addition to medical use, the notes and the flowers are a way for Annie to bring her physical body into the body of her text, an acceptable way for Annie to bring herself into her own entries. In the next chapter, I look at Annie's absence as a subject in her writing. Her marginal menstrual notes and flowers are one place that she is present. It is not insignificant that these conversations happen in the extended marginal space of her diary. Again, her decision as a writer physically foregrounds the fullness of the day, the interaction between text and margin, husband and wife, body and day.

* * *

The movement of Annie's entries — how a typical entry proceeds — is the final aspect of Annie's map that I want to consider in connection to dailiness. In general, her entries move inward at the same time that they move from a limited sense of usefulness to a more complicated one. Here is an example from September 2, 1882:

> Cloudy most of the day and cool. C. worked on the section. I sewed some. Cut out a pair of Pants and roasted Duck. Kept myself busy all day.

This entry begins like most by documenting the weather. If it had been cold or rainy Charley would not have been able to work on the section and there would have been unstated financial consequences. But the day is fair and Charley goes to work on the section. He is working someone else's land so he will be paid by time spent working. Annie documents, with varying degrees of exactness, how much time Charley works for others. In doing so she uses her diary to keep track of how much money he will make. Additionally in this entry, she also documents her, more fleeting, work: the sewing for her brother, the duck that will be eaten, the pants that will be worn. While she receives no financial recompense for this work it is the work necessary to the day. She can remember what has been done and what is still to come.

The final move, however, is inward: "Kept myself busy all day." In comparison to the other information in the entry — information that trades in economies of use — this last line seems unnecessary. She has already documented in more specific ways that she worked hard. Only, in this line, it is not that she was busy but that she kept herself busy. Her final comment is a subtle reminder that Annie must produce, manufacture her own use. Manufacturing and documenting her own usefulness is both a material and rhetorical act. Materially one of the diary's most important tasks is to serve as a repository for moments or activities that could easily pass unnamed but are instead seized and named through the diary's technology. These activities, in particular these consumptive, domestic activities, could easily remain unaccounted for in the same way that minutes were unaccounted for prior to the pendulum.

The diurnal form provides space for not only listing these activities and allowing the diarist to mark a place in space and time, but it also serves as a space for Annie to produce herself. At a slant, by writing "Kept myself busy all day," she reveals her fears at what would happen were she not busy. That she could simply fade away.

It is the diurnal form — and its ability to seize moments — that allows Annie a sense of self that both the high plains and cultural scripts work to erase. Annie claims space in her diary not because it is *her* diary but because it is her *diary*. The diurnal form grants these measured rather than occasioned moments, and Annie is in charge, in large part, of how they get filled.

The Year 1882

Annie remains at her father's house for the rest of the winter. Charley returns on March 29. At the end of April, they move into their claim shanty. It is three miles outside the town of Bridgewater. Annie cannot walk to town and spends most of her days at home. Charley now works on his own fields as well as those of other farmers.

March
Sunday 26
Cloudy and cooler than it was yesterday. I have read a little and tried various ways to make the day seem short but all in vain. I am lonesome. I do wish Charley would come. I am afraid we will lose our claim if he dont come soon.

[March]
Monday 27
Very warm and pleasant. I have not heard from Charley for 10 days. I am disapointed every morning when I wake up and he has not come yet. I am anxious about our Claim. I have not done much today. I got a new Paper and read some. This afternoon I played a few games of Croquet with Johnnie.
A year ago I was suffering fearfully.

[March] 28
Tuesday
Warm and pleasant. I baked a large batch of Bread this A.M. and done up two fine shirts. I am so tired of working this way and for nothing. Wasting time and strength. I hope Charley will hurry home.

Evening — I did not hear from Charley today either. I have not felt
well today. I have not felt much like eating for a week or so: But have
felt worse today. How long the days seem.

[March]
Wednesday 29 /❀/
Cooler. Charley came home this morning. He got here before I was up.
I am so glad. We went down to let the Dr see my ankle but he was
away. I done a good deal of work this afternoon. /❀/

[March]
Thursday 30
Warm and pleasant. Father washed today. Robbie & I Scrubbed and
cleaned the house. Charley went down town to see what he could get
lumber for. He is thinking of buying a little house from Shuck. I have
done a lot of work today and am tired. /❀/

[March]
Friday 31 /❀/
Warm and pleasant. Charley went down town and purchased the
little house we were speaking of buying. We washed up some of
Charlie's clothes this P.M. and in the evening Johnnie Charley and my
self played a few games of croquet. I am very tired this evening too.
The Dr called today to see my ankle.

April
Saturday 1st
It is *very* warm and pleasant. I done a good deal of work today. Made
Ginger Bread &c. Charley went down to our claim and is digging a
cellar. I took a bath this P.M. /❀/

[April]
Sunday 2
Very warm and pleasant. too warm for comfort . It was also very
windy. Robbie Charlie and I went down to the Drs this P.M. He says
my ankle is doing well. Father is sick today.

[April]
Monday 3
Warm and Pleasant. The wind blew so hard today I was frightened.
We churned today. Charley went down town. Mr Croop is working on
our house. I am tired. Part of the Crust came off my Cancer. /❀/

[April]
Tuesday 4
Cooler. I made Bread a lot of it, and washed a little. Charley got some
Paint and Painted the Door.

[April]
Wednesday 5
Cloudy and cool. It rained lightly last night and pretty hard this P.M. I
wish we could get our house moved and were moved into it. This has
been a dismal day.   I remember 7 years ago today. I felt very different from what I do now.

[April]
Thursday 6
Cloudy. It rained hard last night: I have done little today. Neither
Charley or me accomplishes much now days. It seems impossible to
get any one to do any hauling for us. Unless we pay about 2 or three
prices. I am so tired of staying here. /❀/ /❀/

[April]
Friday 7
/went down to the Drs he says my ankle is doing exceedingly well/
It rained hard /nearly/ all fore noon. I am afraid it will put our moving back. I am impatient to go. I feel pretty well now. I have had a bad
cold lately but it is better now.

[April]
Saturday 8
Frequent showers. Part of the time sunny. It rained a good deal last
night. C. started down to the claim but it rained so he came back.
I have not done much today.   Mailed a letter to Hunt.

[April]
Sunday 9

Easter. It rained /nearly/ all last night and has been cloudy all day to-day and snowing part of the time. Father has been sick today. And we ate breakfast up stairs so as not to annoy him. We read some today. I have not felt well at all. /❀/ /❀/

April
Monday 10 /* very very scanty/

Clear. Pleasant. It ~~cleared of~~ froze last night. David and Charley hauled our little Hay stack down to our claim.   Mailed a letter to Walter.   Eve. They stuck in a mud hole with the Hay and had to unload and leave it lying. That is just our luck.

[April]
Tuesday 11 /still very scanty/

Cold and chilly and frosty. I do not feel well. Baked a lot of Bread today. I got a letter from Mrs Ward and one from Miss McKemmie. Charlie got a new Saw today. I felt very sick a little while But took some Chlorodine which the Dr gave me, and soon felt well. it is splen-did medicine.

[April]
Wednesday 12 /scanty/

Cloudy. It seems as though we are never going to get our house moved and get into it. Charley went to town this P.M.

[April]
Thursday 13 /more abundant/

Still cloudy. I wish we could get away from here. Charley started to take some trees down to our claim. I am doing a little washing. Evening. Charley went away this morning and I have not seen him since. I dont see what is detaining him so long. My head aches.

[April]
Friday 14 /scanty/

Clear. I hope it will continue so for some time. Charley came home at 11 oclock last night. He had been teaming for Rodgers. I have a hard head ache.

[April]
Saturday 15
Pleasant. I walked down town to see the Dr, he says my ankle is doing well. I scrubbed the floor this P.M. Johnnie helped me some. Charley went down to our claim to set out trees.
/❀/

[April]
Sunday 16
Pleasant. Charley and I went down to the Shanty this P.M. and got some garden Seeds. It has been very windy.

[April]
Monday 17
Warm. Indications of rain. Mrs Cotie called on me this P.M. C- has been down town all day. They managed to get the house raised. I wish they would hurry and move it. I am afraid it will rain and then there is no telling how long it might be. I made Bread. /❀/

[April]
Tuesday 18
Warm. Charley went down town: Rogers said they would move the house today But I have seen no indication of moving. And I guess they will not touch it today as it is raining hard now. 2 P.M. But there was time enough to do it before the rains began. I am entirely not of patience. I feel like doing something decisive myself.

[April]
Wednesday 19
Clear and pleasant. They started to move the house at 4 P.M. yesterday, took it about a mile and stuck in a run. Charley came home drenched with rain. I went down to the Dr this P.M. My ankle is still doing well.

[April]
Thursday 20
Warm and pleasant. There is no signs of our house being moved yet. I get almost desperate sometimes and feel like going and doing something myself.

[April 22]
Saturday
It was cold and cloudy yesterday. began to rain last night and has rained all day today. *The house is not moved yet.* I guess Charley has concluded to take it to pieces and have it moved any way. I made Bread today. I guess it is good. One of R's calves died today. Charley has gone downtown. /❀/

[April]
Sunday 23 /❀/
I received a letter from Sarah Shepard last night. It was quite a surprise. It has been pleasant all day. I wrote to Mrs Shepard. Charley and David has been working on the house because it was a work of necessity.

[April]
Monday 24
Cloudy all day. Charley and the boys are working on the house. I done a large washing. Johnnie rubbed out a few pieces. I am not near as tired as I expected to be. They got the house moved down and raised today.

[April]
Tuesday 25
cloudy. Charley and David Shingled in the house. I done the Ironing. Patched some. Churned. Picked over Beans. and made a shirt today am tired.

[April]
Wednesday 26
Clear and Pleasant. Charley got His potatoes and vegetables ready to sell today. I worked hard all forenoon and went to see the Dr this P.M. He put some Nitric Acid on my foot. I am very tired tonight. Charley done up all the work.

[April]
Thursday 27
Cloudy. It cleared of [sic] in the forenoon and has been very pleasant all day. Charley went over town to get a team to move our things

down with But I have not seen any thing of them yet and it is 3 P.M.
I made bread today.
Eve. They hauled some Potatoes to town and took down one load.

[April]
Friday 28 /Pleasant/
Rogers Promised to take down the rest of our things today and we
waited for him till noon and then Charley got Jimmie to go. We got
down here about 4 or 5 P.M. It seems very strange down here and not
like home yet. The house will be hard to clean.

[April]
Saturday 29 /Pleasant/ /I am tired/
We were so tired we did not get up early. Charley carried out nearly
all the things and helped me to clean the floor. It was a hard job there
being so much lime on it. It looks pretty well though. C- finished
shingling.   I am glad we have got moved at last.   /❀/

[April]
Sunday 30
Morning cloudy. P.M. Clear and pleasant: I unpacked a lot of things
and tried to get things into order a little But I do not expect to have
things very nice untill we have the kitchen built. Charley went up
home to try and get some one to haul down Potatoes Hay, &c.   /❀/

May 1st
Monday
Pleasant. afterpart of day & cold west wind. Charley set out Trees part
of the day. I blackened the stove it looks well. And done some other
things. /❀/

[May]
Tuesday 2
Clear very cold and windy for the time of the year. C. planted trees.
The Dr called here this P.M. to see my ankle and see how we were
getting on.

[May]
Wednesday 3
Pleasant and warm. I took a good bath today. It rained this eve.
Charley cut seed Potatoes and dug some in the well. /❀/

[May]
Thursday 4 /*scanty/
Clear and warm. we got up very late. I done the washing. C- planted
Potatoes and in the evening went to town when the section men went
up. It clouded up this P.M. /Evening/ C got home at 8. and a few min-
utes later the storm struck us. It raged with terrible violence until 1
A.M. next morning. I was so afraid of the wind I could not sleep untill
after the wind abated.

[May]
Friday 5 /scanty/
It rained slowly all day. Charley shelled corn and cut Potatoes and I
did very little of any thing.

[May]
Saturday 6 /scanty/
Clear. Cool. I scrubbed and cleaned up a little. C- planted a few Pota-
toes. /❀/

[May]
Sunday 7 /not quite so scanty/
It is very cold for the season with a disagreeable east wind. Cloudy. I
do not feel very well. I made Bread and light Biscuits today. I don't
like to do such work on sunday. But could hardly do otherwise. It
rained this P.M. Pretty hard about dark.

[May]
Monday 8 /more abundant — a good deal of pain and general
languor/
It was clear and pleasant this morning but soon clouded up again and
has rained at intervals all day. I done some patching. I do not feel
well. Charley done some tinkering round the house.

[May]

Tuesday 9 /moderate flow/

Frequent Showers this forenoon. P.M. cloudy. I made yeast. Browned coffee cooked Beans &c. this A.M. and sewed some.　　　P.M. I painted the Door & doorframe. C planted Potatoes.

[May]

Wednesday 10

Cloudy with frequent showers. I went up to town with a stranger who was driving through here. Saw the Dr. He put some more Acid on my ankle. Had dinner with the Drs folks. Walked home. Am pretty tired. /❀/

[May]

Thursday 11

Very chilly and cold. I have done a little gardening today. It is too cold for any thing to grow much. Made Potato soup for dinner. Sowed Onion and Parsnip seeds.

[May]

Friday 12

Warmer and more pleasant. I made Bread. Washed. Scrubbed and sewed some more garden seeds. Charley went up home and got our little cow. She is real nice and will soon be giving milk. Watch came with them and is going to stay all night.

May 13

Saturday

Pleasant. Charley done some spading and planted Corn. I sowed some Carrot and Onion seeds. Ironed & c. I am tired. The little cow is not used to being picketed she gets tangled up in the rope and has a good many tumbles.

[May]

Sunday 14

This is the Pleasantest day we have had in a long time. It makes one feel good. Charley went up home to have James bring down the Hay and more of our things. It is a little lonesome to see no one all day long. The Cow and Chickens are all the company I have when Charley is gone. I have read some. things are growing nicely.

[May]

Monday 15

Very warm and pleasant. Charley planted corn all day. we got up
early. I sowed more Onion seeds also some flower seeds. This P.M. I
took a bath. Afternoon took a walk along the RR track. There is a
black cloud in the west. I hope it is not going to storm. The Cow does
not mind the Rope at all now.

[May]

Tuesday 16

Pleasant & Warm. S.E. wind. Charley is planting corn at Jimmies and I
have been alone all day. I have been so drowsy all day I could hardly
keep my eyes open. I wish I had a near neighbor to associate with.
Some woman I like.
I lay down about 6 oclock and slept till Charley came home and woke
up feeling very miserable. I do not feel well at all.

[May]

Wednesday 17

Cloudy and warm. I done a small washing, scrubbed the floor, and
ironed. My head felt very badly this morning so dull and stupid. But it
got better after a while. A stranger coming westward called and asked
the distance to town and a number of questions pertaining to the land
crops climate &c. here. I make a note of it because it is such an unusual thing to see any one. His appearance was not preposessing but
his manners were those of a polished gentleman.

[May]

Thursday 18

It began to rain last night. Rained all night and till noon today. C-
brought Js team Plow & c. down last night to do some plowing. He is
plowing this P.M. He keeps them in Mr Flints stable at night. I cut and
dropped some Potatoes and darned some.

[May]

Friday 19

Cloudy. Rained P.M. We finished plowing the Potatoes and I am tired.
I am sorry it rained this afternoon. C could have got a good deal of
plowing done.

[May]
Saturday 20
Cold and windy. Clear. C plowed this A.M. and P.M. I drove the team
up to Jamses. I got very cold before I got there. I stayed at father's all
night and went down town about noon. /21ˢᵗ/ Johnnie took me
down. did not see the Dr got home at 2 P.M. Johnnie brought me
down about a mile and I walked the rest of the way. It froze last night.
/❀/

[May]
Monday 22
Clear. Cold. It froze last night too. I cooked up a good many things
today. C. planted corn this A.M. and went to town P.M. I have not done
much today.

[May]
Tuesday 23
Pleasant. The little cow had a fine female calf early this morning.
Charley was up nearly all night — the little cow was so sick. we got up
very ~~early~~ late this morning. I concluded to do a little washing this
P.M. and Mrs Chandler Mrs Flint & Miss Chandler called and caught
me in the wash tub. But I am glad they called at all, they seem very
nice. I think I shall like them. I am glad we have them for neighbors.

[May]
Wednesday 24
Pleasant. I sowed a few seeds this A.M. Afternoon I scrubbed &c.
Charley moved the house around and I helped him some. I turned the
crank, put the rollers under &c.

[May]
Thursday 25
Pleasant. Charley carried some rocks to make a Flower bed last
evening. And I finished the Bed today and sowed a few seeds. It looks
first rate. C has gone to town and some other places today. Had breakfast at six oclock. C- got home at 8. P.M. We planted melon seeds
Sweet corn &c.

[May]
Friday 26
Fine & pleasant. Charley finished planting corn and began to plant
Beans. I planted Peas and some choice Beans and hoed some Onions.
/❀/

[May]
Saturday 27
Very pleasant. C. planted beans. I cleaned up the house and P.M.
sewed Flower seeds.

May 28
Sunday
Very warm and pleasant. got up late. Done up the work, read some.
looked round among the crops. Evening Charley and I took a walk.
/❀/

[May]
Monday 29
Pleasant & warm. Clouded up this afternoon. Several fine Heads and
a number of Emigrants have gone west. Charley is working up at
Jimmies. I washed this A.M.

[May]
Tuesday 30
Cloudy, windy and rather chilly. This is Decoration day. I wonder what
is going on today, back home in Wis. There are no flowers in bloom here
but wild flowers yet I hope to have a few flowers.   Charley
took out Rocks until 10 oclock A.M. and then started up to Jimmie's
but came back as it started to rain. A man came here this P.M. to break
for us.   I made Bread and Ironed some also hoed some in the
garden. my ankle which has been looking worse for a few days is
looking better. /* slight/ I have a disagreeable sting in my right side.

[May]
Wednesday 31 /very slight almost invisible/
Pleasant. I wrote a letter to B. Dudley. Charley is working at Jims.
Some emigrants cooked dinner here today.

June 1ˢᵗ
Thursday /still scanty/
Very warm and pleasant. Rodgers came to break today. We had a de-
lightful shower ~~today~~ this eve. We received letters last night from Mrs
Heath and Mrs Child. I have felt very nervous and weary all day. Am
almost ill. Charley has taken out rock and hoed.

[June]
Friday 2 /more abundant/
Pleasant. Rogers broke for us today. I am quite nervous and ill. I set a
Hen today. Some dogs of Rodgers took after the little calf. Watch and
the cow & Charley took after the dogs. I believe they would have /if
let alone/ killed the calf. I made Bread which is not fit to eat.

[June]
Saturday 3 /moderate/
Cool and pleasant. Rather too cool for me. Charley began to dig a cel-
lar. I cleaned up the house and made Bread again. It is good. I planted
a few Squash seeds.
My throat is very sore.

[June]
Sunday 4 /stopped/
This has been a warm beautiful day. David & Robbie came down today
and made us a visit. Watch came too he had only gone home last
night. I do not feel well at all my throat is very sore. it bothered me all
night my whole neck aches. C- has taken cold too.

[June]
Monday 5 /just visible today/
Very pleasant. Charley is working at Jimmies. Mr Wilson came to
break but was too late. I feel better today. I washed the clothes have
very small washings. And afternoon I hoed corn. Am making Bread.
We mailed letters to B. Dudley, B. Heath and B.E.B. Kennedy. /❀/

[June]
Tuesday 6
Warm and pleasant. I done the ironing and baking. had splendid
luck with my Bread. P.M. went over to Mrs Flint's and called on
Mrs Chandler. Mrs Flint and Alice brought me home in the Buggy.
They *seem* real nice people. We made a flower Bed this eve. /❀/

[June]
Wednesday 7
Excessively warm. I transplanted flowers this morn. C- leveled down
an old sod house for a Tomato bed and P.M. hoed. Evening I set out
cabbage and tomato plants. mosquitoes are bad.
/❀/

[June]
Thursday 8
Pleasant. C- planted Beans. I set out some flowers and hoed some.
There was a large herd came by this P.M. They camped near here. And
the boss of the outfit wanted me to make some Biscuits for them
which I did, charging them 25 cts for the job.

[June]
Friday 9
Very hot. I set out some cabbage and tomatoes and planted some
Flower & garden seeds today. C- planted Beans A.M. and P.M. dug in
the well. The herd stayed here till nearly night. Their horses strayed
away and they could not find them for a long time.

[June]
Saturday 10
It looked last night as though we were going to have a severe storm.
But it spent itself south of us and only rained a little here. Watch came
down after we had gone to Bed. Charley got up at 3.30 this morning
to go up to Jims for his team. Watch went with him. He got breakfast
and ate alone and I did went away before day light and I did not get up
till 7 oclock and I felt sick for awhile. I could not do any thing. Could
not eat breakfast and did not get my little work done till 10 oclock.

June 11
Sunday
Hot. Charley finished his work today and took the team home. and
did not get home till late. I read a good deal. /❀/

[June]
Monday 12 /C- planted Beans today/
Pleasant it looks some like rain. I washed this A.M. /❀/ P.M. I slacked
some lime done a few other jobs and about 5 oclock went over to Mrs
Flints and had a chat. Watch seems to be staying over there he is a
nuisance.

[June]
Tuesday 13
It rained a little to day. I have not done much. Charley hoed & c. It
rained nearly all day. It was the nicest rain we have had this season.

[June]
Wednesday 14 /finished planting Beans/
Quite pleasant. This seems like an April day. We have light showers
from fleecy clouds. Charley planted Beans. I set out 100 cabbage
plants.

[June]
Thursday 15
It is very close and warm this morning. I Ironed Baked Beans and
Aired Bedding & c. and Charley hoed. This evening we set out some
more Cabbage plants.

[June]
Friday 16 /we set out some cabbage plants this eve just before the
rain/
Very warm. we had a light shower this P.M. Charley went up to
Fathers. took up the corn planter this morning and got some Butter
also a Paper, and a letter from Frank Hunt. The Small Pox is still bad
in town. The town is quarantined.
It clouded up this P.M. and we had one of the most fearful storms I
ever witnessed. It lasted about an hour. I was so frightened. The storm

came on about dark. It rained some time after the worst of the storm was over. One of our neighbors took refuge here. /❀/

[June]
Saturday 17
Warm and pleasant. Charley hoed. I cleaned the house a little. and made pies & c. We had a shower this P.M. It is just sunset and I am going to Bed. my ankle looks pretty well.

[June]
Sunday 18
Very windy cold for the season and disagreeable. I got up late. Charley wrote some. I read a good deal. Robbie came down this P.M. and brought down my machine carpet &c. and some lumber, also some work for me to do. C- rode up with him and got a setting of eggs. I have not enjoyed this day very well.

[June]
Monday 19
Cloudy and sometimes drizzling. I washed made Bread sewed and done some little jobs also read some. Charley hoed A.M. and worked on the Kitchen P.M. I set a Hen today.

[June]
Tuesday 20
Pretty cool & very windy I ironed &c. I made a pair of Pants. Charley worked on the Kitchen and hoed some. Evening I set out a lot of Tomatoes.
The little Chickens are hatching.

       *   *   *

They spend the summer planting. By fall, they are harvesting.

       *   *   *

September
Friday 1st
very warm and pleasant. I made Bread Turnovers &c. Also ironed. Made a shirt for Charley it is the first I ever made for him. C. worked on the section.
He got home late. Brought a little Duck home with him and dressed it.

[September]
Saturday 2
Cloudy most of the day and cool. C worked on the section I sewed some.
Cut out a pair of Pants and roasted Duck. Kept myself busy all day.

[September]
Sunday 3 /I was dreadfully frightened/
Very warm and pleasant. We did not get up till eight oclock this morning and had breakfast between 9. & 10. It made the day seem very
short. I don't like to over sleep so.
One of the worst looking men I ever saw came in here today. He asked
for a drink then stayed a long time at last C- asked him if he would have
something to eat in order to get rid of him. He gladly excepted [*sic*]
and stayed an hour after that. He talked in such a way that I knew he
was either crazy or a villain. He informed C- that he was a professional Gambler, Pick Pocket & Confidence man. His dinner made him
confidential. I don't suppose he is any better than he calls himself.
Though what was his objective in telling what he was I dont know. /❀/

Sept[ember] 4
Monday
Very pleasant. C was sick this A.M. but went to work any way. I
finished his overalls, Shirt & Vest and done some other little things.
C- came home feeling pretty badly.

[September]
Tuesday 5
Very warm. I heard that Flints were going away soon so I went over
this forenoon to see them. Got back at 12.30. C- did not work today.
He went up town this P.M. /❀/ I milked this Evening and got my
cream ready to churn.
Three years ago Dear Mother was very ill little did I think then that
her trouble would end fatally. What a trying time it was.

[September]
Wednesday 6
Very hot. C- is working for Coolage today. I made Bread, Churned
cooked Beans and Ironed this Forenoon. P.M. did very little.

[September]
Thursday 7
Very pleasant. C- worked at Coolages this A.M. and P.M. mowed at home. I sewed a good deal on my new dress have got it pretty well along.

[September]
Friday 8
Pleasant. C- worked for Coolage thrashing and Haying. Coolage racked up hay here this P.M. I sewed most of the day.

[September]
Saturday 9
It clouded up and rained awhile this A.M. But not enough to damage the Hay much. I cleaned up every thing about the Kitchen. took a bath, and done some cooking also a little Sewing.
It looks like raining this P.M.

[September]
Sunday 10 /*slight/
Very pleasant. We got up rather late this morning. Charley started up town for the mail But met Father & Johnnie he came home with them. They brought down some Butter & c. After dinner we took a ride down to Newtons he was not at home. We have had a few melons today.

It is three years ago today since my mother died. It makes us all feel very badly to think of it. I think that is why Father came down today.

[September]
Monday 11 /scant/
Very pleasant. But rather windy. I sewed a little. Mrs Chandler & Alice came over and spent the P.M.
C- pulled Beans.

[September]
Tuesday 12 /abundant/
Very pleasant. Coolige and Charley stacked the hay. I washed this P.M. It was Hot this afternoon.

A stranger from LeMars called here today for a Drink, his name Manahan.

[September]
Wednesday 13 /moderate/
Hot. I sewed a little after doing my morning work. And P.M. went over to Chandlers and stayed to tea. I got some Flower seeds and a handsome Boquet [*sic*]. Alice played and sung some. I borrowed some lakeside Books. Did not get home till dark.

[September]
Thursday 14
Very pleasant. I churned and made Bread today. And done lots of other work ironing &c. P.M. read a good deal.
Charley Pulled Beans and cut some corn.

/"Where love and high admiration and firm belief have once existed it is a bitter thing to see them broken at a blow."/

Sept[ember] 15
Friday
Very Hot /& windy/. I read and sewed a little before noon and then called on Mrs Coolige. Got very warm and tired before I got home. I would not have gone had I known how hot it was. Read nearly all P.M. Had cold dinner and Supper.   Charley worked at home.

[September]
Saturday 16
Very /Hot/ & windy. I did not do any cleaning up today it is too warm. Only done the work I do every day and put up two jars of Green corn and took a bath. Read some in Lady Marobouts troubles. do not care much for it. Charley worked at home.

[September]
Sunday 17
/✿/ Hot. Gentle breeze all day. I spent most of the day reading and trying to keep cool.
C- done a little work this A.M. and P.M. read and wrote. We are really having splendid weather.

[September]
Monday 18
The weather changed last night and now it is too cold for comfort with-
out a fire. I done my washing and read some. Charley pulled Beans.

[September]
Tuesday 19 /C. went to town got no letters/
We had a little frost last night and today there is a NW. wind and it is
very chilly indeed. I churned and it took me nearly all A.M. the cream
was too cold. I got all tired out. Read some this P.M. in "Hostages to
fortune" it is splendid. Poor Eclitha is going to have trouble. She feels
troubled about something but does not know all that is coming.

[September]
Wednesday 20
Warmer than yesterday. It froze enough last night to kill all the vines.
I am sorry, we would have had plenty of Melons and Tomatoes if it
had held off a little longer. I made Bread Ironed &c. and read more in
Hostages to Fortune. My Pen is getting so poor I can hardly write at
all. /❀/

[September]
Thursday 21
Cold. I did not do much today. C- worked round home most of the day
and P.M. went to town but got no mail. I read a good deal finished
Hostages to Fortune. Warm P.M.

[September]
Friday 22
Warmer. I done a good deal of Patching. C- worked round home. It
froze hard last night.

[September]
Saturday 23
Pleasant and warm. F. Coolige cut some hay for us yesterday. He
worked 3 hours. C- cut corn I have been busy all day. did not do my
usual Saturday cleaning. Took a bath. done considerable cooking. It is
three years ago today since Charley came back to Wis from Leadville.
I dreamed last night I was in Leadville.

Sept[ember] 24
Sunday
Pleasant. My head aches. Robbie came down and I am going up
with him. and will not be home till Tuesday. We started about 4. P.M.
C. went to Cooliges with us. We called at the Drs. He says my foot is
well. We got home about dark. The boys picked Tomatoes after supper and we washed and sliced them. I am tired.

[September]
Monday 25
Very warm. I put up five gals sweet pickles for them today. Jane came
over with the Baby and stayed a while. In the P.M. I called on her.
And at 5 oclock I started down town for the mail but got nothing but
a paper. It was nearly dark when I got home. I am very very tired.

[September]
Tuesday 26
Pleasant. I started home between 7 & 8 oclock A.M. with James who is
going down to our place to stack hay. We went round by town. Got no
mail. Saw the Dr. Got home at 10. They stacked a little hay and it got
so windy they had to stop. They hauled the Beans. I am very tired
tonight too I had a good deal to do when I got home, having been
away for so long. /❀/

[September]
Wednesday 27
Still too windy to stack. I made a few pickles and done a little other
work. C- dug some potatoes. it rained P.M. but not hard.

[September]
Thursday 28
Cloudy. It has been misty and drizzling most of the day. C. went up
town early and got back about 11 A.M. He got the money at last. It is
most welcome. He also got a letter from Walter which he answered.
He also wrote to Gus and sent them money. The lawyers charged an
enormous fee.
It is two years ago today since I started from Leadville. It has been
rather eventful. C. went up town again this evening.

[September]
Friday 29
There was a dense fog this morning. It did not clear away untill quite late. We arose very early and C- went up to Jimmies to get him to haul down some things from town and to stack hay. They did not get here until noon and did not finish the Hay. I cleaned up the Kitchen and done lots of work and read some.

.   .   .

Charley remains home this winter — and in future winters. He works on their property, fixing the henhouse, sharpening tools. In February of the following year, Charley will "conclude" that he should establish a blacksmith shop in Bridegwater. They will move to town in March of 1883, a decision that Anniey does not help make.

3 : Putting Things to Right Generally

It is hard for me to fathom the impact of the pendulum, basically the discovery of new moments in time and space. What would it have been like to have lived at a time during which minutes were invented? I suppose it was similar to the discovery of atoms or even of cyberspace, when suddenly you can no longer think in the terms of what went before, no longer conceive of communication before email. The pendulum's generation of moments in time meant that previously unfilled and unrecognized spaces could then be, in a sense, settled with experiences, with words. They would get filled. Such occupation is akin to the settlement of the West, to the frontier, to the claim Annie and Charley make on the land in Dakota when, as homesteaders, they move into the empty space of the plains and build a home. It is a comparison worth pursuing and one that, I hope, will begin to challenge the consideration of the measured spaces in a diary.

My own experience with living on the plains is limited to the summers I spent visiting relatives in Nebraska and South Dakota and the four years I attended college. Still, Nebraska was never a state I passed through but rather a destination. My parents both grew up on the plains, my mom in South Dakota and my dad on a farm near Cozad, Nebraska. And while the land in the plains states is familiar to them, it is a land that I find ultimately dislocating. I remember being lost one time in western Nebraska when I was in college. It was sometime in the summer and the corn was nearly six feet high. I had jogged too far away from my friend's farm and when I turned around I no longer knew where I was. The dirt roads had carried me far from the familiar. All around me was corn, corn too high to see above, and flatness, unfaltering, unrelenting flatness. There is nothing out there; you have no way to get your bearings. I could not mark my place in space by tree, building, road sign, or even an empty Coke bottle littering the road. The howling wind — now no longer at my back — pushed against me and would not let me move. There is only one other place in the world where I have felt that kind of pressured emptiness and that is the ocean.

Maybe the connection is not that odd either. After all, as Kathleen Norris reminds us, millions of years ago Dakota was an inland sea. It still bears the marks of its oceanic birth. Norris writes, "What makes the western plains seem most like the ocean to me is not the great sweeps of land cut into swells and hollows, or the grass rippling like waves . . . or the sheets of rain that one sees moving in the distance like storms at sea. It is the sound."[1] Hers is a connection I can recognize and feel. The thunderous sound of the wind as it blows with abandon over the fields and the scattered houses. The ponderous sound of the surf passing over your body as you wait beneath the wave.

* * *

There is a moment in my childhood when I grew forever fearful of the ocean. It is a moment well after the years when my brothers and I would play "Rock" for hours at the edge of the shore, our bodies pushed by the surf, tossed along with the bits of shell and other sea debris. It is also a moment far past the age when I would snorkel fearlessly over the Haliewa Trench, happily anticipating the temperature change on my bare stomach as the ocean floor dropped a hundred feet away. Maybe the fearfulness paralleled adolescence and the discovery that something as deeply known as your body can betray you in such visible and uncaring ways. Or maybe the initial betrayal was the military's — the way my dad's naval career forced us to constantly uproot. Perhaps it was the ocean's doing alone, as soft as a flower one moment, so fierce the next.

Growing up in Hawai'i you are taught never to turn your back on the ocean. It is a practice of respect rather than fear. The ocean can change dramatically and without notice. A standing wall of water when before the sea was calm. So you grant that honor and always watch. From an early age you learn that waves arrive in sets of seven and that within each set of seven the waves increase in size, the next always bigger than the last. You also learn that each set of waves also increases through seven sets of seven, the forty-ninth wave, then, being the largest of the series. It seems as though, knowing the ocean's order, you could calculate when it was safe to turn your back, when the sea was done for the time being. Yet, there is always the rogue wave, the great *kahuna*, the one that will take you down, pull you out, roll you over, like the spotted body of an eel bursting from its hole.

And so I know to watch the ocean. As a small child, I could play in rough surf and in water well over my head. Because I knew how to calculate, watch, count, I could get in and out of the water safely. If such vigilance ever failed, I also knew how to dive under the waves that were too big for me, waves that promised to crush me or slam me into the shore. Because if you can get far enough under the churning of the wave there is a pocket of space where the water is calm and undisturbed. You have to go deep, though, to the bottom is best, and lobby against the physical properties of salt water. Above you the wave charges and boils. You can feel the pressure pushing down on you; water-wave tendrils grab at your ankles and hands, trying to draw you into the ocean's mighty works. Sometimes another wave is right behind, you have no time for a new breath, so you must hold onto that head of coral a little bit longer.

While there was always a sense of mightiness as I waited for the wave to pass, clinging to the ocean's floor, I was never really afraid. I thought that as long as you respected the ocean all would be well. Such a belief in the steadiness of bodies — my own and the ocean's — changed one day at Waimea Bay, a beach that still remains my favorite place in the world. That particular day proved to be the first whisper of the ocean's eventual betrayal, the first time that I began to realize that nature follows a path all its own.

Waimea Bay is on the north shore of Oahu. It is as famous for its winter surf as it is for its beauty. When the waves are really up (and really up at Waimea promises a forty-foot wall of water) only a few surfers, brave or crazy, will even go in. The waves on this day were nowhere near that size. I was out playing in them. The other thing you learn about the ocean is that the farther you swim out to sea the less chance you have to be caught in a wave that is breaking (as waves break when they come into contact with the ocean floor). So I was out pretty far. If a wave were to break where I was it would have to be enormous. It would have to be large enough to drag a bottom that was much deeper than anything I could touch.

Diving under waves is tiring. There is the breath-holding and the fight against floating upward and then there is the fact that when the sets get large you must either dive constantly or ride one in. I was in the middle of an increasingly larger set of waves and getting pretty tired. I would have liked to have gone in — I could see my family in their beach chairs on the shore — but felt I had better wait the set out. That was when an enormous wave rose up from nothing. I knew I would need to swim extra deep to be safely out of the wave's grasp. I went as deep as I could and waited, felt the surge of the wave as it moved over my body like a spell of nausea. And I waited and waited and waited for the remaining pummeling and the pressure to pass. But it didn't. Try as I might, I could not get back to the surface. Each new attempt was met by crazy swirling bubbling water pushing me back to the bottom. I thought I was drowning. I could not make it up. I panicked.

Of course, I finally broke through the remains of the wave. Popped up to see the beach cleared of people like the streets after a summer rain. All had moved to higher ground. Soon other heads bobbed up around me and we began swimming for the shore. While it was clear that that wave was the largest the ocean would offer for some time, we all, I think, wanted the security of sand beneath us.

This whisper from the ocean was followed by other moments, including a time when I was caught in a rip current and pulled so far out to sea that I had to be rescued. With each interaction I lost more and more of my authority to be in the water, and these moments eventually accumulated into fear. I now have trouble even playing at the edges of the shore because you never know what might rise from its surface. No matter what knowledge you possess about the patterns of waves or the properties of surf, you are never really in control in the ocean. A natural space, it cannot be fully embraced or known no matter how carefully you watch, how deeply you know, or how far you dive beneath the surface. The *kahuna*, the rogue wave, refuses to be ordered into any kind of measurable system or space. Its presence alone destabilizes the authority I feel by saying: never turn your back on the ocean.

•   •   •

The presence of the *kahuna*, this disruptive force that haunts my attempts to know the ocean, urges me to reconsider how I think about the measured spaces I have been gathering together, spaces whose apparent emptiness I have up to this point qualified as useful: (1) the moments of time created by the pendulum, (2) the empty spaces on the page that define the diurnal form, and (3) most recently and cursorily, the land available to homesteaders with the opening of the frontier. All appear empty, open, and waiting only to be filled. But are they as empty as they seem?

The claim Annie and Charley make on the land is a claim that lies far from the reaches of town. It rests about three miles outside of Bridgewater on a large, empty, grassy field. In settling this space, they domesticate it. They turn it into a home — into, as Annie writes underneath her drawing of the claim shanty, "home sweet home." Prior to such domestication the land, from their own perspective as well as that of other new settlers, was undifferentiated, unrecognizable, and unorganized into anything other than emptiness. The land only became ordered — ordered into endless, even, measured spaces — with the passage of the Land Ordinance of 1785. Enacting what Philip Fisher refers to as the Jeffersonian vision of "democratic social space," this law lay a perfect grid onto the frontier, mapping the country into six-hundred-and-forty-acre sections without pause for natural boundaries or previous claims made by Native Peoples. What was formerly disparate and unknown—the inhabitants, the languages, the climates, the geography— became uniform. With this legislation, the land became ordered homesteads, calibrated spaces of land qualified by an "absence of limits," an "openness," and a "similarity."[2] Land that, now seized, was ready to be put to use.

Tick, tick, tick.

By moving their claim shanty onto the land, clearing the prairie for gardens and crops, and furnishing their house, Annie and Charley seize an empty, measured space and fill it. How similar is their occupation of the land to the way in which the diurnal form allows Annie to seize moments in her day and fill the spaces in her diary daily? Like the technologies of the pendulum and the diurnal form, homesteading (and more specifically Jeffersonian mapping) is a tool that makes the land available for cultivating, for counting. It orders what was previously and apparently empty or unknown. Yet, is such filling so transparent? Are these minutes, these blank pages, these spaces of land simply empty and freely existing, waiting only for a settler, a diarist, or the words "tick, tick, tick" to fill? Or can these spaces only become countable, only be made available for counting after they are first named as empty, open, and ready to be filled? In which case they are not empty

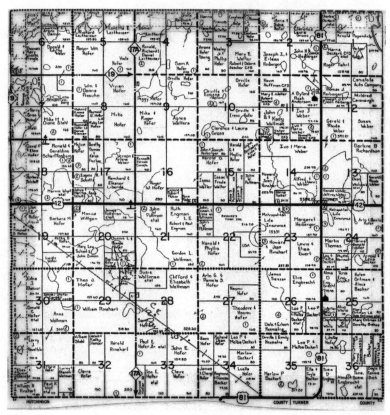

A sectional map of McCook County in South Dakota, 1976.
Charley and Annie Ray homesteaded their 160 acres
on the southwest quarter of Section 28.

but regulated. It is an important question. For the answer will determine the limits Annie is negotiating in her diary, and it will help us understand the nature of the work Annie's diary is doing.

And this is where I have been headed all along. How is the relationship between measuredness and emptiness mutually defining? Empty minutes do not exist until the pendulum measures them into existence. Empty spaces in the diary do not exist until the diurnal form defines their existence. Homesteads do not exist until the land ordinance maps their existence. Spaces of time, like spaces of land, like spaces in the diary only become available for counting, for settling, in opposition to a discourse that names them as existing in the first place. They do not exist prior to naming, to measuring. They are not simply empty. They are bound and charged spaces.

I want to think about how the diurnal form produces these measured spaces rather than discovers them, as well as how the diarist uses and extends the opportunities created by her chosen form. The tension between measuredness and emptiness is one that I think Sherman, in his examination of the rise of the diurnal form, does not name well enough. The pendulum does not seize completely empty spaces that were freely and independently existing, spaces of time only waiting to be discovered by the pendulum. These spaces come into being, quite literally, with the words tick, tick, tick. In the same way, the land that Annie settles does not exist conceptually apart from how it is legally organized. Continuing the parallels, Annie's diary — that free form, blank book waiting to be filled — is not free and empty. Its spaces, too, are regulated by a diurnal discourse, as well as a host of other discourses, those of womanhood, motherhood, and illness. All of these spaces — minutes, land, the pages of the diary — always stand both empty and full.

＊　　＊　　＊

My thinking about the rhetorical outcome of dailiness has been informed, in part, by the work of Ralph Cintron, who explores "discourses of measurement" in his ethnography, *Angels' Town: Chero Ways, Gang Life, and Rhetorics of the Everyday*. I was initially drawn to Cintron's work because he, too, is concerned with rhetorical features of ordinary texts. Rather than a homesteader's diary, though, he is looking at urban literacies, those of a predominately Latino/a community in the suburbs of Chicago. His book is ultimately a study of order — the ordering of society and the ordering of a text, as he works to understand how people make order in their lives.

Cintron sees such ordering as the extension of a system that wants to maintain its boundaries, hierarchies, and privileges. What I find useful about Cintron's work is how his conception of discourses of measurement complicates the apparent "nothingness" of Annie's text. What initially appears simple, orderly, and clean actually strains with the rhetorical effort necessary to maintain its containment. Annie's text, no matter how orderly, how ordered, cannot account for everything. While Cintron focuses on the ways in which these discourses limit an individual, I am also interested in how a writer like Annie might capitalize on the measuredness of the diurnal form in ways that are potentially necessary or even sustaining.

Cintron defines discourses of measurement as the "ways by which a precise order (or the fiction of a precise order) gets made."[3] In suggesting that no discourse exists outside a discourse of measurement, his thinking extends well beyond numbers and explicit kinds of measurement. For Cintron, discourses of measurement make order via texts, gestures, dress, signs, etc., within individuals and communities by concealing the messy reality of an "innerscape" with the mastery of an "outerscape." Their goal is one of "holding the unstable at bay" (210).[4] Cintron looks at a number of attempts to establish order and cleanliness in Angelstown: blacktopping driveways, fencing and manicuring yards, city ordinances about garbage, strict regulations on revitilization, flashy cars, and hip clothes. All work to simplify by ordering out the messy, the complicated, and the unstable. They work to conceal a reality produced by a system that impoverishes and debilitates. In his emphasis on measurement, on how discourses order, we can already see easy parallels to the diary that might include the chronological order of days, the careful replication of form in each entry, the maintenance of margins and legible handwriting, the documentation of time, temperature, weather, the tracking of bodies (the diarist's own and others), the listing of chores, the accounting of money and time, the recording of correspondence and reading, as well as, of course, larger, less literal regulation by both cultural and diurnal scripts.

Significantly, though, what is ordered is never empty. Formerly shapeless spaces — a city street, a body, a diary page — are not actually empty of order but are already circumscribed, regulated by discourses of measurement. Tension exists between what gets ordered in and what gets ordered out. Effort, enormous effort, is required in the maintenance of order, in concealing the mess. In this tension exists the potential for subversion, for agency. Faults are created by the "ordered in" and "ordered out" knocking together, faults that work to collapse the system.[5]

The tension between ordering in and ordering out has a great deal to say for Annie's diary. We have been considering how the ordinary diary is a measured rather than occasioned document. That it is marked by succession, repetition, and an absence of event. Further, we know that the form makes itself available for filling these successive and repetitive ticks of time. But while Sherman suggests that the diurnal form allows a diarist to "seize fugitive phenomena" and make them accessible for experiencing and documenting, Cintron helps us see how these phenomena are never completely fugitive but are already bound by the very kinds of regulating discourses that named them as fugitive in the first place. Second, we know that the rhetorical opportunities afforded by the diurnal form conceal a far more complicated and messy "inner-scape" than what is acknowledged by and within the daily entries. Third, the result of such regulation is the lurking presence of that which was ordered out, a presence that continues to haunt the text and threaten disruption. To return to the ocean for a moment, while waves come in countable sets of seven, and while you can number the waves and never turn your back on the water, the presence of the rogue wave, the *kahuna*, destabilizes the whole system and threatens to reveal how fictive the ordering really is. And fourth, and most importantly for the argument I want to make, the measuredness of things moves us through the day at the same time that it limits our ability to act. Meaning that what is gained in the skillful maintenance of order cannot be dismissed.

In reading Annie's diary, I do not want to lose sight of the fact that Annie gains things by furthering the rhetorical opportunities generated by the discourse of the diurnal form. On the one hand, she is using, ma-nipulating discourses of measurement to maintain a fiction of stability that is culturally and historically mandated. But she is also using (rather than only subverting) these rhetorical opportunities to protect herself. To fully understand the rhetorical work of the diurnal form, I need to highlight Annie's skill at perpetuating the measuredness of things, even as I acknowledge that her skillfulness leads to the continuation of cer-tain damaging fictions.

. . .

In turning to Annie's diary, it is important to keep in mind that Annie, the diarist, is, in Cintron's language, the ordering agent. She is the one mak-ing the order. Writing always entails certain choices, ordering in and or-dering out. Annie exhibits a "will" in making these rhetorical and mate-rial decisions about her diary but it is not a wholly "free will" (231). She is always operating within and between, consciously and unconsciously, certain constraints. On a literal level the constraints of daylight, mate-rials, and time. On a metalevel, the constraints of nineteenth-century perceptions of women, infertility, and the domestic sphere. So when I suggest, for example, as I do below, that Annie makes use of a recycled vocabulary, it is a willful decision though not a completely free one. She devises a rhetorical strategy that is most useful to her while living in a world demanding women remain in certain, confined, and confin-ing spaces. While we cannot determine how limited or unlimited her choices are, we can ask what she gains and loses in the rhetorical deci-sions she makes.

Given this, the place to begin is with Annie's explicit desire for order and the resulting peace of mind such cleanliness affords her. The references to literal ordering are easy to document. There are many entries when she makes comments like "I feel more comfortable now that everything is clean" (January 15, 1884) or "Spent a good part of the a.m. putting a way clothing and putting things to right generally" (July 5, 1881) or "Picked out carpet and put things to right generally in my boxes" (January 16, 1884). References to the "regular programme," "the usual housework," "her Saturday work," indicate a routine that she both appreciates and even requires. Perhaps the most efficient example of the literal measuredness of things is in Annie's references to her menstrual cycle (see chapter 2). Often she will write that she does not feel well "as a matter of course" (as on December 11, 1881). While her language is not an unusual nineteenth-century euphemism, it does succinctly capture the regulation of both body and text.

Sometimes the exactness of her language is almost startling in its rigidity. For example, moments like the one on March 3, 1881, when she writes "Finished R- shirts and darned ~~a lot~~ some socks" demonstrate how important it is to her that she be precise and stand in stark relief to other moments when, as we will see below, she cloaks what is beyond her literal or linguistic control in imprecision and vagueness. She notes with exactness the distance she rode on August 28,1881: sixteen miles; not just that Charley walked home in the rain but that it was seven miles (September 16, 1881); that it began to snow at 4:30 P.M. on December 21, 1881, not simply that afternoon; not that she planted cabbage plants but that there were 100 of them. An entry like the one on January 1, 1884, is not uncommon at all and clearly demonstrates how the measuredness of things literally binds Annie's diary:

> Very cold. It was 22 below this morning. We got up very late and did not have breakfast until 10 o'clock. Mr Kingsbury came at 11. C came a little later. None of Jimmie's could come. Had dinner at 5, all done it justice. Our company stayed until 10 pm. We had some refreshments about 9 . . .

The exact temperature. The time of breakfast. Who visited and in what order. When they came. When they ate. When the guests left.

Annie uses (even expands) the capacity for measuredness afforded by the diurnal form to order her day, literally. In doing so, she creates a fiction of stability, suggesting by what she allows entrance into this entry that this day was a day like any other. That nothing unusual happened. In doing so, she is also participating in nineteenth-century ideologies of womanhood that encouraged domestic tranquility and order.

Hampsten gives extended attention to the "cult of true womanhood" (with its emphasis on stability) and the diurnal form in her study *Read This Only to Yourself: The Private Writings of Midwestern Women, 1880–1910*. She suggests that women in the nineteenth century were invested in assuring that nothing happened within the domestic circle or within the pages of their diaries. In order to maintain the veneer of uneventfulness, women wrote in omission, at a slant, and repetitively, using language to replicate a fictive domestic bliss. Diarists would edit their days, code their concerns, and rely on grammatical structures to convey stability and sameness. Hampsten's work radically revised earlier criticism of ordinary diaries that maintained that such stability was a reflection of a writer's (in)ability. She foregrounds the gender ideologies operating in nineteenth-century America to demonstrate that the absence of eventfulness in an ordinary diary was the mark of female successfulness.

Hampsten's foundational study sheds light on the importance of order and stability for Annie.[6] It helps us read and understand why Annie might literally record the fact that nothing is happening in her day, as when she writes, "It is hardly worth keeping a diary, I have so little to note" (July 30, 1881) or "It seems almost foolish for me to keep a memorandum of my uneventful days but I have little to do and might about do that as anything else" (December 6, 1882). Such nothingness would indicate her success in the domestic sphere. In addition, we can see how cultural messages to maintain stability and avoid disruption appear in the kind of literal ordering Annie employs in her writing — the exact number of miles, the visitors she received and their order, whether she did a washing or a large washing. Annie signifies the sameness of days in the recorded repetition of chores and correspondence.

While Annie, in part, may be keeping her diary in response to nineteenth-century cultural messages about what it means to be a good woman, I think we also need to consider how the diary's connection to temporality equally impacts the form. Dailiness will also produce uneventfulness, regulation, measure, and repetition. Seeing Annie's statement that there "is little to note" in conjunction with the diurnal form's refusal of occasion complicates the work Annie is conducting beyond a single historical image or cultural script and turns us toward questions about her diary as a form of writing. As we will see, such a focus then allows us to see what Annie both gains and loses by replicating dailiness on the page.

By capitalizing on the literal measuredness of her day, Annie engages her diary in the kind of rhetorical work that Cintron suggests all discourses of measurement attempt: "holding the unstable at bay." It is work that requires skill at the same time that it denudes and conceals. The challenge, for readers, becomes one of documenting how other moments, moments not tied so literally into a language of measurement, work equally hard to make order. These less apparent rhetorical strategies are perhaps even more important to Annie in her efforts to order in what she can contain (her daily chores, her visits, her menstrual cycle) and to order out what she cannot (her lack of choices, privilege, and space). In entries like the following, we learn that even the routine of the housework and the dedication to her diary fail to keep the unstable at bay:

[September 1883]
Tuesday 18
Pretty cold. P.M. cloudy. I have not been able to do anything today, but did do the sweeping, dishwashing, cellar work, etc. For all that, I felt very unlike it.

Seeing the way routine and precision are valued by Annie in her writing, it should come as no surprise that the most significant rhetorical strategy Annie employs in her diary is the reduction of possibility and the evacuation of event (occasioned time). If the diary's primary technology is one of seizing and containing measured moments within highly regulated, ordered spaces, then that which is not measured (the detailed and unusual) threatens to disrupt. Annie uses her diary to simplify complicated realities and order out the unstable, while at the same time documenting her usefulness. These strategies can be gathered under the rhetorical umbrella of parataxis, the dominant rhetorical manifestation of dailiness.

Parataxis (from the Greek "to place beside") is quite literally the grammatical equivalent of tick, tick, tick. By definition, parataxis is the placing together of words, phrases, or sentences without the use of conjunctions, in particular subordinating conjunctions (the catalogs found in Walt Whitman's poetry provide an example). As a rhetorical strategy it denies privilege and hierarchy because there is no subordination within the phrases, clauses, sentences, or paragraphs. The reader cannot tell which event within the sentence or the paragraph was the most significant and, therefore, must grant equal weight to all parts. Tick, tick, tick. It is as measured as grammar can get.

Rebecca Hogan has documented the paratactic effects of the diurnal form in her essay "Engendered Autobiographies: The Diary as a Feminine Form," suggesting that an examination of parataxis could inform a new theory for the diary, in particular a new feminine aesthetic. She argues that the piling up of undifferentiated happenings through unsubordinated and repetitive sentence patterns in the diary works subversively to "cross and blur boundaries between things traditionally kept separate."[7] It eliminates perspective based on distance and creates immersion. As we saw above in the work of Hampsten, Hogan examines how a diarist uses parataxis to maintain the cultural requirement placed on nineteenth-century female diarists that nothing happens in a day.

In identifying parataxis as a significant form in women's diaries, Hogan is interested in how the use of parataxis on the part of female diarists serves as an analogy or extension of their lives, that their writerly decisions are connected to gender and, consequently, engender the form. She concludes: "The diary's valorization of the detail, its perspective of immersion, its mixing of genres, its principle of inclusiveness, and its expression of intimacy and mutuality all seem to qualify it as a form very congenial to women/life writers" (105). Rather than see these rhetorical choices in terms of their aesthetic work or their apparent naturalness, I would like to consider how such decisions align with the diary's temporal connection to dailiness, specifically how parataxis as a rhetorical strategy allows the diarist to order her day and her page.

In lifting the ordinary diary outside questions of genre or aesthetics — knowing that Annie's diary will not answer those questions well no matter how "ordinary" the requirements are — we can broaden and complicate the work a diarist might be conducting within the pages of her diary. As Hogan demonstrates, parataxis is a powerful rhetorical strategy. Annie may choose to write parataxically in partial recognition of its power and also to make full use of the measuredness afforded by the diurnal form. What is important, it seems, is that the piling up of sentences, while undifferentiated in terms of privilege, may still remain separated in terms of task. What happens during the day is grammatically evened but it is also grammatically measured. Each recorded event or moment occupies a similar grammatical and syntactic place within the entry while displacing other, less measured, more eventful moments. There is a spacing, a horizontal piling, but it is not a melding. The measured spaces of the diary allow the diarist to rhetorically measure a day into small and equal parts, thereby denying hierarchy and maintaining stability. She does so in order to collect and name them while at the same time limit the impact any one event can have on another. And it is a strategy that ultimately allows Annie to order out what cannot be measured.

Annie relies on parataxis to level her vocabulary. There are any number of reasons that Annie might choose a limited vocabulary. Hampsten suggests that word choice in nineteenth-century diaries is largely a product of class. She maintains that nineteenth-century working-class midwestern diarists relied upon concrete nouns while middle- and upper-class women employed more abstract, imagistic language.[8] Such choice, she says, is a condition of education and leisure time. This discrepancy in language use also leads many readers to value the diaries of extraordinary women rather than ordinary ones (as we have been schooled to appreciate the figurative over the literal). Annie's birth, though, complicates a direct relationship between class and diction. Annie's mother, Lady Joan Ormiston, married the untitled Robert Pringle and they held land in Hawick, Scotland. However, immigration to the United States and, eventually, to the frontier meant that while they might consider themselves culturally upper class, their material conditions were more those of middle or working classes. While I do not know Annie's educational level, I do learn, through her diary, that she reads novels by Dickens, Elliot, and Stowe, that she reads and plays music, that she attends the theater, and that she enjoys the newspaper. However, the words Annie uses in her diary remain common, confined, and useful, far from the highly wrought language of the Victorian novels that she loves, making it appear that her word choice is not simply a reflection of her leisure time, class, or education.

Annie could also draw from a stable and limited vocabulary because she is relying on what sociolinguist Basil Bernstein calls a "restricted code." Drawing on the work of Temple and Bunkers, Brady examines how nineteenth-century diarists use unelaborate language and sentence structure when writing among people who are well known and familiar.[9] Not needing to explain in detail events that are known to all, a diarist might choose to use a sparse vocabulary of shared idioms — in the case of Annie a vocabulary familiar to her and Charley. When writing for another, unknown audience, the same writer might employ what Bernstein calls "elaborated" prose — one that makes emotion explicit and that relies on longer sentences and a wider vocabulary. As we saw in chapter 1, nineteenth-century diarists often shared their diaries with their families. Bernstein's distinction between codes and levels of familiarity help us to understand in terms of convenience why a writer might choose a restricted vocabulary. What I want to consider is what a diarist gains — beyond ease of communication — when she chooses from a confined and stable set of words. What does she need those words to do?

Annie's diary is filled with verbs and verbals. Doing. Making. Waiting. Washing. Every entry documents, often with an understood grammatical subject, the doings of the day. Washed. Scrubbed. Patched. Knitted. Blackened. Made. Sewed. Hoed. Thrashed. The nouns that enter are, for the most part, ephemeral products or results of the verbing rather than the subjects or agents of the action. The extraneous, elaborate aspects of her sentences — those that would propel them beyond, say, the documentation of a chore — are excised, simply not allowed entrance. And what remains within these bare-boned entries simply highlights — grammatically establishes — her weekly routine of work.

June 14 [1881]
Wednesday
Excessively warm. Browned coffee made Bread I washed a few
pieces. It is the first washing I have done since last march. I am
tired. Received a letter from M. T. Kemmerer. Sophie went to
Fathers place and borrowed the coffee mill and P.M. carried a drink
to Charley. I took a bath, I can hardly bear the heat. It rained last
night and is clouding up again.

[May 1882]
Friday 26
Fine & Pleasant. Charley finished planting corn and began to plant
Beans. I planted Peas and some choice Beans and hoed some
Onions.

In addition, the words Annie chooses, here both nouns and the verbs, for the most part, are repeated words. Like the loose pages she writes on, her vocabulary is recycled. Rarely, if ever, does Annie introduce a new or different word to document the day. Charley always hoes. He never weeds in the garden or tends the corn. Annie always patches. She never repairs. They go up town or down town. They never set out for town. She chooses from a stable and useful vocabulary. It is a vocabulary that is certainly concrete rather than abstract, reliable rather than malleable, spare rather than waxing. But such selection is not a result of her educational status as much as it is a rhetorical strategy Annie employs to reduce the options, to eliminate mess. By paring down and recycling her vocabulary, Annie keeps the unstable at bay.

Given the strategy she adopts it should not be surprising that there are very few adjectives — the words that Anne Carson says serve as the grammatical latches of the world, tying each noun down in a specific and unique way. Without such latches we are forced to operate at a certain level of generality and commonness. Patching is never qualified — washing is only a load or a large load. Annie employs metaphoric and descriptive language very rarely and usually only to describe the natural world — the shape of a cloud, or the way the frost clings to the grasses. It is not that she does not appreciate beautiful things — she remarks on whether the dress she makes is smart, if her hat is first-rate, she reads beautiful works of literature and enjoys playing the guitar — it is more that adjectives create a kind of detail that could swell her language beyond what she can and wants to control.

These limitations of language — her recycled diction and pared down sentences — work to exclude or order out possibility. For example, the work Charley does in the fields is typically limited within the diary entries to hoeing or threshing. Such a limitation in vocabulary has nothing to do with class, position, talent, or ability, but rather that when Charley goes out to the field for the day it signifies more than simply another day of work. On one level, Charley is engaging in an infinite number of complicated tasks, some of which Annie could name and others that she could not. So how he spends his days is somewhat a mystery to her. In addition, both his work and his social position allow him to leave the house while she cannot. (She writes on July 3, 1882: "This is such a lonesome place to live. I hardly see anyone. Charley can go to town occasionally. But I cannot.") Her confinement speaks both to the separation of spheres as well as to the fact that she physically cannot walk the distance to town while Charley can. By going into the field, he leaves her alone for the day with only the cows and chickens for company (she writes on August 18, 1882, "The loneliness is sometimes almost unbearable. It dont seem as though my life is of any use at all"). Her loneliness accumulates into depression and anxiety.

By continually reducing Charley's work in the fields to the verbs "hoeing" or "threshing," Annie brings a messy and complicated reality under control, regulation by a word. In essence, she reduces the complexity of her own position, her own loneliness, to a phrase: Charley hoed. In taking the measure of the day, she orders in what is controllable (that Charley is working) while ordering out the messy (that she is sad, lonely, and trapped). It is not that she does not have the time, leisure, education, or ability to write in more abstract and metaphoric ways. It is not that she is writing in a way that Charley might recognize. It is that the words required to do this work, to contain the reality of living on the plains in a claim shanty, must be as refined as the teeth of a rasp.

*　*　*

Annie reveals a similar desire to order the outerscape of her entries in the way she regulates her sentences. Simple, occasionally compound, but almost never subordinated, they too replicate her strategy of containment through parataxis. Short, simple, and repetitive, Annie intentionally uses only the number of words necessary to hold a place within an entry, to document a moment in the tick, tick, tick of diurnal time. They rarely unravel anymore. In addition, and maybe more significantly, her sentences often function without subjects or agents — assigning all domestic tasks grammatically as well as literally to one person, the rarely present subject, Annie. "Am tired." "Worked hard of course." "Washed & Made bread." "Am not well, Am decidedly unwell." This lack of grammatical subject is partially an outcome of diary writing — the one writing being the same one doing. Additionally, it can and does point to larger cultural instructions about when and how women can appear even in their own writing. But the lack of subject also speaks to her desire to continually operate at a certain level of generality, so general that this work could be ascribed to anyone. She knows what she has done that day and is therefore not forgoing the advantage of documenting work that typically passes unnoticed. But listing her chores without naming a subject provides the additional rhetorical benefit of lifting her daily work beyond a particular situation and settling it within a kind of routinized, subjectless cycle. It further eliminates grammatical latches and brings her work to the same semantic level as Charley's hoeing with the same promise of ordering out the mess.

Parataxis also allows Annie to contain potentially disruptive moments or events within a routinized, measured sequence, thereby deflating their status as events and denying their ability to matter. In this case, what might typically get ordered out makes an appearance in the text but it is so completely measured, so deftly contained that it is easily missed. Here is an example of how such deflation works within an entry.

[June 1881]
Wednesday 29
Cool A.M. but grew hot during the day. Johnnie came down and plowed our potatoes. Everything is growing finely.

Charley sent the Dr to see me. He made a careful examination and left more medicine. I am losing my hair. It is nearly all gone now. But the Dr thinks he can save some of it.

Ransacked my trunk and looked over a lot of old dresses trying to find something suitable to wear on the 4 of July if I go out that great day.

Again, the paratactic effect is an evening out of both grammar and content. It is difficult to say what was most significant about this Wednesday: harvesting? evidence of a good crop? the expense of medicine? her hair? the fact that she has few clothes? the anxiety/excitement about the upcoming holiday? When I read it I am always most shocked by her loss of hair. Such a response is largely a product of my own values and of a literary training that encourages me to assign meaning and worth to the juxtaposition of radically different ideas. Annie seems to be writing against that precise, literary reading. By embedding a potentially troubling and upsetting event within the other measured moments of the day, she demands of herself and her text that her baldness not destabilize her efforts to maintain control.

Parataxis appears as well between entries — sometimes to greater rhetorical effect. For example:

June 1st [1881]
Wednesday
/Pleasant./ I went to town Monday. Had dinner at the Doctors and got some more medicine   J & J moved over home. Fathers got a new stove. Tuesday I helped about the churning and done a good many other jobs. and had a severe head-ache in the evening.

Have not done much today, and feel pretty well. Charley is working on the house. The team father was working ran away today.

June 4 [1881] /*/
Saturday
I do not feel as well as usual. We are getting ready to move. It is very warm.

June 5 [1881]
Sunday
Moved into Davis house. I am very tired. We are very much crowded. and have not got all our things here yet. The house is small. I think we will be comfortable.

These entries awe me. June 1 is the first time that Annie mentions this house. By the fifth, two entries later, they have moved. "Had dinner at the Doctors and got some more medicine" has the same grammatical structure and occupies almost the same position within the entry as "Moved into Davis house." They are syntactically and physically identical. Yet, one would imagine the two events were experienced quite differently. The ways in which both events receive the same grammatical attention conceals or denies the reality that such a sudden move represents. It is subtle, almost magical, the way Annie uses language to, in her words, "put things right generally."

Finally, the progression between entries is also paratactic and assures the ordinary diary produces no event, creates no occasion. Climax requires the simultaneous privileging of certain events and deprivileging of others in order to propel action forward. It requires that the writer modulate how events unfurl. Annie works rhetorically to forestall climax, to deactivate the emotional release of closure by containing disruptive, eventful moments within the tick, tick, tick of the day. Such refusal of closure — a refusal that is replicated globally in the way the diary itself refuses closure — occurs repeatedly, especially in the first year of her diary, and it again points to the ways Annie can conceal her fears and anxieties by capitalizing on the diurnal form's ability to convey measure rather than occasion. Consider the following example.

In 1881, when Annie returns from Leadville to spend the winter without Charley, she brings a young girl named Sophie to help out and keep her company. This arrangement does not work at all. Apparently

Sophie is willful and stubborn. Annie whips Sophie at least once and refers to her as a "pest" at other times. The frustrating relationship between Annie and Sophie is revisited often at this period in Annie's diary. The topic functions almost like the words in her recycled vocabulary, reducing possibility. She and we both recognize it like we would the churning or the ironing. In the summer of 1881, Annie and Charley have finally been sent the money for Sophie's return trip to Colorado. Given the emotional upheaval Sophie's presence has caused up to this point, one would think her departure would be a climactic moment. Yet here is how Annie documents the day:

> July 24 [1881]
> Sunday
> Pleasant. As soon as the morning work was done Charley went over to town to get a bill changed for Sophie. She took a bath washed her hair and dressed while I packed her trunk. Then I bathed and dressed. In a short time Johnnie arrived with Lizzie for me to ride up home on, as we were all invited up there for dinner. Waited quite a while for C to return and then went off without him. When we got there, Father was making a Pudding for dinner. Had dinner about 1 oclock and partook heartily. Mr & Mrs Babcock & the baby came over about 3 o clock and stayed till eve. Father and I got Mothers clothes ready for me to bring down here and take care of. It was so sad. It always made me or any of us feel sad to see things Mother used to wear. We ate Supper with Father too. And then R hitched up the horses and brought us home. Sophie seemed to feel quite badly towards evening, and when she was bidding them good bye. We started to the Depot at 10 oclock. The train came at 11 and S was soon aboard and off. I often feel sorry for the little girl and sincerely hope she will get through all right, went to bed at 12 P.M.

This entry is a wonderful example of how Annie actively dismantles occasion. Sophie's departure on the train is not the central event of this entry. In fact nothing is. The dinner, Charley's late arrival, the visit from the Babcock's, collecting her mother's clothes, Annie's feelings about Sophie, and the time she and Charley got to bed *all* receive the same attention as Sophie's leave taking. Annie rhetorically decenters the entry and does not allow what was potentially a relief to achieve any climactic pull. We are almost left in the same place as when we began.

Sometimes such deactivation accumulates into complete denial. In the following example, the movement toward a climax — and in particular the emotional catharsis that accompanies a climax — is not so much decentered as completely denied. This usually works between entries (in particular when she is waiting for Charley to come home, waiting for the house to be moved to the claim, and waiting for the threshers to come). I will be looking at an example early in Annie's diary.

When the diary begins in January of 1881, Annie is working for her room and board at a boarding house in Plankington, Dakota. Charley has gone west to find work as a blacksmith and it is one in a series of winters in which Annie is separated from him. The winter of 1881 is a harsh one. Powerful blizzards blow across the plains. Annie and others are stranded in Plankington. The snow is too deep for trains or wagons to get through. Many of her initial diary entries document being stranded — in fact they replicate being stranded. But they also deny the release at being rescued. What follows is the chain of references to the blizzard. These references do not represent the complete entry for the given day nor do they represent all the entries Annie made during this time period.

January 21: The stage did not come.

January 25: It seems as though we are elected to stay here. This blockade is said to be the worst of the season — no trains to Mitchell since last Wednesday.

January 26: The R.R. is blockaded worse than ever.

January 29: Trains have not got through yet.

January 30: It is snowing hard this eve.

January 31: When will this end — I can hardly bear to stay here any longer and can not get away.

February 1: R- & I started to Mitchell this P.M. After we were down about 4 miles, Granger thought it would be dark long before we got there and that we had better come home so here we are.

February 2: Quite warm and pleasant. Trains have not got through to Mitchell since Sunday No chance to get home yet. I am so tired of waiting to get home and for Spring.

February 3: Sudden change — very stormy and cold. . . . The prospects for getting home are not better. The blockade is worse than ever. And coal almost gone.

February 5: Still storming — quite warm — Trains still at Algone and men tired of shoveling out. No prospects of getting home for some time.

February 6: The horses could not pull the loaded wagons through the drifts. . . . I wish I was home, I can hardly stand it any longer.

February 7: Am tired of everything here.

February 8: Jan. 30 was the last time I had a chance to go home.

February 9: The stage got through today.

February 10: This waiting is almost beyond human endurance. And there is no telling when it will end. It may be a few days a week or a month before we can go.

February 11: Traveling is almost impossible.

February 15: All the people round here are nearly out of coal and flour.

February 16: I wish we could get home.

February 20: If all goes well we will be in Mitchell tomorrow night.

February 21: Got to Mitchell at sunset. May not get home for a week. The trains will not be through for some time.

February 23: Home. Pleasant — that is not very cold. Started from Mitchell this morning without breakfast. Dined at Alexandra. Dinner was good But I did not eat much, my head ached. . . .

For over a month Annie documents being trapped in Plankington. We learn that fuel and food are short. Travel has ceased by foot, wagon, and train. Annie wishes the winter to be over, to be home, to be gone from the Granger's. Reading these entries, the evidence begins to build. We feel Annie's frustration. We desire release as well. Yet, such a climax is completely denied. Going home is not rhetorically heightened in any way. She is just there. "Home." Weather, her meals, her health — information documented every day — occupies its customary position. Not

only has nothing moved forward — the expectation of movement results in feeling as though you have moved back. Annie does not create
a plot — we do. She resists at every level the kind of highlighting, detailing, elaboration, and suspension required in telling a story. Instead
she controls her own reception of events (and ours) through parataxis.

By limiting her vocabulary, reducing possibility, and containing
potentially disruptive events within the measuredness of her entries,
Annie assures that nothing happens. And she does this *so well* that you
are almost soothed into believing that life on the plains is really that
measured and ordered. You become seduced by what Steven Kagle and
Lorenza Gramegna call "the illusion of control," the diarist's ability to
persuade herself and others that nothing is really happening at all.[10]
The fiction of a precise order works you over like the wind on the prairie
grasses. It causes you, along with Annie, to momentarily forget what
such ordering has ordered out. That is, until the order is disrupted:

> November [1882]
> Monday 6
> Clear and warmer. We overslept this morning and It was late when
> Charley got away to his work at Fathers. I get rather melancholy
> when I stay alone all day and see no one from sunrise till long after
> dark. I keep thinking, thinking. I think anyone must have a strange
> nature who can /forget/ anything which happens to be unpleasant
> to remember. As some people profess to do. Some people talk as
> though they could forget their whole past lives if they had a mind
> to. For my part I can forget *nothing* which has once been impressed
> upon my mind. Particularly anything which has caused me much
> *joy* or *sorrow*. As far as I can see, there is most of pain and sorrow
> in our lives. If we were only sure of *eternal* happiness beyond the
> graves, who would cling to life.

The appearance of this entry seems to suggest that Annie does not always order out her pain. Here she is expressing the very feelings that
are concealed by the hoeing and the washing. It is in these moments,
though, when Annie names her suffering and alludes to pain that far exceeds the number of chores or even the extent of her loneliness, that you
realize the amount of work she had been conducting every single day.
The regulation, the reduction, the repetition become even more meaningful rhetorical choices when illuminated by the sadness and anxiety
they have fought to contain. Ordering is never complete. It is never a

successful rhetorical choice — though it may be the only rhetorical choice. While Annie does "put things right generally," she never puts them right completely. However, even when disruption occurs in the diary, Annie strategically attempts to contain that which threatens to unmake both her and her text.

* * *

What gets ordered out, then, is not eliminated. It remains. And like the *kahuna*, it continues to haunt, to threaten the fiction of order. As I wrote in the previous chapter, Annie's diary is a haunted text. Most obviously, it remains the only trace of a vibrant, living being. Her apparently ordered, uneventful, and plain entries are equally haunted by what has been ordered out. Annie is trying to keep the unstable at bay, trying to keep the ghosts away. She is successful much of the time — meaning she successfully orders out what she cannot contain or she is able to bring the ghosts in by shrouding them in measuredness. However, her success depends on physically writing over or rhetorically concealing a reality that is working to take her apart, a reality she herself sometimes refers to as the "grim specter" (September 8, 1881).

On the very few occasions when Annie literally writes about this specter she is referring to an affair Charley had with the mysterious M. H. The affair, though, is simply one form the ghost can take. The "grim specter" becomes metonymic of all that is ordered out, and its presence haunts her text much more often and less literally. What Annie orders out, and what returns to haunt her text, encompasses more than the messy reality of an unfaithful husband. Its presence signifies all the anxieties and concerns generated by being a childless woman, alone on a prairie, at a historic moment that denies women choices and that contains them physically and politically. These anxieties erupt at times in Annie's diary, sometimes quite openly like when she writes on September 8, 1881, "I am suffering from great mental depression," or on October 5 of the same year, "I feel just like flying to pieces." Most often, though, the ghost is less visible; it enters as an absence, a contradiction, or concealed in the cloak of ineffable language.

* * *

At times, the ghost haunts an entry as merely something that Annie has crossed out but not eliminated all together. Saying that Annie crosses out what she cannot rhetorically contain needs complication, of course, for it might not be Annie who is crossing things out and there could be multiple reasons for censorship in nineteenth-century diaries (see chapter 1). Most often what gets washed out or crossed out, though, is conducted in the same ink color; so for my purposes at this moment I am attributing much of the censoring to Annie while at the same time acknowledging that such decisions might not have been hers. One of the first instances in which Annie censors herself is on January 20, 1881:

> Morning Cloudy — P.M. Pleasant. I felt very cross all forenoon. Everything I touched seemed to go wrong. Felt like scolding someone But did not and am glad of that. I do not think people are always to blame for their feeling so at times. ~~I wonder if Charley is thinking of me.~~

I find this entry fascinating. Just a few days prior to this Annie has hinted at the fact that she misses Charley, but then writes "But I am unwise to feel like this." Missing her husband, wondering if he is missing her is open, dangerous territory, a place where the wise would not go. We learn later in the diary that Charley has already betrayed her with at least one other woman, M. H. Wondering if he is missing her is akin to wondering if he is remaining true to her. His infidelity coupled with the fact that he might not care for her is a reality that, if acknowledged, threatens to sweep her away, drown her. It works to unwind what she has fought so hard to contain. Yet, hope lingers. Annie attempts to bring this ghost in, to inscribe it within the noneventful and usual. But almost as quickly she ushers it back out. Its energy, its import, however, literally remains, haunting the entry. Unlike previous instances of crossing out — "darned ~~a lot~~ some socks" — her editing has little to do with precision. She cannot measure in the instability of desire — her own or Charley's. So instead of writing directly about her relationship with Charley, Annie documents his presence in her life through their measured exchange of letters in the mail.

There are other moments when Annie censors that which potentially could destabilize both her marriage and her well-being. In August of 1881, Annie comes as close as she dares to naming Charley's deceit. The entry from August 23 is one of the longest in the diary and over half the entry is crossed out. Unlike the above example, where Annie still toys with a messier reality in simply drawing a line through the troubling sentence (so that it is still legible), what she crosses out in August is so unthinkable that it cannot be ordered out by a single strike through. In that entry, she refers to the past wrong done to her as something she tries to conceal but that, like a ghost, always makes its way back into her mind, her life, the pages of her diary. Here the censoring is final. How different this act of inscription is than the one above where she nestles the potentially disruptive reality of losing her hair in between her chores.

> Tuesday, August 23
> It did not rain much last night. There are indications of rain this morning it is thundering both in the north and South. Walter dropped a few words last night which brought to my mind some olden memories which were it in my power ~~I would blot out of my mind forever. I can not put it away from me. My heart aches with bitterness and indignation and a sense of the wrong done me which can never be~~ [crossed out and illegible] ~~The ones having~~ [crossed out and illegible] ~~can never in anyway atone for such a wrong.~~ [crossed out and illegible] ~~They have lost my faith and confidence in mankind. I had too much confidence. How blind I was not to see through it all. Especially~~ [crossed out and illegible for remaining twenty lines].

Unlike losing her hair or being alone on the plains, the pain of the past cannot be measured into the day. She has tried to "blot it out of [her] mind forever" but it still threatens to wash over her. Because it cannot be regulated by a word like "hoes," or ordered among the washing and ironing, or simply crossed out with a single line, she orders it out completely by willing it not to exist.[11] These are examples of a physical ordering out. We know that she was thinking about what troubles her, that she was willing to write about it at least initially, but that other forces in her life (her own prudence, her fear, her own ambivalence) compel her to cross them out. We can wonder about the therapeutic value of the initial inscription, but we can only know for certain that these moments could not remain within the pages of her diary. What is harder to see are the moments when the ordering out occurs before the destabilizing event or thought even makes it to the page. Here the ghost is harder to detect. I see its presence in entries like the one from July 4, 1881.

> After breakfast we began to get ready to go to B[ridgewater] to celebrate this "Great day." It took some time — Then the boys came down and we rode over with them.
> There was nothing new on the program. /we/ enjoyed our selves pretty well Had dinner at Shucks. I was introduced to several ladies: The singing was quite good.

We found an old carriage vacant — took possession for an hour or two and found it a most comfortable place to rest and watch the surging crowd, and study faces. There is nothing I like better for a past time. This is very different from all other celebrations I ever attended.

Annie has been looking forward to the Fourth of July picnic. She has spent time finding something to wear and has been preparing picnic food for the past few days. Such preparation would typically signify "eventfulness"— like the preparation she makes for Burns' Anniversary or for the threshers to come. However, in documenting this "Great day," she begins by saying that there was "nothing new on the program." Her enclosure of the holiday, this great day, within the routine or program of all her other days is a familiar enough rhetorical move. In line with other uses in the diary of "usual" and "uneventful," such a statement by Annie signifies control over the "outerscape" and over her writing, that the fiction has been maintained. However, unlike most of Annie's entries, this one appears to have been written at different moments. The space between the sentences is a technique Annie usually reserves for changes in tone, subject matter, or writing situation (see chapter 2). It appears that this entry may have been written in several stages — in particular, the final section detailing the carriage comes as almost an afterthought. In addition, unlike other entries this one does not proceed chronologically. Both the nonlinear aspects of the entry, combined with the detail surrounding the abandoned carriage, push this entry into occasioned time rather than measured moments.

Most significantly, Annie ends this entry by saying things are no longer routine. Something has happened. She writes, "This is very different from all the other celebrations I ever attended." And we are left to wonder about the contradiction. Are things the same or has something caused a disruption. The point may seem unconvincing — after all it is just a contradiction. But when you consider that the contradiction rests within the language of the "usual" and the "different" and the accompanying costs that each status brings, the ambivalence seems much more significant. Was the day a day like any other? Or is she indicating an anxiety through opposing language? It is not surprising that the following day Annie writes that she is "putting things to right generally." Although she is literally referring to their wraps and clothing, she is also trying to clean up a more metaphoric mess, trying to return to measuredness within her day and within her writing.

That which threatens the fiction of stability, the ghostly presence that disrupts, is signaled again by imprecise language. Such moments stand in stark relief to the measured language Annie is usually at pains to employ: time, weight, distance, amount, anniversaries, expenditures, weather, dates, correspondence, visits, and deaths. As I stated above, Annie relies on a recycled vocabulary that works to reduce possibility, to reduce reality to a single word, "hoes," for example. It is a vocabulary equally governed by precision, a literal means of making order. This dedication to a set of words and their specific meanings gives Annie the ability to measure her day, to cement what she can control. Imprecise language works toward the opposite effect — releasing the meaning and potential of language, allowing multiple possibilities to coexist. Like contradiction, it signifies a break with the measured by complicating the reading — hers and ours.

By imprecise language I mean abstract nouns like "thing" or indefinite adjectives like "some." Appearance of such language often signals her struggles with the ghost. What such language gets for Annie is a kind of distance that blurs or conceals her connection to what she writes about as well as her emotional investment. For example, on July 13, 1881 (after the Fourth of July picnic), she writes:

[July 1881]
Wednesday 13
Very warm, but breezy. Fixed up some clothes for Sophie. The Dr called to see how I was getting along. I am feeling well most of the time.
Charlie went up to Father's to try and get them to do some breaking for him. Some things are rather discouraging.

The final sentence is both elliptical and vague. We have no idea to what she is referring, though we can guess maybe her health or the fact that they do not own a horse and plow and must rely on others to break sod for them. Whatever it is that is troubling makes it into the measuredness of her day under the veil of imprecision but only to haunt what has been more efficiently measured. It hovers, syntactically detached from time or place as well as physically detached from the rest of the entry.

The following comes several days later:

[July 1881]
Friday 29
Quite windy. But pleasant. Charley worked up at Fathers 2 or 3
hours this A.M. & went to town this P.M. for mail. I sewed a little.
Things in the garden are looking well. and I hope they will continue so. Other things are discouraging enough. My health is still
improving which is one blessing I am truly thankful for.

Again, we do not know what is discouraging and its vague presence
weighs heavily against the precision of the weather, the amount of time
Charley worked, and her health. The presence enters but is not named.
Such moments, passing references to "some things," are not given the
recognition or the paratactic position of the mail or the washing. They
simply hover in the entry, suggesting by their vagueness all that cannot
be contained.

Sometimes Annie uses vague language to speak more directly about
her own situation. In these instances, more than in the above examples, the entries are ghosted with the fact that Annie cannot write directly about her feelings, that she is limited in choices. The closest she
can come to naming her fears is to dilute her references beyond their
ability to be traced. While it is a way for Annie to write about herself at
a slant, the references only appear in opposition to what she is working
hard to measure. For example, she writes later in 1881:

November 1st [1881]
Tuesday
Windy & cold. The Butcher came & got two cattle. I am very sore &
lame especially my right arm. It hurts me to do any thing. Rode
Lizzie over to town this P.M. I expected a letter from Charley but
did not get one. What a hard, hard life some people have. One
week ago C & I went down to our claim.

It is fairly clear that the "some people" whose lives are difficult is a reference to her own — to the fact that Charley has left again for the winter. She refers obliquely to herself in other examples like this one from
the same month:

Nov[ember] 27 [1881]
Sunday
This is a beautiful day. We had what is called a transparent morning.
The air all day has been as soft and balmy as on a summer day. We

could see for miles further in every direction than we usually can. Jane & the Babcocks were here this P.M. also Walter who took dinner with us. I expected a letter from Charley. Robbie went for mail. But I was disappointed. This is the third November Charley & I have lived apart. What strange hard times some people have. I wonder what Charley is doing and where he is.

Again, the abstract and vague "people" stands in for herself and stands out in contrast to the rest of her ordered day — precise down to the day's weather and the number of winters they have spent apart in their married life.

The ghost does make figured appearances in Annie's entries — or more specifically appears in figurative language. The appearance of figurative language in conjunction with an ordinary diary signals the disruptive capabilities of the ghost. As I have said, Annie does not use many adjectives, let alone metaphoric language. The elaborative potential of adjectives or figures of speech (those as imprecise and veiled as metaphors) are the very kinds of mess Annie is constantly working against. Yet, they appear. And when they do they, like contradiction and imprecision, point to the looming presence of all that has been ordered out.

Metaphors and other kinds of imagistic language create layers of meaning, multiple and potentially irreconcilable ways of seeing and being in the world. They complicate meaning. They allow for messier realities to exist. The appearance of metaphor, then, signals Annie's recognition of all the incompatibility between her diary and her life. It allows her to allude to a situation without naming it.

The metaphors Annie uses are repeated. In this way, as with her strategy of using a recycled vocabulary, she does work to contain them within the measuredness of the diurnal form. Still, the sheer openness to interpretation is so striking in comparison to her daily work that their presence replicates, for the reader, the disruptive force they represent. Typically they appear at the end of an entry, though they can also begin an entry or erupt in the middle. The most often used metaphors include: the "grim specter," the "affair rankling in [her] heart," "the veil which hides from [her] view nearly the whole of the one trial and disapointment of [her] life," the fear that she is "wasting her life," and — as in the following example — the comparison of her life to the weather or the seasons.

[October] 18 [1881]

Tuesday

This is a lovely day. I wish it could be like this all the time it is so warm and pleasant. But that cannot be. The seasons are made up of warmth & cold. Clouds & sunshine. So is life but there seems to be far more clouds & storms than sunshine. I washed, scrubbed and baked beans today. Charley went down to our claim today to start putting up a shanty. Mrs. Shuck brought back the machine today and said she had not been able to make it run. She paid me a dollar for the use of it. I went to town this eve and mailed letters to David, Miss McKemmie, Walter & a card to Mrs Ward. I do not feel quite well.

In this example, the removed reference to the difficulties in her life extends from the measured documentation of the weather and moves just as easily into scrubbing the beans. The few recycled metaphors that Annie uses reveal, in their multiplication of meaning, a messiness of living on the plains that no amount of grammar, language, or measuredness of days can work to contain. Less metaphoric, but equally imprecise, repetitive, and loaded are other standard phrases that she uses, including: "I wish some things were different," "I am thinking, thinking, thinking," and "I feel strange." All appear at moments when Annie seems closest to writing about the reality of living alone on the plains, closest to confronting the ghost. And they ache with the effort.

Only *worked all day*. I wonder where Charley is and what he is doing. I have a bad cold.

I have been thinking, thinking, thinking. Have heard it said that we never stand still — But either grow better or worse. I wonder if I am as good as I used to be.

[January 27, 1881]

It has been severely cold today. Wrote a letter to Mrs Ward and one to Miss Virgile. Some way I feel down-hearted and lonely. The way seems so hard and dark.

[February 27, 1881]

These phrases, these metaphors, bear meaning and point to bigger, messier, uglier realities than those that can be inscribed in ordinary writing. The words "I feel strange" represent such an enormous distance from "Washed & Made Bread" that it is impossible for either her or us to really transgress the space. So much rests in both. The first holds all that cannot be said. The second the skill required to say the rest.

Finally, the longest, and perhaps most dramatic, appearance of the ghost occurs in Annie's dreams. Dreams function as a kind of free space for Annie, a blank wall that is less ordered and regulated than "real" life. She cannot help what she dreams. Therefore, she does not have to control her dreams. While she certainly can choose whether to document the dreams in her diary, they allow her the ability to speak about the unspeakable. Annie mentions her dreams four or five times in the space of four years. Once or twice it is only to say that she dreamt the previous night, or that she had bad dreams, or that the dreams kept her awake ("My dreams were of an unpleasant nature," February 13, 1881). On another occasion she mentions that she dreamt she was dying ("I dreamt last night that I was dying. I thought I was drawing my last breath. It was a strange sensation and I was glad when I awoke," December 21, 1881), and on another she dreams of suicide and murder ("I had horrid dreams last night of murder Suicide &c.," January 30, 1882). These references remain relatively sparse and unconnected to each other or to the rest of the entry. More importantly, they are ordered into the measuredness of the day. For example, the dream of dying on December 21 is preceded with the exact time it began to snow and her sewing projects and is followed by, "Worked over & packed Butter. Had vegetable soup for dinner."

By the middle of 1882, the random quality of her dreams begins to change — as does her ability to contain them. Annie mentions on August 17, "I dreamed again one of the old dreams which has become a nightmare to me." It becomes more apparent that her nightmares are related to each other in some way and illuminate a specific event. Whether or not Annie actually has these dreams or whether she is making them up is of little importance. What is important is that dreams, as less regulated spaces of the imagination, and her writing about her dreams allow Annie to acknowledge a reality that is too threatening to name openly in her diary. It is not insignificant that Annie begins to refer to her dreams as "The Dream" in August of 1882. This is the same time that Annie and Charley have their "long talk" about a "very painful subject." It is also the period of time containing the long and mostly censored entry when she comes closest to naming Charley's deceit (August 23). The close positioning of the dream and his infidelity begin to signify each other, and her nightmares start to name the cause of her sadness more specifically.

Then on March 2, 1883, out of nowhere, Annie records a dream in the single most occasioned, storied, descriptive, and lengthy entry by far in four years of diary keeping. It stands out so starkly against the other entries that it seems written by another person for another purpose in an altogether different kind of space. Here is that entry in entirety:

Friday, March 2
Very pleasant and warm. The beautiful spring like weather makes me feel like staying on the farm. March came in like a lamb this year. I wonder if it will go out like a lion. C. has gone to town today. I read some in the "Brownie O' Bodsbeck". Done a little sewing and made some paper flowers. I dreamed last night of being in the old log school house at Slabtown. At some kind of gathering. C. was there also M. H. I saw her getting ready to go before the meeting was out. At the same time noticed C. putting on his wraps. I felt my heart sink with a vague fear and anxiety. I went to him and asked him where he was going. He looked at me angrily and seemed much annoyed. And with out him giving me a direct answer I knew he was going with her. I remonstrated with him (because I thought I had a right to as I was his wife). He accused me of being small and jealous. Said if I was not I would not want her to go alone so far. It seemed two or three miles. But I knew it was because he liked her so well he was going so they went away up the Slabtown hill and through the woods over towards Pigeon Creek. I followed at a distance of about 50 yds. The night seemed so dismal, cold and dreary. And I felt cold and weary and my heart ached so hard. After a while I got to talking with C. and crying. It seemed as though I was begging him to do different. He was vexed at me for following and wanted me to go away from them. I asked him if I might not talk to her and he said I could. So I got her to go back along the road a piece so he would not hear and I sat down on an old log and crying all the time, I told her how much misery their intimacy had caused me and how different I had expected life to be from what it was and how happy I used to be at first before they knew each other. I wanted them to stop. But she was not sorry, she did not care for my misery. She did not care for my rights. They found pleasure in each

others society. That was all they cared for. She looked thoughtless and happy and I thought how hard hearted she was. My tears did not move her. Then I went away back alone in the dark. With my heart aching. Then it seemed that I went to the School house and began to hunt up my books and things as I used to do the last day of school. Some things I could not find, some of my books were torn. I found some pretty vases among some old rubbish on one of the windows. I wondered if they belonged to anyone. I thought if I knew no one would care I would take them they were so pretty. One was broken. But I left them there. All the time I was getting ready to go, my heart was aching and with my sorrow, it never went out of my mind what ever I done I felt so lonesome and my eyes smarted with the tears I had shed. I thought I had never seen her before and that I studied every feature of her face, every word and gesture to get the right idea of her character. I started along the road up towards my old home. But never dreamed of reaching there or anywhere else. I just seemed to wander around and then after a while I woke. Felt somewhat depressed after such a dream. I have suffered as much in my dreams and been as happy too in dreams as I ever was in reality. And I like to dream. They seem like revelations sometimes. Other times they seem prophetic and one often seems in a different world altogether.

So much could be said about this unusual entry. Its length alone is staggering — fifty-some lines in comparison to the average entry length of only seven lines. What I find most interesting is how this entry stands in opposition to all the others in terms of the work it must do. While it begins as most of her entries do, with the language and style of measuredness, it quickly turns to occasion, as if the dream is too large, too unsettling to be contained within the chores. In fact it is a doubly occasioned entry, as it describes both the occasion of the dream and the occasion within the dream. There is a modulation of information, a narrative with a setting (the schoolhouse), characters (Charley, Annie, and the mysterious M. H.), and a plot that reaches its climax. Unlike the entry documenting Sophie's departure, emotions are named. Annie and Charley have an argument and state their feelings. Annie claims the right to be angry, even if her claim is marooned by her own parentheses: "(because I thought I had a right to as I was his wife)." No longer is it simply "some people" whose life is hard, it is her own "misery" and "heart aching." She writes herself out in her dream in a way that she cannot in her days. The fiction of a dream, the blank wall a dream provides, means that things no longer must be limited and controlled by language. Adjectives — "dismal," "cold," and "jealous" — swell her sentences beyond the general and the measured, inviting the complexity, possibility, and fullness of language into her writing as well as into her life. At the end of her dream, she has not "put things to right generally." Instead she is unable to find what she is looking for and is wandering aimlessly around. How far we are from washing a large load.

This dream is the most haunted entry in Annie's diary. It is also, significantly, the least ordinary writing that she conducts. It does not heed the rules of diurnal discourse by unfolding in endless, paratactic, and open ways. Rather it breaks such measuring and allows Annie to write herself out in a less regulated and, arguably, more "real" way. Only because the entire occasion is situated within the fictions of a dream can it remain within the pages of the diary. Unlike other, more censored entries — censored both literally and rhetorically — Annie details her fears and acknowledges by name the forces that are working to take her apart. Ultimately, the dream is the same ghostly presence that haunts other entries via imprecise language, contradiction, and crossing out. It is just a more dramatic example.

* * *

I hope the danger in that last sentence is apparent. The danger in claiming that the most storied and literary writing Annie produces is also the most dramatic. In the dream entry Annie comes closest to naming her reality and closest to a literary form most readers would recognize and respect. I would argue, though, that the drama of this entry is only apparent when you recognize the kind of work Annie has been conducting every single day in her diary. The reason that the ghost of all that Annie orders out can be traced is because the tools and vocabulary exist for naming all that has been ordered in. Annie puts to use the measuredness of the diurnal form in a rhetorically strategic and powerful way. She is not a plain writer. Her entries are not boring and uneventful. They pulse with the effort of a writer who has capitalized on the rhetorical opportunities of the diary and who extends the potential of dailiness. And they document the experience of a woman who is physically and emotionally worn from living on land that churns like the sea.

Why not . . . level the concept of high art
and recover another sort of art, one that is
not dressed in prestige but that names,
nevertheless, an aesthetic or crafting that underlies
the practices of everyday life. . . .
RALPH CINTRON, *Angels' Town*

4 : Making Ordinary Writing

It is late April, 1969. For the past few weeks, sparse desert flowers have begun to appear along the cactus-rimmed roads of Kingsville, Texas, a town in the south of the Lone Star state, a town known mostly for its naval base. The flowers rise open-faced and brimming with the promise of new life after a short, mild winter, one noticeable only to the locals. Within several months, somewhere in the hot middle of summer, the roads will be filled with June bugs the size of small mammals. Those who have lived in Kingsville for at least one summer already know that when driving these June-bugged roads, they need to turn the radio up in the car to drown the sound of the bodies crunching beneath the tires. But this is not yet. Now it is spring. And in rhythm with the rest of the natural world, the obstetrics ward of the Kingsville County Hospital is filled with women giving birth to their own open-faced bundles.

A man races into the waiting room reserved for expectant fathers. He is tall and thin and strong, wearing a dark suit with a narrow, plain tie. A few short hours before he had been at the hospital and then left. Having made sure his wife was safely in the hands of the doctors, he rushed home to shower and change from his cotton pants and T-shirt. When his first child came into the world, he wanted to be wearing a suit. Now, shaving cream still clinging to the lobes of his long ears, he has returned, suited, and takes a place in the waiting room with the other fathers. The total trip has taken only a little over an hour. What he doesn't know now is that the waiting has only begun.

*   *   *

Recently, I spent some time looking back through the writing note-books I have kept during the making of this text — a set of four spiral-bound books used to help me think through my ideas and to clarify my questions. As I paged through the notebooks, I was struck by a number of things — not the least of which is how much my project has changed. In my earliest notes, Annie's diary figures very little. My pages are filled with attempts to define the power of story and the reasons that story matters. Lists and lists of possible stories to tell, stories that I can no longer even remember, are interspersed with quotations that wend a history of what I was reading at the time. These moments are so far from — really the complete opposite of — where I would eventually end: the making of ordinary writing. Looking at these pages now, what I appreciate is the way my notebooks remember these efforts, record these attempts. They document the transparent process of thinking, by naming all that would typically pass unnoticed and unmarked. In them, I watch as ideas are taken up and dropped. I can see a scholar enter my head for a week and divert my attention, like a fallen tree limb across a river, until I eventually realize that I have left the banks of my own questions in pursuit of theirs.

My journals also document the equally elusive making of a text, spe-cifically the making of this book. The ways ideas trail off, halt, or pile up testify to the fact that writing is always partial, that it comes from many places, and that it ultimately results in a temporary set of decisions rather than a seamless text. The pages are mostly filled with what has been left behind. For it is only when I am most empty, most blocked that I fill these pages in desperation. Once I have what Ann Berthoff calls an idea to think with, I leave, only to return a few days later, having reached another end. In this way, these notebooks document the mid-dles of my project — the working through rather than the crafting of.

They also reveal the dailiness of making a text. Along with the quo-tations, the outlines, and the anxiety ("I am a fraud" or "How will I ever figure out what to write"), come my bank balance, a telephone number without a name, flight information for a job interview, and the list of points I want to remember to make when I call my landlord back to lodge a complaint. As with Annie's diary, there is no spatial hierarchy in my notebooks. The vet appointment and a critical citation about the everyday occupy the same space. My days come and go in these pages.

Really, reading now what I wrote then I am thrilled by how — in the writing of a text about the making of ordinary writing — I have also succeeded in producing ordinary writing of my own. Thrilled because years ago I would not have known what I had nor had the tools to read it. A few years ago, these notebooks would surely have been tossed.

.   .   .

In this final chapter, I want to consider ordinary writing more broadly and to suggest at least three outcomes that result from learning to read a text like Annie's diary, a piece of ordinary writing. In short, I will suggest that reading ordinary writing (1) illuminates more clearly the making of both subject and text and in so doing reveals the partiality of all texts, (2) complicates the site of ordinary writing beyond simple considerations of the ordinary that work to either idealize or demonize that site, and (3) ushers ordinary writing into conversation with lifewriting and in so doing demands a broader definition of what counts within that field. Before turning to these outcomes, though, I want to summarize the defining attributes of ordinary writing in general as well as what I have learned specifically about ordinary writing from reading Annie's diary.

From the beginning I have defined ordinary writing largely in terms of what ordinary writing is not. This is not because I want to privilege categories like the literary or affirm ultimately useless dichotomies, but rather because the only way we can talk about the ordinary is through negation. The ordinary disappears as soon as we approach it. Because the ordinary rests as a backdrop against the more extraordinary, storied moments in our days, we can only see it as the frame, as that which surrounds the other, nonordinary moments in our lives. That the ordinary is "made up of everything that doesn't stand out"[1] does not mean we can't define ordinary writing, but it does mean that much of the way we define it will depend on defining what it is not. I have used the metaphor of the stream to describe the ordinary but the image of white space in a painting is also useful. When we view a picture, our eye pays attention to the colors, to the forms. We don't typically see the ways in which the white space, the ordinary, defines these figures, causes them to appear through negation. To say ordinary writing is not literary writing, then, does not privilege the category of literary writing as much as it names the reality that most writing is not literary. The limit of the literary, though, is also what makes ordinary writing so powerful and pervasive. It is everywhere, like air.

Ordinary writing is also defined by its status as the discarded, or maybe I should say more clearly its status as the disregarded and hence easily discarded. Miller writes in *Assuming the Positions* that ordinary writing is "writing we choose not to see."[2] We choose not to see it because we have been taught not to see it. We value differently. Our prejudices, assumptions, forestructures cause us to sweep past that which is so present. In the introduction to his study of people and their diaries, Thomas Mallon tells a story about returning home after the death of his father. Cleaning out his father's closet, Mallon comes across boxes and boxes full of canceled checks. Unlike most of us, Mallon's father never threw a single canceled check away. When what is typically discarded is instead saved, we glean a measured performance of a life in process: the grocery store, a pair of shoes, electricity, the hospital bill for the birth of his son, Thomas. The checks capture the in-between moments of a life. They document the experience of being in the days.

As a result of my work with ordinary writing, my office has begun to resemble the curbside piles my family used to pillage when I was a child. I hesitate to throw anything out, realizing that the act of tossing is equally an act of valuing, that I am largely in charge of what becomes the ephemeral, the ordinary in my life. So I have bank statements dating back to 1987 — statements that trace my marriage and divorce in the changing name on the account. And I have begun to save random notes to myself and others, as well as the datebooks in which I record appointments. In used bookstores, I find myself more taken by the notes left in books and the notes written within books than I am by the books themselves. Most recently, I discovered a dictionary in which the insides of the front and back covers were marked by tiny, faded penciling. While I could not actually read the writing, I did realize that this text was not random but made, and that, given time, I could read the work of the one who made it.

Of course the question becomes, is ordinary writing still ordinary when it is saved? Literally speaking, no. Something cannot be both ephemeral and saved. But this very paradox points to a third attribute of ordinary writing — it was not supposed to be here but it is. That is what makes it an opportune site for contemplating the ways in which ordinary choices by ordinary writers at ordinary moments reveal the complex set of negotiations constantly undertaken by writers, by people living in the world. As a document not meant to last — not meant to stand in or withstand a public — it demonstrates more readily — less craftedly — the work of the writer and the inadequacies of writing. We glimpse what we should not be able to see and, as a result, we learn how individuals make texts, make subjects, and ultimately make culture every single day.

Hence, we can define ordinary writing as a text that is not literary, is not noticed, and one that should have been discarded but that instead somehow remains. As I write in the introduction, though, a text is not intrinsically ordinary but rather assigned to the ordinary by its context. I don't think I can emphasize this point enough. People are always asking me what "counts" as ordinary writing. My response is to ask where the writing was found and how it works rhetorically rather than to focus on what kind of text it is. Notes, diaries, cookbooks, letters, memos, messages, and lists can all be ordinary writing, but they may just as easily not be. Questions of genre in many ways fail us in thinking about ordinary writing. And limitations of genre — literary, autobiography — are the very concepts that perpetuate the invisibility of texts like Annie's because they ask questions that neither text nor writer can answer well. There are many, many diaries that are far from ordinary. Diary writing as a genre is not automatically equated with ordinary writing. A diary like Annie's, however, becomes ordinary writing when the context surrounding and informing the writer and the text define it as unmarked, unreadable, and without value. We can then only access that writing once we learn to ask questions attuned to the measured hum of the ordinary.

When we learn to read ordinary writing, we discern additional, more particular attributes — features that not only reveal it as existing in the first place but that allow us to see ordinary writing as a complicated and made text. What we learn, for example, is that ordinary writing, as writing that documents the in-between, unmarked moments of our daily lives, takes the *measure* of all things. It is not an occasioned document, a document shaping an occasion, but is produced and remains in the middle. What we learn about the temporality of the ordinary diary becomes metonymic of the fact that ordinary writing is always in the moment rather than about the moment. Even though ordinary writing may not be diurnal in the ways an ordinary diary is — not kept every day — ordinary writing is written every day and always in the moment. In the same ways that Pepys's recorded carriage fares represent his passage through the city and Annie's financial accounts along with the weather and the meals duplicate her complicated, layered experience of time and space, the canceled checks Mallon's father saves document the unmarked moments in his life, as the list of errands

I made only yesterday — the list I have since tossed — marks mine. None of these documents tells a story. They can be made to story, but their own work — their rhetorical work — is to take the measure, not render the occasion.

That ordinary writing is defined in large part by its temporality should not be surprising. The everyday — that which passes unnoticed — is unmarked primarily *because* it is boring, repetitive, and cyclical.[3] It is not a reflective space but an immediate one, where the subject is immersed in the rote, repetitive, and mundane. The temporal register of ordinary writing assures that the text remains open rather than closed, fragmented rather than whole, nonnarrative, unframed, and halting. If a moment were not a part of this repetitive, measured hum, it would become a noticed, marked, and narrated occasion that begins and ends *at the very moment it leaves and returns to the ordinary.*

For example, the journals that I kept when writing this book are marked by the middles of my project. They record the ordinary and contain the discarded, the unused. When I have an idea, I leave my journals — often in midsentence — to write the nonordinary text that you are reading right now. If I could intertwine these two texts, I could begin to have a sense of the fluidity with which our lives and our texts vacillate between the marked and unmarked moments of our days. It could potentially look like this:

---

documenting the ordinary is a methodology → refuses closure

Sept. 16

mom cell
817-563-2242

I was talking with Rona last night about my next chapters. She asked me what I most wanted people to know about Annies diary — which is sort of the same question I am always struggling with — why is this important. Cintron is able to say his work on the everyday is important because it is closer to the <u>real</u> — the rest is all about order — maybe what I want to suggest is that by studying the ordinary we can see that it is no more real than anything else but equally important in terms of making us who we are — how we want to be — so I would look @ the structuring of the ordinary — how it gets constructed — how Annie <u>uses</u> her wtg to fabricate a self the way one might choose their politics or their clothing — it is one more way of being in the world

---

My fear is that one day I will decide that I know Annie — but really I can never know her — the diary seduces me as it hints at trauma into thinking I know who Annie is — but by delighting in the messiness

Have you ever been swimming in glacial water — water turned milky blue or deep maroon by minerals and deposits seized by the glacier as it ponderously made its way across a continent? You would have been high atop a mountain, maybe in the Canadian Rockies or in Montana, where glaciers, now in retreat, still press down on the earth's crust. And it would have been in the summer — late August perhaps — the sun warm and still and bright, making you feel as if a dip in this remote glacial tarn is just what your tired body needs at this point in your day. Maybe you would have tested the water with your hand before undertaking the arduous process of unbooting. And your fingers would have said, yes, get in. Off come boots, wool socks, and liners made dank by sweat and three-day-old dirt. Off comes your shirt, shorts, underclothes — your body not quite so warm, a tiny breeze lifting over the pass. Still the water waits, still.

By intertwining these two texts (a page from my notebook and the start of chapter 2), I can see myself write my way into nonordinary writing. My writing thrums along — nonhierarchical and nonlinear — shepherding into the same space what I am reading, how I want to diverge, an important conversation, and my mom's new cell phone number. When my thoughts turn to my ethical responsibility as a writer, I leave that page to make this text. I remember where I was when I was writing this entry — sitting in a house in Evansville, Indiana, where Michael was teaching poetry. Stuck and staring, mulling over failure and the lure of story, my eyes fell on a picture of Michael sitting near a glacial tarn that we swam in several summers ago in Glacier National Park. Story, a story, moves me along, pulls me from the nonnarrative march of the ordinary and into a moment. I then inscribe that moment as a clear, whole, wrought text. What was invisible, partial, halting on the page becomes, for my reader, a round image, a unified moment, a story to caution against the woo of story.

＊　＊　＊

But more important than being able to identify or define ordinary writing is all that we gain when we learn to read it. Developing tools to read ordinary writing allows us to see that ordinary writing, while measured and open and fragmented and boring, presents just as complicated an intersection of writer, text, and context as any form of writing. What we first might take as simple, unsophisticated, and plain becomes one of the few opportunities to access the ways in which subject and text are made every day by ordinary people.

For example, we see Annie construct her text in tune with the cultural scripts that surround her as well as her own sensitivity to the capacities of the diurnal form. On a daily, almost hourly basis, we see Annie work at performing — in her writing — the kind of woman that she feels she should be — the woman inhabiting the literature she reads, the woman her mother taught her to be, the woman whose concern for others is always uppermost. At the same time, in the way that Annie decides how she will use her diary and how she will set boundaries and create conversations within and between the pages and the entries, we discern more agency and control than that typically granted ordinary writers or even nineteenth-century women. Such boundary setting complicates our understanding of Annie as both a woman and a writer. She is neither fully confined nor fully free, and quite often she appears to be in charge at the same time we read of her confinement and despair. In the same entry even.

How different — how simplistic — our understanding of Annie would be if we only relied on writing made by others rather than Annie's own production. For example, Annie lingers as a shadow in her own obituary, a text written by the Rev. A. C. McCauley who describes himself, in his "Beautiful Tribute to Mrs. C. A. Ray," as her "beloved pastor for 46 years." He spends two columns speaking about Annie's father and brothers and husband, referring specifically to Annie only in reference to her physical health — "Mrs. Ray has never been very strong" — or when noting her work for the church. This column reads little differently than the tribute written a year earlier in the same newspaper when she and Charley celebrate their fifty-first wedding anniversary. Only in this article Annie does not even have the status of being deceased. There is little direct mention of her. Charley and his successes as an entrepreneur dominate the text. I find it hardest to read when the author, at the beginning of the article, writes that "the Tribune extends to [Mr. and Mrs. C. A. Ray] its heartiest congratulations on having lived together for so unusual a period." I find myself wondering in such a small town as Bridgewater what makes the period so unusual, the length or the circumstances. Given only these texts, Annie remains absent and feeble.

It is, then, significant that Annie negotiates her identity in *her writing,* by her hand. Her use of parataxis to reduce possibility and her work to order out what she cannot or does not want to name are clearly not the strategies of an unsophisticated or uncomplicated writing subject. Her diary documents more than her daily chores. Rather, it documents her performance of identity — largely through gaps, absences, and emptiness — and ultimately comments on how a woman in the nineteenth century replicates and resists cultural directives naming how and when women should write, think, feel, and appear. While we need to keep in mind Leigh Gilmore's caution that autobiographical identity and agency are not identical to agency in real life, we cannot fail to miss the fact that what we have when we read ordinary writing is anything but simple, static, and known.[4]

In addition to offering an unexpected example of a complex text and writing subject, ordinary writing actually illuminates the work undertaken in other, nonordinary texts. I will be examining this point more fully below, but for now I simply want to name the fact that ordinary writing offers a lens for reexamining all texts. Because ordinary writing is not seamless or whole — a result of its middleness and immediacy — it illuminates more clearly the ways in which all writing is made and therefore partial. Like all texts, ordinary writing represents a set of temporary and tentative decisions made by a subject whose identity is equally contested. Unlike crafted, literary texts, the choices made by the writer are more visible in ordinary writing because the writer is not working to create a narrated whole and may even be — as in Annie's case — actively working against such closure. We can see and name those decisions in large part because of the opportunities (or constraints) of ordinary writing — the fact that there is no space for reflection or closure. Ordinary writing will always reveal the seams.

Before detailing the three outcomes reached by reading ordinary writing — before moving to assert an order in my own text, to claim closure, to say that this is what we have when we are done, to say this is why my story matters, to suture the remaining seams — I want to remember and record once again that the study of ordinary writing is a study of failure. When we freeze a moment, create an occasion, we no longer hold the ordinary. When we frame the unframed, narrate the nonlinear, say we know what we have, we have, in fact, already lost it. As Rita Felski, quoting Maurice Blanchot, writes, "The everyday escapes . . . it belongs to insignificance" (78). To ignore this point hurls us into believing that what we have is whole and knowable.

And it is not.

* * *

The young man has been waiting for hours in the tiny room. Other new fathers have already come and gone. As a man used to being in charge, only recently released from his tour of duty in Southeast Asia where he served as a legal advisor, he does not wait well. He also has an innate distrust of doctors, mostly because they possess a knowledge that he does not. While he has delivered calves and colts as a young boy on his family's farm, he knows nothing of delivering a baby. Even given his own ignorance, though, he knows that this long period of waiting cannot be good.

Hours later his wife's doctor appears. He bursts into the waiting room, having not even taken the time to change his blood-soaked scrubs. The doctor is sweating and out of breath, as if he has been the one in labor. The young man — stunned by the material fact of his wife's blood — finds himself rehearsing over and over the patterns created by the mint green fabric and dried blood on the doctor's smock. Clouds, flowers, buildings, snakes. The man does not hear every word the doctor says but by highlighting the key terms comes to understand that things have gone badly in the delivery room. He learns that he must now choose to save either his wife or what could be/would have been his daughter.

The Kingsville County Hospital waiting room is empty and the dark suit now seems painfully out of place. News like this should be met less formally. It could appear to someone on the outside, a bystander, that he came to the hospital prepared to mourn.

Faced with the possibility of losing the woman that he loves, the young man chooses his wife. In so doing he also chooses to let the daughter go.

◦   ◦   ◦

When we write, we make texts. *Not freely but willfully.* All texts. Even those ordinary ones. Writers, as makers, choose — on a continuum from the word to the example — what to put into their texts as well as what to leave out. What remains is both the substance and the shadow of these choices. Ordinary writing makes these choices by the writer more explicit because, as texts, they claim little craft and even less coherence. If writing is always a reduction of the world, of possibility, into a pattern or an order, then the work of a writer like Annie is a meta-reduction. In her refusal to narrate her days into story and in her attempt to reduce all that might work to overwhelm her — both in terms of language (adjectives and metaphors) and example (Charley's deception) — she leaves only the barest of patterns, the absolute distillation of both language and experience. What remains in her text puts into greater relief the decisions all writers undertake on their way to making an ordered text.

To suggest that texts are merely illusions of coherence, confidence, and the known is certainly not a new idea. Our postmodern world begins with the instability and partiality of language and perception. But in pointing to examples of just how partial knowledge can be, we often look to writers who intentionally — for rhetorical or aesthetic reasons — perform the postmodern predicament. Ethnographies serve as excellent sites to study the partiality of making because reflexive ethnographers highlight their inability to render what they see. Good ethnographic writing is equally about the making of a subject and the making of a text. Cintron suggests that ethnography is always a failed expectation — it reveals the failure of making, the inability to account for everything. Kamela Visweswaran, too, explores the assumptions inherent in doing ethnographic work in her *Fictions of Feminist Ethnography*. Visweswaran feels that neat and tidy ethnographies can and do betray their subjects because the ethnographer appears so certain of what he or she is observing, a certainty that is translated into a closed, known whole. Hesitation, gaps, and questions often do not find their way into professional ethnographies. Like much literary writing, closure is assured, if only because the writer must revise toward an end. Writing against such certainty, Visweswaran tells the same story, the same ethnographic moment, in several different ways, including fiction, to express the number of possibilities found in the act of writing — all the various sediment produced in the distillation of the world. Each story tries to give the feel of something said. Each in a different way.

Visweswaran's writing is far from ordinary. It shares little in common with Annie's diary or ordinary writing in general. Visweswaran is not only a talented writer and gifted prose stylist, she has a great deal of formal education and the desire and training to write for an academic community. In addition, Visweswaran is foregrounding the partiality of knowing and of writing intentionally — by reproducing the fragmentedness of knowledge in her text. So while she presents multiple possibilities without choosing one, she does so to make a point about the gaps in reading, writing, and knowing. She is in charge of when and how the gaps will appear.

Other writers are equally invested in producing a fragmented text, a move James Seitz suggests can help readers see the gaps inherent in the act of reading. Seitz's essay, "Roland Barthes, Reading, and Roleplay: Composition's Misguided Rejection of Fragmentary Texts," is compelling because it argues for the potential in reading what he calls fragmentary texts — texts that either acknowledge or display the gaps that characterize their reading, gaps that, in fact, characterize all reading.[5] He appreciates the ways in which such writers call attention to their gaps, to the fact that meaning is always only partial. What Seitz envisions is the ultimate legitimation of the fragment within the fields of composition and literary studies, where the fragment is no longer degraded but seen as a reality of the act of reading, as a rhetorical choice. He concludes by suggesting "that we renew and extend our forms of writing and reading so that fragmentation or 'lack of control' becomes a site for exploring a *characteristic* rather than simply an abuse of language" (824).

But Seitz is only considering fragmentary texts that acknowledge their fragmentation, texts that playfully foreground their gaps. He examines professional writers who work to help their readers see — perform for their readers — the illusion that an ordered text creates. What about a text, like Annie's, that is not performing fragmentation for aesthetic or rhetorical effect, but is, nonetheless, not whole, always partial, only fragments. In many ways, I would suggest that her text, even more than the fragmented texts found in current anthologies or valued by Seitz, reveals the gaps that exist in the reading act. More to my point, they reveal the gaps in the writing act as well. A piece of ordinary writing, like Annie's diary — more than polished, professional texts — reveals the maker or reveals the making more clearly because the seams that show are not crafted but are rather the very seams that result from the continual construction of identities and texts.

For example, recall this entry of Annie's that I looked at in chapter 3.

Cool A.M. but grew hot during the day. Johnnie came down and plowed our potatoes. Everything is growing finely.

Charley sent the Dr to see me. He made a careful examination and left more medicine. I am losing my hair. It is nearly all gone now. But the Dr thinks he can save some of it.

Ransacked my trunk and looked over a lot of old dresses trying to find something suitable to wear on the 4 of July if I go out that great day. [June 29, 1881]

As I suggest in that chapter, Annie is concerned with ordering both her world and her text. She works to order, through strategies like repetition and a limited vocabulary, what she can manage and to order out what she cannot control. Here we see the ways in which she inserts both the destabilizing and debilitating reality of cancer (a disease that unmakes literally and metaphorically) within the mundane hum of the ordinary. Her loss of hair becomes entwined with the very ordinary list of weather, crops, and clothing — to suggest that all of these items are part of the regular cycle of her day. She demands that the nonordinary become ordinary in order to maintain a stable sense of self, text, and world.

How different our understanding of this writer, this woman, would be if I had told a story about Annie's battle with cancer. What if I had written that at twenty-six, medicines, doctors, and illness are wasting her, are erasing her. What if I had told you that illness dominates her life, that she defines herself by illness, even that illness allows her to figure in a way that good health does not. I could write pages about the need for her to matter through her cancer. But such stories would stitch together an argument that is seemingly more sturdy and dominant than Annie's actual experience of either her days or her illness. Cancer does not define her. Illness is not her only narrative. By looking at her ordinary writing, we see how a writer negotiates the randomness and insistence of unmaking through textual making. Her identity as it appears on the page is made and unmade. Her work in her text like our work in the world is seen in the powerful stitches that hold us together until the next entry.

Because ordinary writing is not crafted, coherent, and whole we can more easily see her work. We can name her choices. And in naming them, we see how she uses writing to make her day and her identity, revealing through writing the fact that all of us work to keep together what we know is falling apart. In addition to the fact that there are few elements in ordinary writing, the measure of ordinary writing also provides an excellent model for seeing how texts are made — because it remains open. The ordering of an ordinary diary is more apparent largely because the writer never gears up for an ending. She never knows when her last entry will be her final one. Anchored in measure, ordinary writing remains in the middle, not allowing the ordinary writer to gain critical distance from the text, the kind of distance that allows for universals, for generalizations, and for reflection. Revision, distance, closure, these are the moves writers make to cover the seams of their choices. These are the very tools that the ordinary writer can never obtain.

All writers make ordered texts. All writing is a reduction of possibility. No writing can account for everything. All texts contain gaps, holes, and the residue of the discarded. Some writing conceals these gaps more deceptively than others, appears seamless. Even those writers who foreground the fragmentary nature of text making still assert an order, still tie the particulars into the general. In professional writing, published writing, literary writing, the work of the writer, the production of the text, the choices made are harder to see. Harder to name. More even than professional writers who perform the multiplicity of possibility, ordinary writers expose the inability of writing to cohere. What ordinary writing — the starkest reduction, the fewest elements, the most seams — teaches us is how all writing requires establishing a tentative and illusory order. In doing so, we are thrown back into the literary, the crafted, and the whole. Only now we read differently. We are more suspicious.

* * *

And what of that which the young man cannot see. What is happening in the other rooms of the Kingsville County Hospital? What, for instance, is happening in the delivery room now that the doctor has returned with the father's decision? No one can say. The mother, the doctor's patient, has long been unconscious. Perhaps from the drugs, or the pain, or the grave amount of blood that pools beneath both body and bed, she has slipped into a comatose state. The baby, the daughter, six weeks premature, is wedged in the birth canal, doubled up, her rear end first. The doctor, too, is not able to say for sure what has gone wrong. In his mind, he reviews his decisions, questions his choices, and considers the options that remain. At moments the delivery room has been noisy and panicked. There were the pain-filled screams of the then-conscious woman, the shouted commands of the doctor, and the urgent questions from the nurses. Now, as the doctor studies the rear end of the baby and considers how best to remove the body, it is as quiet as a library. The baby is a test question he works to get right.

In the end, he chooses to fracture. With confidence born from a decision reached, he breaks her collarbone swiftly and in so doing severs nerves in her neck. No longer worried about the fact that the umbilical cord has wrapped around the baby's neck, denying her oxygen for long periods of time, he pulls the broken body out with forceps.

Father waiting. Mother unconscious. The body of the baby is dumped into a bucket on the floor and shuttled across the linoleum into an adjoining room. With renewed vigor, the impediment removed, the doctor begins to suture the woman's gaping wounds.

* * *

Dear Great Billie,

The second weekend you and I were supposed to sit together with a tape recorder capturing your words, you were, instead, unconscious in the ICU. Your skull was in fragments following a fall down the stairs, a fall from which you never got up. What were you thinking about as you drifted away from us? My mother sat with you every day and says that your face showed all these expressions. That you were thinking, dreaming, moving in your mind. What were the moments you revisited? I want to think they were the ordinary moments of your life. Maybe giving your son a bath, pruning your wisteria, eating grapes. I want to think they were not the violent, unhappy, extraordinary moments by which we, as a community, tend to want to define our lives. The loss of your husband, breast cancer, an only son who lives far away. I hope that you were equally recounting the spaces in-between.

Accidents seem to generate the preponderance of narratives by which I define my past. Hospitals, edifices standing in everyday witness to the extraordinary moments of beginning and end, are the setting of so many of my stories. When I visited you in the hospital, a month after your fall, I did not want to go. As my mom said, who would? Yet, she was more used to being there. She knew to wear sweaters against the air-conditioning, that you didn't need to check in at the nurses' station, and where to buy a paper with the *New York Times* crossword puzzle. A few years before, in the very same hospital, she sat with her mother as she died. And a year after your death, again she would hold the hand of one dying, this time her father as he left the world. In visiting you every day for two months, the hospital, your accident, became her ordinary. A routine. Moving your limbs like drying the dishes, picking up one, rotating, and setting back down.

What I wanted from my mom before seeing you was the assurance that you would look the same, that I would recognize you as my Great Billie, that nothing extraordinary would have altered the constancy of a woman who, at the age of two, I named as Great. The thing is, though, you were a stranger. And I will never recover from that fact. You on the bed, a crumpled, balding, empty body, clad like a baby in diapers and a smock. That moment of seeing you, that moment of expecting my Great Billie, is held in my memory as one of mere motion: your mouth, a mouth, moving without words, eyes drunkenly rambling in and out of focus, puppeted limbs that thrashed and jerked. I could see glimpses of you in the shadows and light playing across your face as on a field when clouds pass over the sun. There were moments when you clearly recognized me, would brighten for a second — like you had opened the door to your house and there I was standing before you, a surprise visit from Ann Arbor. But mostly there was detachment in your face.

My mom and I talked to you. Asked you questions, showed you pictures of your son, your sister, your nieces, your great-niece. We held your hand to the leaves of the plants in your room, hoping to encourage life and spring. We touched your face with the fur of a stuffed kitty and watched your expression warm at the touch. We asked the hospital's beautician to set your hair. Sometimes you would respond to our questions — not with words but with sounds in the shape of words. The tone following the well-known edges of conversation. The trace, the feel, even in the end, of something being said. Mostly though, you murmured, leaving the world in a sea of syllables, measured, warming, and gentle like the surf.

Two years ago, almost to the day, you died. An end. I, too, am ending, am finally finishing these words, words you encouraged me to write, words of Annie's that run the risk of being lost. In the end, words are really all that remain. Words of condolence, congratulation, joy, appreciation, sorrow, anger bobbing upon an ocean of words that appear ordinary, simple, and without worth. You have shown me that we must be accountable for each and every one. Because often you do not know what matters until long after it has been lost. Love, Jennifer

*   *   *

I have suggested that the ordinary is a devalued site in large part because we have been taught to see and to privilege the nonordinary, in particular the literary. In tracing the changing embrace of autobiography, I have demonstrated how nonliterary texts like diaries have been accepted into the folds of autobiography only when they have revealed an adequate number of literary symptoms. Only when diarists prove themselves to be more than "lovably artless chroniclers of their little lives" do they become lifewriters. In suggesting that the ordinary is devalued for aesthetic reasons — for not rising to the level of art — I have named merely one way in which the ordinary gets defined and, thereafter, devalued. But the ordinary bears a long tradition of being equated with deprivation and an equally long connection to gender.

The ordinary and terms like the private, everyday life, and the domestic are not interchangeable concepts. Yet, they are united — historically and theoretically — as spaces marked by the immediate (or immanent), the ephemeral, the repetitive, the natural, and the mundane. In this section, I am going to use these unequivalent terms as more or less equivalent. I am not interested in pulling apart the distinctions as much as I am interested in the dichotomous treatment of these spaces and in their gendering. In my work, I have chosen to use the term "ordinary" to describe the kind of writing that comes from the unmarked moments of everyday life. My choice in the use of "ordinary" versus "everyday" or "commonplace" stems from reasons that will become clearer below — namely that current conceptions of the everyday idealize the space as a site of resistance and not also as a site of safety. I also prefer how the term's etymological connection to order prefigures the idea of the ordinary as a site of construction, of ordering, as well as the term's etymological connection to succession. Even though, given these reasons, I use the term "ordinary" almost exclusively elsewhere, in this section I have made the decision to move freely between the term "ordinary" and terms like "the everyday," "everyday life," "the domestic," and "the private." For my purposes, these terms collectively refer to what Felski calls in *Doing Time* "the essential, taken-for-granted continuum of mundane activities that frames our forays into more esoteric or exotic worlds" (77).

As Felski points out, the everyday is a democratic concept. All of us are, she writes, "ultimately anchored in the mundane" (79). The majority of our days are spent performing mundane activities. We eat or sleep or use the bathroom. We write a note or ride the bus. Yet, even though the mundane accounts for much of our time, these activities typically proceed not only unnoticed but, when noticed, devalued. The everyday has generally been seen as an impoverished space. Because it requires very little reflection to repeat mundane activities like brushing your teeth, what occurs in the thrum of the ordinary is often seen as nonintellectual. We can see this bias operating, for example, in the ways in which scholars prefer diaries that are reflective and reflexive rather than immediate. We can also see this bias at work in the ways housewives are constructed by the media as vapid and silly (for example, the late-1980s show *Scarecrow and Mrs. King*). The ordinary is something that must be transcended if any critical work is to be done.

Critical work is seen and valued in the form of product. In the ordinary, nothing is produced. Nothing is made to rest in the public. Nothing is erected. Nothing gets created. The note left on the counter is thrown away, the answering machine messages are erased, gas is used to drive to the grocery store, and dinner is eaten in the space of fifteen minutes. Unlike extraordinary works — say, for example, art or philosophy — which testify to being in the world, which transcend the ordinary and the mundane, the ordinary is marked by consumption. We eat, we wear, we toss, we clean, and we use the mundane that surrounds us. We save, we frame, we preserve, and we honor the nonordinary in our lives. Philosopher Hannah Arendt (among others) argues that progress, that civilization, is measured by the works, the products, we place in the public sphere. Progress is measured by acts and action. A space like the private, for her, is a space of deprivation because nothing can be made there. Things can only be consumed. Iris Marion Young writes in her essay "House and Home: Feminist Variations on a Theme" that "if building is the means by which a person emerges as a subject who dwells in that world, then not to build is a deprivation." She adds later that the "subject expresses and realizes his individuality through taking on projects — building a home, organizing a strike, writing a book, winning a battle."[6] When subjectivity is connected to that which transcends the ordinary, those who remain in the mundane are rendered invisible.

While the everyday may indeed be a democratic concept — we all put our pants on one leg at a time after all — it has not been applied democratically. Men are able to leave the mundane behind, knowing that home and wife wait, like a womb, for their return. Historically, women have been tied to the consumptive, repetitive, fixed sphere of the domestic while men have moved freely between public and private worlds. As feminists have shown, women's connection to the everyday has worked to disempower and confine. Much of the connection between women and the domestic is based in biology. Felski points out that everyday life is "above all a temporal term" (81). It is marked by cycles and repetition. The cyclical nature of women's bodies — menstrual and birth cycles — replicates the cyclical nature of the day and the repetition of the mundane. Such a connection has been used to suggest that women are essentially made for consumption rather than production. In the modern, Western world where progress is linear rather than cyclical, women's connection to the domestic disenfranchises them completely.

We can see the ways Annie's own sense of self is invested in the domestic. Literally, her body and her work become indistinguishable when she tracks her menstrual cycle alongside her daily chores. The passage of time is also tracked by the cycle of chores; certain days are given to washing while others are for scrubbing or cleaning or blackening the stove. These chores are completed only to be repeated the following week, the following month, the following year. Annie's chore schedule is not simply about having a schedule as much as it is about having a sense of self-worth. I have shown that she takes the measure of her feelings by how much work she has accomplished in the day (for example, she writes on January 15, 1884: "I feel more comfortable now that everything is clean"). Chores undone work to undo her. Because her work is consumed, she uses her diary to record her worth by very accurately recording her completed work (to the number of socks darned in one afternoon). I conclude chapter 2 by looking at a passage in which Annie writes "Kept myself busy all day." The danger she alludes to is the fact that if she is valued and values herself only through consumptive acts then she must generate her own sense of worth as well as record it. This is not the case with Charley. As I write now my feet rest on the footstool that Charley made for Annie. The sewing projects she kept inside the footstool no longer remain. The cover she made for the footstool has long been removed. Charley remains in my living room (literally underfoot), as well as in legal documents that I have, in business transactions, in newspaper articles, and in property deeds. Examining Annie's diary, it is not at all surprising that feminists have decried the domestic space and its connections to patriarchy.

But rather than abandoning the domestic and the everyday, feminists have reclaimed these spaces. And the everyday, the mundane, and the ordinary have become sites of resistance. Within feminism and cultural studies, attention is being paid to the ways in which individuals are able to subvert systems like patriarchy on the level of the particular. Only by looking at individual actions can we begin to see ways in which cultural scripts get misread, reread, or rewritten. Sidonie Smith and Julia Watson have an entire collection of essays dedicated to the ways in which everyday autobiographical acts allow individuals agency. For example, Kay Cook in her essay "Medical Identity: My DNA/Myself" describes the empowerment she achieves by looking at her medical records while the doctor is out of the office. She argues that the medical profession coauthors our bodies — from tests that invade our bodies to medical records that record them — and then keeps this information from us. Unlike other forms of autobiography — letters or diaries — we have little control of how our bodies are inscribed within the medical system. By reading her medical record, she reclaims what should have already been hers. She resists, on a small level, the medical authoring of her body. Essays like Cook's, testimonies, memoirs, and ethnographies are all attempts to get to the level of the particular, the daily work an individual undertakes as she moves through the day, to see the ways in which identity is formed with and against these cultural scripts. What is important to note, though, is that acts of resistance are where identity formation occurs. Therefore, the everyday (according to these theorists) becomes idealized as the space where these important, agentive moments occur.

But here is my concern. When I read Annie's diary, I do see acts of resistance (for example, she records her "novel account" amidst the list of Charley's blacksmith tools), but I also see work being done to construct the familiar through order — work that is not so much resistance as much as it is reproduction of an order that she seems to need or desire. While I would never suggest that the reproduction of cultural scripts that imprison is in any way empowering, I do think there is a certain amount of reproduction of the domestic and the everyday that is familiar, safe, and ultimately nurturing. Felski points out that representations of everyday life either demonize or idealize that space. There is either entrapment or resistance — nothing in between. Young, too, wants to complicate familiar spaces and value the safety and preservation such a space can bring.

For Felski, the repetition found in the everyday does not have to doom the subject to a fixed sense of self. She writes that "repetition is one of the ways we organize the world, make sense of our environment, and stave off the threat of chaos" (84). She further suggests that home can be a complex rather than static sense of place. It can serve as a place to act from. Seeing the familiar — the ordering into the familiar — as a value, as a way of preserving rather than imprisoning complicates the work of ordinary writing. Annie's attempts to order her house, her body, and her text, while limiting in the ways she then equates her worth with her work, also serves in equally important ways to inscribe stability. She maintains the familiar through her ordinary writing and draws strength from the fact that her diary is here today as it was yesterday. As I say in both chapters 2 and 3, I do not want to lose sight of the fact that Annie gets things by maintaining succession and repetition. She does not simply reproduce measure, she furthers it. And that work is not necessarily only about resistance. It is also about making and remaking the familiar every single day.

· · · ·

Dear Mom,

The other day I was thinking about how we used to go camping on weekends when the three of us were little. We would bike home from school on Friday and the van would be full — camping gear, groceries, horseshoes, bug repellent, and the Tupperware of Chex party mix. The wayback would be stacked with body boards and that bright orange beach chair. All we would have to do is put on play clothes and jump into the already crowded car. I can't remember if we would wait for Dad to come home or if he would just meet us there. I want to say we would drive out early and Dad would come later. That giant green canvas tent already standing. It has taken me twenty-five years to recognize the fact that you were behind all of that. That someone, you, had to put all those things into brown paper bags before we could carry them to the campsite. That someone, you, had to make sure we had forks, knives, matches, ketchup, and cream of tartar for the Portuguese man-o'-war stings. That someone, you, remembered the tent, the tent poles, and the stakes. It was not something I was taught to notice as a child.

Which is why I think I originally felt that the quilt you made a few years ago should be hung on the wall rather than draped on a bed. It just seemed like we had eaten all your other work. Dad has books on the shelves containing papers or briefs he has written. Our scrapbooks are stuffed full of awards and finger-painted pages. But we wore out all the clothes you made, ate all the Chex party mix.

I love that quilt. Both of my prom dresses are in it, and the brown overalls you made out of that funky fabric Grandfather brought back from Germany. The peach-and-white striped material that I used to make a jumper the summer you taught Stacy and Karen and me how to sew. And the silk Dad brought back from his trip to Korea — I think you finally made it into a suit for yourself when you went "back to work." Even though the quilt is pieced together with all of these scraps of material and even though you made it to fit the Jenny Lind bed because that yellow spread was so ratty, it didn't matter. All my feminist impulses said don't let my mom be an absence, save the quilt from cat pee and drooling guests.

Have you ever read Alice Walker's short story "Everyday Use"? It is a story of two daughters — one who has gone to the city and found "ideas," the other who remains connected to "home." The city daughter wants the family quilt to go in a museum, while the other daughter recognizes its value in its use on a cold night. I was the city daughter. I wanted your work to be marked and hung — not in a museum but maybe the living room — rather than rest unmarked on the guest bed. I thought that the living room wall gave it value while the guest bed did not. Annie's diary has taught me this is not so, that often whether something matters has little to do with whether it is saved and more to do with how it is used. Which only makes me want to say thank you. Not only for loading the car but also for letting me sleep under the quilt. Love, Jennifer

*　　*　　*

The woman's wounds are almost closed. The blood loss has been stemmed and color returns almost like magic to her cheeks. She will live. Nurses and other doctors shuffle in and out of the room, carrying trays and charts and rubber gloves and tools. Some are helping to stitch the woman back together at the seams; others are on their own business. It is a little after 6 P.M. when an older green-scrubbed doctor who has recently begun his shift walks through the adjoining room and sees the bucket containing the discarded baby on the floor. He does not know that it is a baby. He just sees a form. Intuition, experience, hope, or the universe nevertheless causes him to stop and wonder. Then, he makes a choice. From what will forever be known as the Dead Baby Bucket, the doctor pulls the baby out. It is bloody and broken but — and this is what he cannot believe, this is what cannot be believed — it is breathing. The dead baby is breathing.

.   .   .

In chapter 1, I trace the ways in which equating the diurnal form with autobiography has resulted in the devaluation of ordinary writing like Annie's because it contains very little story matter. Expectations of plot and coherence have worked to exclude ordinary writing from the genre of autobiography for its lack of unity and reflectivity. Yet, clearly ordinary writing has something to say about the ways in which individuals render their experience of space and time. Diary scholars have long argued that the diurnal form is the more authentic form of autobiography because it captures the openness and immediacy of a life in progress. What we learn from reading ordinary writing is how the unmarked moments of our days equally and fully participate in the continual making of identity and the making of texts. We learn how Annie constitutes a sense of self in her writing not because she tells us stories but because she uses her writing to produce a usefulness that would otherwise remain unobtainable. It seems only obvious to add that if we continue to consider only writing that stories as lifewriting then a writer like Annie leaves even less than nothing behind.

Currently, one of the central debates in the study of lifewriting is how (or even whether) to draw the line between fiction and nonfiction. It began with the understanding that the self at the center of an autobiography is a fiction and has swelled into a discussion of how "true" autobiography itself has to be or even can be. Recent questioning of authenticity — for example, Binjamin Wilkomirski's *Fragments: Memories of a Wartime Childhood* and Rigoberta Menchu's *I, Rigoberta Menchu* — challenge the value and presence of "truth" in autobiography. As Timothy Dow Adams writes, the fictiveness of autobiography seems to be a given.[7] Which is one reason, as Adams further suggests, that the term "autobiography" is slowly being replaced with the more comprehensive term "lifewriting." As autobiography becomes more performative and less a specific form or genre of writing, more texts are being included under the umbrella. What is interesting to me in these discussions is that even though autobiography is considered more and more performative or fictive it is not, at the same time, becoming less and less fictionlike. Story still patrols the borders of lifewriting. And while lives are narratives — Adams, quoting Oliver Sacks, writes, "It might be said that each of us constructs and lives a 'narrative,' and this narrative *is* us, our identities . . . for each of us *is* a biography, a story"[8] — I see no reason why the forms of lifewriting must be equally regulated by the elements of fiction. Our lives may be stories but the writing that evidences our days does not have to be.

In her essay, "Whose Life Is It Anyway? Out of the Bathtub and into the Narrative," Marlene Kadar lists the features of lifewriting. The first is that "Life writing comprises texts that present a simple or complex narrative, a narrative exhibiting some features of narrativity, some of which may indeed be deferred, fragmentary, or disunifying." The second is that "These life-writing narratives may otherwise be viewed as having Aristotle's beginning, middle, and end."[9] That the first two attributes of lifewriting are concerned with the coherence and narrativity of the text is obviously a concern. Kadar herself, and the writers Kadar includes in her collection, are most interested in considering examples of literary fiction that qualify as lifewriting. The examples for the most part come from literature. This is not surprising. So much of lifewriting is entwined with fiction. What I find striking is that while Kadar is critical of the genre of autobiography — critical of the fact that autobiography proper is insistent on a unitary subject, an insistence that has proven to exclude women and women's lived experience — she is not equally critical of autobiography proper's insistence on a unitary text. Even though Kadar allows for the fragmentary text within her definition of lifewriting, she is in fact referring to postmodern, metafictional texts that are crafted fragments. There is little space in Kadar's argument or in her collection for a text that comes to us as nonliterary, fragmented, and open. There is little space in her argument for the fact that the experience of life is equally about the experience of the in-between and that we do, in fact, have texts that document the undocumented, the unnoticed. They, I would argue, more than crafted narratives reveal the ways in which we, as individuals, make ourselves and make our culture—from, through, and against other cultural scripts—every single day.

Take, for example, my own diary. Not the one I have kept as an adult, but the one I kept ever so sporadically as a child, the one I received at the age of eleven, the one with the girl dressed in blue on the cover. I consider this diary in relation to the field of lifewriting at length in an article entitled "Inscribing Ordinary Trauma: The Diary of a Military Child."[10] Here I only want to highlight how often decisions about whose life counts when and how severely limit our understanding of lives in writing. In the field of military lifewriting, it would initially appear that the war stories that get recorded, and therefore those whose experiences have been heard and remembered, are the stories of the soldiers — the ones who carried the guns as well as the wounded. Samuel Hynes, a leading expert on military lifewriting suggests that in order to understand what war is like "we must turn away from history and its numbers, and seek the reality in the personal witness of the men who were there."[11] His use of the masculine pronoun is not insignificant, for Hynes claims that only soldiers have the experience necessary to tell the tale of war. In particular, only male soldiers. Female soldiers, nurses, officers, and civilians are completely erased from "The" tale of modern war. It is, sadly, a very familiar stance.

Hynes is an exception, though, in the trajectory of recent scholarship. Recently scholars have shown that, while soldiers' stories are important, soldiers are not the only ones with war stories to tell. For example, nurses and civilian participants also bear stories — which only document more fully the reaches of war. Even still, gaps in military lifewriting continue to exist — absent are stories by military wives, those by children from other countries left behind by American soldier/fathers, and narratives by gay servicemen. By far, one of the largest gaps is the writing by and about military children. At first, perhaps, such a gap may seem quite appropriate. After all, children of U.S. military personnel do not fight wars. They have not enlisted, do not train, test, shoot, order, strategize, or deploy. Yet, it is for this very reason that their lifewriting must count. They do not choose to serve, yet, their lives, often from birth, are conscribed by both the possibility and the paraphernalia of war.

A diary like the one I kept as a child all too often fails to count as lifewriting for reasons beyond the authority to write, reasons that gather under assumptions about the form of lifewriting. Given the terms set forth by Kadar, my diary, like other examples of ordinary writing, would most likely fail to register as lifewriting. The words I inscribe are far from narrative and I am certainly not using the fragment for aesthetic or theoretical purpose. There are not enough entries to even produce the piling up that sometimes passes as something said. They, like Annie's diary, quiver with all that cannot be said, all that must be maintained, contained in support of war.

Military childhood is spent in paradox. Unlike a civilian child, a military child grows up in a culture rooted in the possibility of war. At the same time, the trauma induced by the possibility of war is with great effort made ordinary by the military. For example, the paraphernalia of war — missiles, guns, tanks — is made as ordinary as a fire hydrant or shrubbery. The extraordinary passes as the ordinary for the military child. Yet, the trauma of living under the threat of war is not at all ordinary and shares similarities with (is not equivalent to but shares with) the trauma induced by battle. Traditional definitions of trauma — like traditional definitions of lifewriting or the literary — fail to help us in considering the position of the military child because they focus on extraordinary, cataclysmic, one-time events that completely unmake an individual. The experience of the military child rests somewhere in between the extraordinary experience of being in battle and the "ordinary" experiences of civilian children for whom war is both abstract and remote. Unlike their parents who have preservice memories that act as counternarrative to which they can compare the military experience, military children have no other touchstones outside their lives in service. For the military child, the possibility of war is the only ordinary. Further, that possibility is actively made ordinary by a military that must cultivate a community willing to make the ultimate sacrifice. Yet, while the possibility of war is very ordinary, it is nevertheless also staggering. The fact that war is a concrete, immediate possibility (one that fathers and/or mothers prepare for every day) throws the shadow of the battlefield across the daily experiences of children from military homes, moving their everyday experience more securely toward the pole of trauma. We can see these half-articulations at the level of text.

One entry by way of example. One that, importantly, has been informed by my reading of Annie's diary, the first ordinary writing I worked to read.

October 5, 1983:
Life is hard right now. I have no friends. I miss my old ones. I probably can't get contact lens and I feel very low at times. . . . I think there may be a nuclear war which we will deserve because the world is falling apart. . . .

What strikes me most about the above entry, an entry whose literal inscription I no longer recall but an entry whose content, the fear of war and the loss of moving, remains indelible, is the way in which the extraordinary possibility of nuclear war is embedded within the context of the everyday: a teenager's desire for contacts before she starts a new school. The two concerns become equalized within the space of the diary entry. One is not more meaningful than the other. Both bear equal weight.

When I was growing up, dinner table conversation often ranged from what we had done in school that day to why Reagan's Strategic Defense Initiative was so crucial. No boundaries were drawn between what would typically count as the private and the public. Both were dinner talk and dinner talk rambled freely between the two. In the same way, nuclear capability was not something that I read about in my textbooks or heard about at school. It was seen in my daily drives around the base or to and from school. My best friend's father captained a nuclear submarine. On dependents' cruises (day-long cruises on which the friends and families of the submariners could participate), my friend and I would sing in the narrow halls of the submarine trying to outmatch the booming aftershock of a blasted torpedo slug. There was nothing remote about mutually assured destruction. I felt the weapon's power reverberate in my chest. The fact that the war and the everyday would meet in my diary is not unusual. They met in my world.

In the above entry, nuclear destruction erupts from the entry — both syntactically and thematically. The entry comes in telegraphic fragments, rather than narrative. I do not reflect on what it means to learn as a child to love others but to see daily evidence that some need to be guarded against, need to be threatened, indeed, need to be destroyed. I do not name what it feels like to be a girl who cares about her appearances in a world that is "falling apart." Rather I reinscribe the conflicted position of a military child: where the extraordinary and traumatic possibility of war must be contained, must be made ordinary, by those living in a community where nuclear holocaust serves as table talk and fathers leave for months and months to live under the sea.

Several of the entries in my early diary, while hinting at the fact that what I am experiencing is not ordinary, insist that all is regular, that all is the same. In these entries I see the work I undertook on a daily basis as a child to reproduce military scripts that gave me the message that all is well, that this missile is like this mailbox, a thing on the side of the road. It was an enormous undertaking. Growing up in the Cold War, I was surrounded by military presence and power. To deny military children the position of lifewriter, as documentarians of an experience that does not begin or end on the battlefield, assures we will never fully understand the reaches of war, never fully understand the costs of being a military superpower. More to the point here, though, to deny an ordinary writer the status of lifewriter misses how the reaches of war are tested, felt, made, and remade in the pages of the diary of an eleven-year-old girl.

Reading ordinary writing through an appropriate lens results in nothing less than the reconsideration of the field of lifewriting. Lives are not stories. They contain stories — occasions marked by being narrated — but they also contain all that white space. For example, I have a friend whose grandmother recently passed away. Cathy was the only living relative and drove immediately to her grandmother's house when she had heard what happened. When Cathy arrived that afternoon, she found the house exactly as it stood the moment her grandmother had died. While I do not know all the details, what I imagine is that the breakfast dishes remained on the table, the place she had been sitting when she died. The coffee pot was turned on. And a newspaper sat on the table, open and covered with bits of shredded wheat. While her grandmother's death is extraordinary, it interrupted the very ordinary of her life. Her grandmother's day up until her death would likely have remained unnarrated, untold. Because it turned out to be her final day, we mark it as an occasion.[12] My point is that the writing produced from a life — what we mean when we say that a document is an example of lifewriting — should account for the fact of the in-between.

The field of lifewriting — a life in writing — must account for what passes unnarrated. Only look to see what we have learned of one woman's life — how one woman makes herself and her text every single day. Only think of what would have been missed had the only access to Annie been the initial story I told of deceit and loss. Charley's affair is, indeed, a part of Annie's life. But that story cannot stand in for Annie's life. We can never actually tell another's story, but we can fail to move beyond story and into that which does not seem to matter yet is the majority of matter in our lives.

*　*　*

For the next thirteen years, the mother and father watch their daughter for signs of mental retardation, seizures, and physical disabilities. With each milemarker of childhood — sucking, sitting, crawling, walking — they anxiously wait for signs of normality. As new parents who are already nervous about the responsibilities of caring for a tiny life, they are doubly burdened by the fragility of this child. She arrives home from the hospital bandaged and for the first six months of her life, she never stops crying. It is a lot for new parents. Until adolescence, every fall is accompanied by the catching of breath, a moment of waiting, and release.

Like all parents, this mother and father fill scrapbooks full of photos. Only what they take pictures of, what they document, are even the most ordinary moments in this child's life — crawling on the grass, sitting in a stroller, underneath the table, lying on the floor — the moments of a child's life that would often pass unnoticed. These moments somehow seem the more remarkable simply because they almost did not occur.

*　　*　　*

Dear Annie,

I have been thinking a lot about whether I am failing you as well as whether I am failing the words that remain a hundred years later. I guess it all depends on how you define failure.

I think many might see your diary as failing — failing to inspire, to persuade, or to perform, failing to be literary enough. Others might see what I have done with your diary as failing to be scholarly in the ways I honor stories as much as criticism, failing to be objective in my familiarity with you, evidenced even at the level of how I refer to you as Annie rather than Ray, and even failing to cling tightly enough to the claims postmodernism makes about the illusion of authorship and agency.

That seems like a good thing, though. I think I may want to fail. I remember reading a poem once about aspen trees in the fall and the way the wind tries to shake the dying leaves to the ground — the last line says that all the wind succeeds in doing is making music, "the noise of failure growing beautiful." We have to start recognizing the failure in all acts of meaning-making from the literary to the ordinary — as well as the attendant beauty. Love, Jennifer

*　　*　　*

This text is almost made. Unlike Annie's diary, in these final paragraphs I cannot help but know my end, consider closure, stake my claim. As maker of this text, I have tried to be fully present, to name my choices, to expose my seams, to refuse to bind and hold and have. But even in that I have failed. The pressure to be smart, sophisticated, and rare is so powerful. I want you to understand me. So I tell stories.

I come from a family of storytellers. Perhaps because we are a military family, perhaps because I have no tree in a backyard somewhere that was planted on the day I was born and has grown with me for thirty-odd years, or perhaps because my family can claim no place as home, the stories told again and again at our gatherings root us to each other and to our past. In many ways this book questions the power story has on us — the ways in which assumptions about the storied exclude so much of the lived. Yet, we cannot talk about who we are and what we think and feel outside of narrative. That is the bind. It is not that the ordinary is more or less useful or important or present or pretty than the extraordinary. Nor that storied is more or less compelling than what passes unnarrated. We do not have to choose, for choice is always about reduction and if anything Annie's diary flings the doors open wider.

Furthermore, we cannot choose. Mostly because we can never hold the ordinary. We can never say this piece of writing or this moment in time is ordinary for it has — in our naming — become remarkable. We call it out and it disappears into story. Which means that Annie's diary is not truly ordinary and that Annie is not an ordinary writer. Ordinary writing, like this text, like any text, is illusory at best. I failed before I began.

What we can do is always question what we hold. Think about the work of story in the world. For ordinary writing ultimately casts the light back onto more privileged writing, writing that is storied, crafted, and whole. Only now we see differently. We read these texts as reductions, as the residue of choices, as that which moved out from the ordinary and was marked. We read all writing for what it is — a collection of decisions, a text that reveals the writer's negotiation between making and unmaking. We ask about the in-between, the absent, the unsaid. We are wary of occasion and seek measure. Annie has given us so many tools.

And so, ironically, I tell stories — some of them extraordinary, none of them ordinary, all of them crafted — in my defense of the ordinary. In the hope that in the telling, I have fragmented the knowing, reproduced the hesitation necessary to even see ordinary writing, and called attention to the fact that I am the maker of this text. My stories, like my text, though, eventually end. Mine ends this way . . .

* * *

I have carried the knowledge that I was born from the Dead Baby Bucket with me my entire life, thankful every day for the choices made on my behalf. While in many ways the fact the doctor found me is extraordinary, I think it is equally important to name and recognize that, like Annie's diary and like ordinary writing, the fact that I am alive is not so much extraordinary but rather the ultimate in ordinary. For I, too, wasn't supposed to be here, but I am.

Notes

INTRODUCTION:
STORIES THAT MATTER,
THE MATTER OF STORIES

1. Laurie Langbauer, "Absolute Commonplaces: Oliphant's Theory of Auto-biography," *Margaret Oliphant: Critical Essays on a Gentle Subversive*, ed. D. J. Trela (Selinsgrove: Susquehanna UP, 1995) 126.

2. Amy Shuman, *Storytelling Rights: The Uses of Oral and Written Texts by Urban Adolescents* (Cambridge: Cambridge UP, 1986) 74.

3. See Lather and Smithies, *Troubling the Angels: Women Living with HIV/AIDS*; Felman and Laub, *Testimony: Crises of Witnessing in Literature, Psychoanalysis, and History*; Alcoff, "The Problem of Speaking for Others"; and Behar, *Translated Woman: Crossing the Border with Esperanza's Story*.

4. Linda Martin Alcoff, "The Problem of Speaking for Others," *Who Can Speak? Authority and Critical Identity*, ed. Judith Roof and Robyn Wiegman (Urbana: U of Illinois P, 1995) 98. For more on interpretive responsibility see Gesa Kirsch, "Multi-Vocal Texts and Interpretive Responsibility," *College English* 59.2 (February 1997): 191–202.

5. A discussion about the matter of ordinary writing is always a paradoxical one. While it can be said that the matter of ordinary writing — in the case of an ordinary diary, the washing of clothes and the baking of bread, for example — has historically not mattered, I am also suggesting that ordinary writing lacks matter, lacks content. This, of course, does not mean that ordinary writing is not as complex as writing that matters more or writing that is more mattered. The ordinary writer makes her text in view of different goals and with different needs. In many ways, as we will see, she may be writing against content.

6. While considerations of temporality, specifically the difference between measure and occasion, here will focus on the diurnal form and its historical connection to dailiness, the final chapter will demonstrate how writing in a moment rather than of a moment is actually an attribute shared by all ordinary writing. At that point I will consider how the ordinary (temporally rooted in the repetition, rote, and cycles of the everyday) informs the rhetorical work of ordinary writing.

7. I should note at this point that, obviously, both men and women produce ordinary writing as well as ordinary diaries. I focus on women as ordinary writers because of the intimate (and historically devalued) connections between the ordinary, the form of the diary, and women's roles. As I will argue in chapter 2, female diary writers were the ones who realized most successfully the diary's relationship to dailiness, thereby extending the work of their chosen form.

1. In an essay entitled, "Inscribing Ordinary Trauma: The Diary of a Military Child," I consider my first diary in more detail and make the argument that I am actually working to ensure that my diary remains ordinary given the extraordinary possibility of war that unsettles me as a military dependent. I also visit this point briefly in chapter 4, in relation to what I learn from reading Annie's diary.

2. While the term "diurnal form" can refer to any form of writing that is produced daily — meaning newspapers, travelogues, magazines, even epistolary novels — I am using the term to refer specifically to a personal diary kept every day. Sherman argues that the personal diary is the initial diurnal form that historically informed other manners of daily writing (e.g., the daily newspaper). Even with this distinction, the diurnal form is a capacious category. Its reach extends from diaries resembling the one I will read, what I call an ordinary diary, to the diary literature produced by well-known diarists like Anaïs Nin. The fact that one term must account for both Annie's and Nin's work illuminates the need for multiple reading strategies.

3. Margo Culley, in particular, looks at the connections between diary writing and the domestic sphere in her book *A Day at a Time: The Diary Literature of American Women from 1764 to the Present* (New York: Feminist P at CUNY, 1985). She writes: "As the modern idea of the secular diary as a 'secret' record of an inner life evolved, that inner life — the life of personal reflection and emotion — became an important aspect of the 'private sphere' and women continued to turn to the diary as one place where they were permitted, indeed encouraged, to indulge full 'self-centeredness'" (4). Seen as the province of women writers, diary writing became devalued. Prior to that period, men were apt to keep diaries as a "record of public life" (3). As we will see, these published texts by famous men became the descriptive models for diary literature. More recently, in "The Cultural Work of Diaries in Mid-Century Victorian Britain," Kathryn Carter charts the connections between the nineteenth century romantic conception of the self and the "golden age" of the diary, arguing that while women were encouraged to keep diaries, they were denied the model of romantic subjectivity that spurred the diary explosion. She looks at published diaries in particular and the disastrous consequences women faced when they placed their diaries in the public sphere.

4. Diane Freedman uses the term "not genre" to describe the private writings of American women in the nineteenth century. Her point is that many women did not have access to more privileged and public forms of writing and therefore sought and explored "less formalized and predetermined" forms like the diary and letters. The determination of these women to write has resulted in a "legacy of not genres." Diane P. Freedman, *An Alchemy of Genres: Cross-Genre Writing by American Feminist Poet-Critics* (Charlottesville: UP of Virginia, 1992) 83. Esther Captain takes the point even further by suggesting that historically diary writing has been considered "*almost not* writing, only seeing, experiencing, registering, and reproducing: a sort of verbal duplication of life itself"

(emphasis in original). Esther Captain, "'Written with an Eye on History.' Wartime Diaries of Internees as Testimonies of Captivity Literature," *Tydskrif-vir-Nederlands-en-Afrikaans* 5:1 (June 1998): 2.

5. Quoted in Harriet Blodgett, *Centuries of Female Days: Englishwomen's Private Diaries* (New Brunswick, NJ: Rutgers UP, 1988) 261–62.

6. Suzanne L. Bunkers and Cynthia A. Huff, "Issues in Studying Women's Diaries: A Theoretical and Critical Introduction," *Inscribing the Daily: Critical Essays on Women's Diaries*, ed. Suzanne L. Bunkers and Cynthia Huff (Amherst: U of Mass P, 1996) 1.

7. Cynthia Huff, "Reading as Re-Vision: Approaches to Reading Manuscript Diaries," *Biography* 23.2 (Summer 2000): 506.

8. Told another way. My friend Mary is both a longtime feminist and a Roman Catholic from the cradle. I have asked her — politically — how she can be both, given the church's patriarchal stance on so many social issues. She says she sees two options. One can either work from the inside, trying to instill change patiently and through preestablished channels. Or one can work on the outside, disregarding the former structure completely, forming a new church. She has chosen the former. Metaphorically, I am choosing the latter.

9. This is obviously an oversimplification of the forces at work in the academy that resulted in a paradigmatic shift in the evaluation of what counts as "literature." While New Criticism as a theoretical approach experienced a decline in popularity in the 1970s, more than the rise of feminist theory should be credited. For example, the field of cultural studies has turned attention to the ways in which everyday acts and everyday texts replicate and resist institutional forces. The theoretical work of Michel de Certeau, Clifford Geertz, and Pierre Bourdieu, in particular, has been highly influential in terms of the kinds of texts that receive attention. In addition, scholars like Janice Radway, bell hooks, and the authors in the edited collection by Sidonie Smith and Julia Watson, *Getting a Life: Everyday Uses of Autobiography*, investigate many everyday sites, sites that would traditionally have been overlooked (like television talk shows), to illuminate the complex of forces at work. Additionally, literal changes in the academy's demography have directly influenced the texts that are valued. The fact that women, scholars of color, gays and lesbians, scholars from non-Western countries, and those from working-class backgrounds are gaining stronger and stronger voices within the academy has also meant changes in the definition of what is worthy of study.

10. Examples of early collections of excerpted diaries include Arthur Ponsonby's *English Diaries* and *More English Diaries* and William Mathews's *British Diaries 1442–1942*. In addition, several articles were published on the diary. For example, in 1972 and 1973, respectively, Earl Miner and Steven Kagle published articles theorizing the diary. And in 1970 Robert Latham and William Mathews released the first edited volume of Samuel Pepys's diary with a critical introduction by Mathews. However, 1974 does mark the year when the first *full-length* diary studies were issued — and more to my concern — the year when feminists began their work with diaries.

11. As we will see in the next chapter, Sherman sets out a somewhat similar chronology. He, though, is more interested in examining how the historical context of the seventeenth century gave rise to the diurnal form. He sees that period (rather than the nineteenth century) as the most significant in the generation of the diary as a distinct form of writing. Like Fothergill, though, he attributes writers in the late eighteenth century and the early nineteenth century with a movement toward a more personal form of diary keeping, a movement toward what he calls a "diurnal narrative of the self."

12. Robert A. Fothergill, *Private Chronicles: A Study of English Diaries* (Oxford: Oxford UP, 1974) 32. Emphasis mine.

13. Mary Jane Moffat, Foreword, *Revelations: Diaries of Women*, ed. Mary Jane Moffat and Charlotte Painter (New York: Random House, 1974) 3–4. Emphasis mine.

14. Arnold's oft-cited remark is found in the preface to *Literature and Dogma*, 1873.

15. Earl Miner, "Literary Diaries and the Boundaries of Literature," *Yearbook of Comparative and General Literature* 21 (1972): 47.

16. Elizabeth Podneiks, *Daily Modernism: The Literary Diaries of Virginia Woolf, Antonia White, Elizabeth Smart, and Anaïs Nin* (Montreal: McGill-Queen's UP, 2000) 10.

17. Judy Nolte Temple and Suzanne Bunkers, "Mothers, Daughters, Diaries: Literacy, Relationships, and Cultural Context," *Nineteenth-Century Women Learn to Write*, ed. Catherine Hobbs (Charlottesville: UP of Virginia, 1995) 198.

18. Consideration of the diary as either a public or private document is, clearly, not a conversation about the text itself as much as it is a consideration of the mobile relationship between text, writer, and reader. While a woman's position within a historical and social context is one marked by varying access to the public, the diary, as a document, is not intrinsically public or private. As I examine below, the theoretical understanding of writing as a social act has greatly reconfigured the way we examine a "private" document like a diary. In addition, in the remaining chapters I continue to use the term "private writing" as a conceptual category, while recognizing that a diary is never truly private. I find the term useful in distinguishing between diary writing and other personal writing conducted by women at the same time period, for example letter writing, commonplace books, or women's club documents.

19. I am loosely calling on Hannah Arendt, who suggests that the private is a place of de*privat*ion. It is "to be deprived of the reality that comes from being seen and heard by others, to be deprived of an 'objective' relationship with them that comes from being related to and separated from them through the intermediary of a common world of things, to be deprived of the possibility of achieving something more permanent than life itself." Hannah Arendt, *The Human Condition* (1958; Chicago: U of Chicago P, 1989) 58.

20. Many scholars should be credited with demonstrating that the diary is more than private. See in particular Lynn Bloom, Margo Culley, Elizabeth Hampsten, Suzanne Bunkers (especially "Diaries: Public *and* Private Records

of Women's Lives"), Temple and Bunkers. More recently, work by Elizabeth Podneiks, Kathryn Carter, and, in particular, Molly McCarthy blurs the boundaries between the public and private. Cinthia Gannett suggests that diaries were privatized (and feminized) by a nineteenth-century culture that relegated women to the private and then encouraged them to keep diaries for their own self-improvement and as family histories.

21. Suzanne Bunkers, "Diaries: Public *and* Private Records of Women's Lives," *Legacy* 7.2 (Fall 1990).

22. Lillian Schlissel, *Women's Diaries of the Westward Journey* (New York: Schocken Books, 1982) 11.

23. Though this, too, is a tricky line. As Blodgett reminds us in *Centuries of Female Days*, while many women in the mid to late nineteenth century indicated that they were keeping daily diaries as family records for their children (a motive for writing that was authorized by Victorian culture), in fact the shield of a sanctified future audience allowed them the space to write about themselves, space they were not automatically granted. Blodgett, chapter 2. Elizabeth Podneiks adds another, wonderful layer of complexity by demonstrating how women writing diaries for publication in the early twentieth century could use the veil of the "private" to write about socially taboo topics in a public way. In both instances, we see ways in which women subvert their roles within the domestic/private space to conduct important and powerful work.

24. Molly McCarthy, "A Pocketful of Days: Pocket Diaries and Daily Record Keeping among Nineteenth-Century New England Women," *New England Quarterly Review* 73.2 (June 2000): 288.

25. Jane H. Hunter, "Inscribing the Self in the Heart of the Family: Diaries and Girlhood in Late-Victorian America," *American Quarterly* 44.1 (1992): 60.

26. The turn-of-the-century lock and key does not mean contemporary diarists write with any more reassurance that their words will remain "private." Bunkers relates her fears in having her diaries potentially subpoenaed by a judge during the custody battle between her and her child's father over their daughter Rachel. Rachel's father was trying to prove that Bunkers was an incompetent mother. He thought her diaries would suggest at least that — and Bunkers worried about how her diaries would be interpreted in a court of law. The shear length of her diaries saved her. The judge chose not to read through volumes and volumes of words. Bunkers retained full custody but no longer writes in her diary without the fear of someone looking over her shoulder.

27. Judy Simons, *Diaries and Journals of Literary Women from Fanny Burney to Virginia Woolf* (Iowa City: U of Iowa P, 1990) 10.

28. Cinthia Gannett, in discussing the connections between composition and journal writing, looks at how diaries are social. Citing the work of George Summerfield, she argues that journal keeping is not private (individual) but "a social act, albeit displaced." Cinthia Gannett, *Gender and the Journal: Diaries and Academic Discourse* (Albany: SUNY Press, 1992) 31.

29. Karen Burke LeFevre, *Invention as Social Act* (Carbondale: Southern Illinois UP, 1987) 39.

30. Anne Ruggles Gere, *Writing Groups: History, Theory, and Implications* (Carbondale: Southern Illinois UP, 1987) 6. Diary writing as a social, rather than private, act is also explored by Jeanne Braham who, quoting Jane Marcus, writes, "If we agree that the writer resurrects herself through memory, then the reader also resurrects the writer through reading her. This *collaboration* is a re-production of woman's culture as conversation." Jeanne Braham, "A Lens of Empathy," *Inscribing the Daily: Critical Essays on Women's Diaries*, ed. Suzanne L. Bunkers and Cynthia Huff (Amherst: U of Mass P, 1996) 57.

31. Margo Culley, Introduction, *A Day at a Time: The Diary Literature of American Women from 1764 to the Present*, ed. Margo Culley (New York: Feminist P at CUNY, 1985) 8.

32. Elizabeth Podneiks, "'Keep out/Keep out/Your snooting snout': The Irresistible Journals of Elizabeth Smart," *a/b: Auto/Biography Studies* 11.1 (Spring 1996): 57, 58.

33. *Daily Modernism* 43.

34. Lynn Z. Bloom, "'I Write for Myself and Strangers': Private Diaries as Public Documents," *Inscribing the Daily: Critical Essays on Women's Diaries*, ed. Suzanne L. Bunkers and Cynthia Huff (Amherst: U of Mass P, 1996) 35.

35. Culley 10. In addition, Bunkers ends her essay "Diaries: Public *and* Private Records of Women's Lives" with a list of questions we should ask diarists that include questions of purpose, shaping, audience perceptions, and intention. Suzanne Bunkers, *Legacy* 7.2 (Fall 1990): 24.

36. Most recently, attention has shifted toward consideration of the diary as lifewriting, a more inclusive category that many feminist scholars prefer over autobiography. I consider Annie's diary in relation to the field of lifewriting in chapter 4.

37. For an excellent summary of the evolution of the field of autobiography in relation to women's studies, see the introduction to *Women, Autobiography, Theory: A Reader*, edited by Sidonie Smith and Julia Watson (Madison: U of Wisconsin P, 1998).

38. Estelle C. Jelinek, *The Tradition of Women's Autobiography: From Antiquity to Present* (Boston: Twayne, 1986) xii.

39. What is significant to me about Blodgett's rejection of the autobiographical lens is that she offers instead the category of literature as a more appropriate framework for the diary. In her essay "Preserving the Moment in the Diary of Margaret Fountaine" she writes, "A diary seems to be real life going on rather than being, as in autobiography, life retrospectively shaped to a coherent whole." Harriet Blodgett, *Inscribing the Daily: Critical Essays on Women's Diaries*, ed. Suzanne L. Bunkers and Cynthia Huff (Amherst, U of Mass P, 1996) 156. She goes on to suggest that the diary would be better served if read as literature. To support her point she looks at the diary of Fountaine who, as Blodgett admits, "fortunately" had a knack for the literary (164).

40. Roy Pascal, *Design and Truth in Autobiography* (Cambridge: Harvard UP, 1960) 3.

41. Wayne Shumaker, *English Autobiography: Its Emergence, Materials, and Form* (Berkeley: U of California P, 1954) 120.

42. Suzanne L. Bunkers, "Reading and Interpreting Unpublished Diaries by Nineteenth-Century Women," *a/b: Auto/Biography Studies* 2.2 (Summer 1986): 16.

43. Sidonie Smith and Julia Watson give 1980 as the approximate date when women's autobiography is first acknowledged as a field. Sidonie Smith and Julia Watson, "Introduction: Situating Subjectivity in Women's Autobiographical Practices," *Women, Autobiography, Theory: A Reader*, ed. Sidonie Smith and Julia Watson (Madison: U of Wisconsin P, 1998) 5.

44. Suzanne Juhasz, "'Some Deep Old Desk or Capacious Hold-All': Form and Women's Autobiography," *College English* 39.6 (February 1978): 664.

45. Moffat 5. Emphasis mine.

46. Blodgett, *Centuries of Female Days* 96.

47. Elizabeth Hampsten, *Read This Only to Yourself: The Private Writings of Midwestern Women, 1880–1910* (Bloomington: Indiana UP, 1982) 2.

48. Suzanne Bunkers, "What Do Women *Really* Mean? Thoughts on Women's Diaries and Lives," *The Intimate Critique*, ed. Diane P. Freedman, Olivia Frey, and Frances Murphy Zauhar (Durham: Duke UP, 1993) 211.

49. Judy Nolte Lensink (see also Judy Nolte Temple), "Expanding the Boundaries of Criticism: The Diary as Female Autobiography," *Women's Studies* 14 (1987): 43.

50. Felicity A. Nussbaum, "Toward Conceptualizing Diary," *Studies in Autobiography*, ed. James Olney (Oxford: Oxford UP, 1988) 134.

51. See, for example, the Winter 2001 issue of *Biography*, which is dedicated to the question of perfomativity and autobiography and includes two articles on diaries.

52. Juhasz makes this distinction in her essay considering how the term "fragmentation" circulates in literary circles — particularly the work of modernists like Virginia Woolf. She suggests that the diary as a form does not fit within a modernist conception of fragment — a piece of a whole. Rather a diary entry, the fragment, "is complete in itself" ("'Some Deep Old Desk'" 666). In my reading of ordinary diaries as fragmented texts, I have come to appreciate the distinction Juhasz makes between a fragment that comes from a whole and a fragment that never adds up to something.

53. Geneva Cobb-Moore, "When Meanings Meet: *The Journals of Charlotte Forten Grimké*," *Inscribing the Daily: Critical Essays on Women's Diaries*, ed. Suzanne L. Bunkers and Cynthia Huff (Amherst, U of Mass P, 1996) 140.

54. Fothergill claims that a successful literary diary is a "book of the self" (43). Thomas Mallon goes as far as to say that "diaries are the flesh made word." Thomas Mallon, *A Book of One's Own: People and Their Diaries* (New York: Ticknor and Fields, 1984) xvii. And Trudelle Thomas highlights the diary as "the book my days are writing." Trudelle Thomas, "The Diary as Creative Midwife: Interviews with Three Writers," *Inscribing the Daily: Critical Essays on Women's*

Diaries, ed. Suzanne L. Bunkers and Cynthia Huff (Amherst, U of Mass P, 1996) 169.

55. Judy Nolte Temple, "Fragments as Diary: Theoretical Implications of the *Dreams and Visions* of 'Baby Doe' Tabor," *Inscribing the Daily: Critical Essays on Women's Diaries*, ed. Suzanne L. Bunkers and Cynthia Huff (Amherst, U of Mass P, 1996) 78.

56. Caren Kaplan, "Resisting Autobiography: Out-Law Genres and Transnational Feminist Subjects," *De/Colonizing the Subject: The Politics of Gender in Women's Autobiography,* ed. Sidonie Smith and Julia Watson (Minneapolis: U of Minnesota P, 1992) 119.

57. There are important ways in which Annie's diary is also not an "outlaw." Annie writes from a position of relative privilege. She is educated, middle class, and white. She also has the time (limited though it may be) to keep a diary and the material conditions that allow her to do so. Her diary, an ordinary diary, and diaries like hers are outliers to the diary canon given the limits and conditions currently placed on the diurnal form, but they are insiders when measured by the diarists' social and intellectual capital.

2 : TIME, DAYS, AND PAGE

1. Of course, all writing is subject to the possibility of hyperperformative readings — of violence to, and disregard for, the text — because interpretation is always a negotiation between text and reader at a specific time and place. And I am not suggesting that the kind of text predetermines the kind of reading in any essential way. More that certain texts are culturally constructed and physically constructed in ways that make them more or less vulnerable to hyperperformative readings. As Kaufman points out, an interpretation is the result of a complicated dialog between text and reader and largely a matter of the reader's presumed authority as well as the specific site of reading (the "kind" of reading being privileged — academic, personal, etc.). That an ordinary diary is more vulnerable to readers who assume too much authority is really not surprising at all given the historically delegitimated, unauthorized position of the diary, the diarist, and women writers in general.

2. Susan Miller, *Assuming the Positions: Cultural Pedagogy and the Politics of Commonplace Writing* (Pittsburgh: U of Pittsburgh P, 1998) 13.

3. I should add that the desire to produce simplified readings is not limited just to textual interpretation — who did what to whom, what should the final voiceover say, how should we organize the writing in the margins — but also with what we want to say about our interpretations. For example, Temple cautions against "the feminist fallacy" when reading diaries — imposing feminist consciousness and theory onto a diarist who lived historically outside such a frame. Gaps and silences can be filled in by readers who want to see resistance and agency in spaces that represent reproduction and constraint. Thus sacrificing the form of the diary for political and intellectual agendas can harm more than help. This is not to say that ordinary diaries are not spaces for resistance and empowerment — rather that the general abundance of empty spaces and

open endings can invite equally open and ungrounded readings posing as "right readings."

4. Stuart Sherman, *Telling Time: Clocks, Diaries, and English Diurnal Form, 1660–1785* (Chicago: U of Chicago P, 1996) xi.

5. Sherman suggests that Pepys's diary is the first diary that is diurnal in form. It becomes the model for his study.

6. Sherman looks at Frank Kermode's book, *A Sense of an Ending*, to demonstrate how stories follow a ticktock structure. Sherman relies on Kermode's argument to describe the kind of filling, the plot, a "time when," that is expected of narrative. We anticipate the tock as soon as we begin a story. Plot, by design, is occasioned — there is an event, a problem, a need at the center of the narrative that must get worked through. Plot is the working through. Occasioned diaries mimicked the ticktock structure of larger narratives and the ticktock of the clock. They missed the measured, in-between moments that both the pendulum and the diurnal form seize and make available for filling.

7. Sherman 22. I should note here that Sherman does not consider self-knowledge the same thing as self-discipline. He carefully distinguishes his understanding of the diary as a form for documenting the self from a Foucauldian notion of discipline. For Sherman, such knowledge grants autonomy not subjection (101–107).

8. Cinthia Gannett, in drawing distinctions between diarists writing within domestic versus public spaces, writes that "all men, regardless of class, write in a larger circumference than women" (68). Gannett suggests such access makes it easier to say what men's diaries are "about."

9. It is, of course, not this simple. The fact that never in my life was a repair person called for any reason at any time testifies not only to my dad's ability with tools but to his ingenuity. Many a time, he would find a creative solution to a practical problem. Still, the sheer number of my father's tools, their specialization, and the need for me to know how and when to use a tool, as well as the danger inherent in working with those tools was a radically different experience than I had working with my mom.

10. I hint at the idea of the diary as a haunted text merely to keep in mind that the diary is always a reduction of the real. Though it aims to be exhaustive and to replicate the fullness of time, it can never account for everything. While the text bears the traces of Annie and of her days, it maps neither fully. In the next chapter, I consider the diary as a haunted text. Below, I suggest that the physical fragility of the material text further evidences its ghosted state.

11. For a more extensive discussion of how commercially produced texts reproduced in their inscribers gender and national ideologies see Huff's essay, "Textual Boundaries: Space in Nineteenth-Century Women's Manuscript Diaries." In addition, McCarthy's essay "A Pocketful of Days: Pocket Diaries and Daily Record Keeping among Nineteenth-Century New England Women" does an excellent job of describing how women negotiated the spaces provided by commercially published diaries.

12. I hesitate to use the term "content" because Annie's diary is not only

limited in "content," but, as I argue in the next chapter, she is actively writing against "content" as we might understand it. My point here is only to demonstrate that while the "what" of Annie's diary may appear quite culturally determined the "how" of her diary is more within her charge.

13. Significantly, for the remaining year and a half, Annie keeps her diary on various similarly sized pieces of paper. These are mostly long ledger sheets folded into quarters and taken from the account books of Charley's blacksmith business. She also writes on ruled paper and a page from what appears to be an accident report from the railroad. Below I consider what happens in her writing when Annie moves from the ledger book to the loose sheets.

14. Molly McCarthy, "A Pocketful of Days: Pocket Diaries and Daily Record Keeping among Nineteenth-Century New England Women," *The New England Quarterly* 73.2 (June 2000): 295.

15. Margaret K. Brady, *Mormon Healer and Folk Poet: Mary Susannah Fowler's Life of "Unselfish Usefulness"* (Logan: Utah State UP, 2000) 172.

16. Many diary studies document the fact that nineteenth-century ideologies of womanhood left women with little voice and little room. For overviews in particular see Blodgett and Hampsten. Gannett describes how the diary becomes representative of women's "physical and discursive experience" often providing the only space for expression. Bunkers and Temple trace the ways in which women were culturally muted in the public sphere and more connected in the private in their diaries. And Lensink's book *"A Secret to be Burried"* gives extensive attention to the ways in which women were silenced even within their diaries (e.g., only being permitted to talk about their bodies when pregnant).

17. For example, Blodgett in *Centuries of Female Days: Englishwomen's Private Diaries* writes that "for any woman who feels lonely or isolated by her circumstances, the diary provides a needed listener" (5). And Jeanne Braham in her essay, "A Lens of Empathy," looks at the ways in which both writing and reading a diary recreates "women's culture as conversation" (57).

18. I am defining margins very broadly to include any textual markings that exist outside the body of the daily entries — whether those markings are in the top margins, the left margins, or even hovering just outside the frame of the entry. Also, my comments about margins apply primarily to the entries in the bound book. The loose papers that make up the final year and a half of her diary do not have explicit margins. For the most part, Annie covers the entire page of these papers with her entries and does not allow the creation of marginal space.

19. The actual entries (as well as the margins) indicate that Annie would at times compile an entry throughout the day. She would indicate a change in the time and/or place by starting a new line or by leaving a large space between the words. November 1, 1882, provides an example of a revisited entry:

> It has been quite cold and windy all day. We got up very early and
> Charley started at 6 to Father's to work again.   It is after 7 and he is
> not home yet. I sewed a good deal today. Wrote a letter to Miss Murray
> of London, Eng. and done ever so many jobs have been busy all day.
> /❦/

There are other reasons Annie would choose to begin a new line — often to mark a transition between tone or rhetorical intent or to record an anniversary.

20. I should note here that Annie might censor her entries but she does not, for the most part, edit them. Revisiting is a continuation of the conversation, not an emendation. Annie exhibits no sense that there is a "correct" way to write in the days.

21. I proceed cautiously here. It is my informed sense that Annie is tracking their sexual relations. I do not know for sure. As Brady cautions in *Mormon Healer and Folk Poet*, in working with diaries, with private writings in general, there is "a danger in taking any piece of writing out of its immediate and extended contexts." She goes on to remind us "how powerful the voice of the ethnographer can be in any retelling" (197).

3 : PUTTING THINGS TO RIGHT GENERALLY

1. Kathleen Norris, *Dakota: A Spiritual Geography* (New York: Ticknor and Fields, 1993) 40.

2. Philip Fisher, "Democratic Social Space: Whitman, Melville, and the Promise of American Transparency," *Representations* 24 (Fall 1988): 65. One of Fisher's overarching points, that such mapping orders as well as erases, reverberates in the discussion below.

3. Ralph Cintron, *Angels' Town:* Chero *Ways, Gang Life, and the Rhetorics of the Everyday* (Boston: Beacon P, 1997) 210.

4. It is interesting to note the similarities in language between the primary task of a discourse of measurement as one of "holding the unstable at bay" and Gannett's identification of the effort on the part of scholars "to keep the diary at bay" (39). In such a comparison the diary represents the same threat to decency as the one a garbage ordinance staves off.

5. An example from Cintron's book may be helpful. Chapter 4 is titled "A Boy and His Wall" and forms the central chapter to his book. It is a case study of a boy named Valerio. The chapter depends on the extended metaphor of walls — walls that separate cities as well as walls in houses. These walls are "symbols of confinement, of the deep fissure that [separates] those who have more power and socioeconomic standing from those who have less" (99). But while walls confine, Cintron writes that they also heighten the desire to scale, becoming blank spaces for the imagination, places for people to "subvert what pains them" (99). Valerio has covered the walls of his room with pictures of fast cars, marines, and famous sports stars. In order to protect himself, he has surrounded himself with images that, in his words, give him power because of their strength, speed, courage. By "writing himself out" on the walls of his rooms Valerio is practicing a literacy denied him by the educational system, for in school he has been labeled "LD." He fails to read or write "well."

Cintron spends time and energy trying to make sense of Valerio's learning disability. The diagnosticians and counselors are of little help. They can only offer the evidence that Valerio has trouble naming objects, finding the right word. Cintron concludes that Valerio's struggle is one that results from straddling two languages. It is a messy struggle, one not easily diagnosed and ordered by tests or by the educational system. Instead, "LD," a label seized by his teachers, his parents, and even Valerio himself, is used to clean up and organize a much too messy reality. The discourse of disability, a discourse of measurement, works to order Valerio into a system and, at the same time, order out or conceal the more difficult reality of being bilingual. That which is ordered out reappears in Valerio's desire to write himself out in images, to take charge of the walls that contain him.

6. Since Hampsten's initial study of midwestern diaries in connection to "true womanhood," more has been written about "the cult of true womanhood" and the effects on the private writings of women. Work by Helen Buss and Frances Cogan, in particular, demonstrates how "true womanhood" as an ideology was not the single cultural message available to women — nor even necessarily the dominant one. These multiple messages, while differing in some degree from each other, remain connected in their desire to circumscribe women's lives.

7. Rebecca Hogan, "Engendered Autobiographies: The Diary as a Feminine Form," *Prose Studies* 14 (September 1991): 100.

8. Chapters 2 and 3 of *Read This Only to Yourself* address intersections between class and language most closely.

9. See in particular "Mothers, Daughters, Diaries: Literacy, Relationship, and Cultural Context" by Temple and Bunkers as well as the last chapter in Brady's book *Mormon Healer and Folk Poet*.

10. Steven E. Kagle and Lorenza Gramegna, "Rewriting Her Life: Fictionalization and the Use of Fictional Models in Early American Women's Diaries," *Inscribing the Daily: Critical Essays on Women's Diaries*, ed. Suzanne L. Bunkers and Cynthia Huff (Amherst: U of Mass P, 1996), 43.

11. Another example appears on September 15, 1881. In this entry she is referring to her brother-in-law, Walter. It is not clear what the friction between Annie and Walter is, only that she cannot openly write about it. These lines, like those few I have recovered from the August 23 entry, are censored but not enough to be unreadable. The entry reads: "There is a piercing North wind this morning and it seems very cold although it is not freezing. I got up pretty early to get breakfast for W. as R. wanted him to go down with him. They started about 9 oclock. I am so glad we are going to have some breaking done at last. ~~It is a great relief to have W. absent for one day. I wish he was away all the time. I wish that he had never come.~~ I made Bread and browned Coffee and repaired some clothes. The wind has gone down this eve and I am glad. It made such a dismal sound. I am so lonesome tonight. I can hardly bear it — to think of staying alone is dreadful. I do wish Charlie was home. We got a letter from Milt and one from Gus."

1. Laurie Langbauer, "Absolute Commonplaces: Oliphant's Theory of Auto-biography," *Margaret Oliphant: Critical Essays on a Gentle Subversive*, ed. D. J. Trela (Selinsgrove: Susquehanna UP, 1995) 125.

2. Susan Miller, *Assuming the Positions: Cultural Pedagogy and the Politics of Commonplace Writing* (Pittsburgh: U of Pittsburgh P, 1998) 1.

3. Rita Felski, *Doing Time: Feminist Theory and Postmodern Culture* (New York: New York UP, 2000) 81.

4. Amy Wink quotes Leigh Gilmore in her essay "Narratives of Resistance: Negotiating the Altering and Altered Selves in the Diaries of Henrietta Baker Embre and Tennessee Keys Embre," *a/b: Auto/Biography Studies* 13.2 (Fall 1998): 201. Wink's work is of particular interest to me as she considers how and when women use their diaries as "weapons of resistance," specifically in the way diaries serve as repositories of evidence.

5. James Seitz, "Roland Barthes, Reading, and Roleplay: Composition's Misguided Rejection of Fragmentary Texts," *College English* 53.7 (November 1991): 820.

6. Iris Marion Young, *Intersecting Voices: Dilemmas of Gender, Political Philosophy, and Policy* (Princeton, NJ: Princeton UP, 1997) 137, 148.

7. Timothy Dow Adams, *Light Writing and Life Writing: Photography in Autobiography* (Chapel Hill: U of North Carolina P, 2000) xi.

8. Adams xii.

9. Marlene Kadar, "Whose Life Is It Anyway? Out of the Bathtub and into the Narrative," *Essays on Life Writing: From Genre to Critical Practice*, ed. Marlene Kadar (Toronto: U of Toronto P, 1992) 159.

10. Jennifer Sinor, "Inscribing Ordinary Trauma: The Diary of a Military Child," *Arms and the Self: War, Military, and Autobiography*, ed. Alex Vernon (forthcoming from Kent State UP).

11. Samuel Hynes, *The Soldiers' Tale: Bearing Witness to Modern War* (New York: Penguin Press, 1997) xii.

12. Another way to consider just how little of our lived experience is narrated is to think about the dinner table conversation. You rehearse for your partner or your children the events of the day: a conversation, a phone call, a meeting, the traffic on the drive home, a story you heard on the radio. Even though these are ordinary parts of your day, by choosing to describe these moments — as opposed to all the other moments — you mark them as nonordinary, as special. They become the narrated story of your day. The in-between moments go unmarked. Even though these moments are equally about both your day and your sense of self, they are not turned into a story.

Bibliography

Adams, Timothy Dow. *Light Writing and Life Writing: Photography in Auto-biography*. Chapel Hill: U of North Carolina P, 2000.

Alcoff, Linda Martin. "The Problem of Speaking for Others." *Who Can Speak? Authority and Critical Identity*. Ed. Judith Roof and Robyn Wiegman. Urbana: U of Illinois P, 1995. 97–119.

Allemendinger, Blake. "Anastasia of Oregon." *Arizona Quarterly* 51.1 (Spring 1995): 111–31.

Applegate, Shannon. "The Literature of Loneliness: Understanding the Letters and Diaries of the American West." *Reading the West: New Essays on the Literature of the American West*. Ed. Michael Kowalewski. Cambridge: Cambridge UP, 1996. 63–81.

Arendt, Hannah. *The Human Condition*. 1958. Chicago: U of Chicago P, 1989.

Behar, Ruth. *Translated Woman: Crossing the Border with Esperanza's Story*. Boston: Beacon P, 1993.

Bettelheim, Bruno. "The Ignored Lesson of Anne Frank." *Fields of Writing: Readings across the Disciplines*. Ed. Nancy Comley et al. New York: St. Martin's P, 1994. 649–59.

Blodgett, Harriet. *Centuries of Female Days: Englishwomen's Private Diaries*. New Brunswick, NJ: Rutgers UP, 1988.

———. "Preserving the Moment in the Diary of Margaret Fountaine." Bunkers and Huff. 156–68.

Bloom, Lynn Z. "'I Write for Myself and Strangers': Private Diaries as Public Documents." Bunkers and Huff. 25–37.

———. "Escaping Voices: Women's South Pacific Internment Diaries and Memoirs." *Mosaic* 23.2 (Summer 1990): 101–12.

Bloom, Lynn Z., and Orlee Holder. "Anaïs Nin's *Diary in Context*." *Women's Autobiography: Essays in Criticism*. Ed. Estelle C. Jelinek. Bloomington: Indiana UP, 1980. 206–20.

Brady, Margaret. *Mormon Healer and Folk Poet: Mary Susannah Fowler's Life of "Unselfish Usefulness."* Logan: Utah State UP, 2000.

Braham, Jeanne. "A Lens of Empathy." Bunkers and Huff. 56–71.

Bunkers, Suzanne L. "Issues in Studying Women's Diaries: A Theoretical and Critical Introduction." Bunkers and Huff. 1–22.

———. *In Search of Susanna*. Iowa City: U of Iowa P, 1996.

———. *"All Will Yet Be Well": The Diary of Sarah Gillespie Huftalen, 1873–1952*. Iowa City: U of Iowa P, 1993.

————. "What Do Women *Really* Mean? Thoughts on Women's Diaries and Lives." *The Intimate Critique*. Ed. Diane P. Freedman, Olivia Frey, and Frances Murphy Zauhar. Durham: Duke UP, 1993. 207–21.

————. "Diaries: Public *and* Private Records of Women's Lives." *Legacy* 7.2 (Fall 1990): 17–26.

————. "Subjectivity and Self-Reflexivity in the Study of Women's Diaries as Autobiography." *a/b: Auto/Biography Studies* 5 (Fall 1990): 114–23.

————. "Midwestern Diaries and Journals: What Women Were (Not) Saying in the Late 1800s." *Studies in Autobiography*. Ed. James Olney. Oxford: Oxford UP, 1988. 190–210.

————. "Reading and Interpreting Unpublished Diaries by Nineteenth-Century Women." *a/b: Auto/Biography Studies* 2.2 (Summer 1986): 15–17.

Bunkers, Suzanne L., and Cynthia A. Huff, eds. *Inscribing the Daily: Critical Essays on Women's Diaries*. Amherst: U of Mass P, 1996.

————. "Issues in Studying Women's Diaries: A Theoretical and Critical Introduction." Bunkers and Huff. 1–20.

Buss, Helen M. "A Feminist Revision of New Historicism to Give Fuller Readings of Women's Private Writings." Bunkers and Huff. 86–103.

Captain, Esther. "'Written with an Eye on History.' Wartime Diaries of Internees as Testimonies of Captivity Literature." *Tydskrif-vir-Nederlands-en-Afrikaans* 5.1 (June 1998): 1–15.

Carter, Kathryn. "The Cultural Work of Diaries in Mid-Century Victorian Britain." *Victorian Review* 23.2 (Winter 1997): 251–67.

Certeau, Michel de. *The Practice of Everyday Life*. Trans. Steven Rendall. Berkeley: U of California P, 1984.

Cintron, Ralph. *Angels' Town:* Chero *Ways, Gang Life, and Rhetorics of the Everyday*. Boston: Beacon P, 1997.

Cline, Cheryl. *Women's Diaries, Journals, and Letters: An Annotated Bibliography*. New York: Garland Publishing Co., 1989.

Cobb-Moore, Geneva. "When Meanings Meet: *The Journals of Charlotte Forten Grimké*." Bunkers and Huff. 139–55.

Cogan, Frances B. *All-American Girl: The Ideal of Real Womanhood in Mid-Nineteenth-Century America*. Athens: U of Georgia P, 1989.

Coles, Robert. *Doing Documentary Work*. Oxford: Oxford UP, 1997.

Cook, Kay K.. "Medical Identity: My DNA/Myself." Smith and Watson. *Getting a Life*. 63–85.

Crowther, Barbara. "Writing as Performance: Young Girls' Diaries." Jossleson and Lieblich. 197–220.

Culley, Margo, ed. *A Day at a Time: The Diary Literature of American Women from 1764 to the Present*. New York: Feminist P at CUNY, 1985.

————. "Women's Vernacular Literature: Teaching the Mother Tongue." Hoffman and Culley. 9–17.

Davies, Gayle R. "Women's Quilts and Diaries: Creative Expression as Personal

Resource." *Uncoverings: Research Papers of the American Quilt Study Group* 18 (1997): 213–29.

———. "Women's Frontier Diaries: Writing for Good Reason." *Women's Studies* 14 (1987): 5–14.

Felman, Shoshana, and Dori Laub. *Testimony: Crises of Witnessing in Literature, Psychoanalysis, and History*. New York: Routledge, 1992.

Felski, Rita. *Doing Time: Feminist Theory and Postmodern Culture*. New York: New York UP, 2000.

Fisher, Philip. "Democratic Social Space: Whitman, Melville, and the Promise of American Transparency." *Representations* 24 (Fall 1988): 60–101.

Fothergill, Robert A. *Private Chronicles: A Study of English Diaries*. Oxford: Oxford UP, 1974.

Freedman, Diane P. *An Alchemy of Genres: Cross-Genre Writing by American Feminist Poet-Critics*. Charlottesville: UP of Virginia, 1992.

Gannett, Cinthia. *Gender and the Journal: Diaries and Academic Discourse*. Albany: SUNY, 1992.

Gere, Anne Ruggles. *Intimate Practices: Literacy and Cultural Work in U.S. Women's Clubs, 1880–1920*. Urbana: University of Illinois Press, 1997.

———. *Writing Groups: History, Theory, and Implications*. Carbondale: Southern Illinois UP, 1987.

Hampsten, Elizabeth. *Read This Only to Yourself: The Private Writings of Midwestern Women, 1880–1910*. Bloomington: Indiana UP, 1982.

Hoffman, Leonore, and Margo Culley, eds. *Women's Personal Narratives: Essays in Criticism and Pedagogy*. New York: MLA, 1985.

Hogan, Rebecca. "Engendered Autobiographies: The Diary as a Feminine Form." *Prose Studies* 14 (September 1991): 95–107.

Huff, Cynthia A. "Reading as Re-Vision: Approaches to Reading Manuscript Diaries." *Biography* 23.2 (Summer 2000): 505–23.

———. "Textual Boundaries: Space in Nineteenth-Century Women's Manuscript Diaries." Bunkers and Huff. 123–38.

———. "Writer at Large: Culture and Self in Victorian Women's Travel Diaries." *a/b: Auto/Biography Studies* 4.2 (Winter 1988): 118–29.

———. "Private Domains: Queen Victoria and Women's Diaries." *a/b: Auto/Biography Studies* 4.1 (Fall 1988): 46–52.

———. *British Women's Diaries: A Descriptive Bibliography of Selected Nineteenth-Century Women's Manuscript Diaries*. New York: AMS Press, 1985.

Hunter, Jane H. "Inscribing the Self in the Heart of the Family: Diaries and Girlhood in Late-Victorian America." *American Quarterly* 44.1 (1992): 51–81.

Hynes, Samuel. *The Soldiers' Tale: Bearing Witness to Modern War*. New York: Penguin Press, 1997.

Jelinek, Estelle C. *The Tradition of Women's Autobiography: From Antiquity to Present*. Boston: Twayne, 1986.

———, ed. *Women's Autobiography: Essays in Criticism*. Bloomington: Indiana UP, 1980.

Johnson, Alexandra. *Leaving a Trace: On Keeping a Journal: The Art of Transforming a Life into Stories*. Boston: Little, Brown and Company, 2001.

———. *The Hidden Writer: Diaries and the Creative Life*. New York: Anchor Books, 1997.

———. "The Drama of Imagination: Marjory Fleming and Her Diaries." *Infant Tongues: The Voice of the Child in Literature*. Ed. Elizabeth Goodenough, Mark A. Heberle, and Naomi Sokoloff. Detroit: Wayne State UP, 1994. 80–109.

Jossleson, Ruthellen, and Amia Lieblich, eds. *Making Meaning of Narratives in the Narrative Study of Lives*. Thousand Oaks: Sage Publications, 1999.

Juhasz, Suzanne. "The Journal as Source and Model for Feminist Art: The Example of Kathleen Fraser." *Frontiers* 8.1 (1984): 16–20.

———. "Towards a Theory of Form in Feminist Autobiography: Kate Millet's *Flying* and *Sita*; Maxine Hong Kingston's *The Woman Warrior*." Jelinek. 221–37

———. "'Some Deep Old Desk or Capacious Hold-All': Form and Women's Autobiography." *College English* 39.6 (February 1978): 663–68.

Kadar, Marlene. "Whose Life Is It Anyway? Out of the Bathtub and into the Narrative." *Essays on Life Writing: From Genre to Critical Practice*. Ed. Marlene Kadar. Toronto: U of Toronto P, 1992. 152–61.

Kagle, Steven Earl. "The Diary as Art: A New Assessment." *Genre* 6.4 (1973): 416–27.

Kagle, Steven E., and Lorenza Gramegna. "Rewriting Her Life: Fictionalization and the Use of Fictional Models in Early American Women's Diaries." Bunkers and Huff. 38–55.

Kaplan, Caren. "Resisting Autobiography: Out-Law Genres and Transnational Feminist Subjects." *De/Colonizing the Subject: The Politics of Gender in Women's Autobiography*. Ed. Sidonie Smith and Julia Watson. Minneapolis: U of Minnesota P, 1992. 115–38.

Kaufman, Rona. "Navigating the Limit Points of Reading." Unpublished.

Kirsch, Gesa. *Ethical Dilemmas in Feminist Research: The Politics of Location, Interpretation, and Publication*. New York: SUNY, 1999.

———. "Multi-Vocal Texts and Interpretive Responsibility." *College English* 59.2 (February 1997): 191–202.

Langbauer, Laurie. *Novels of Everyday Life: The Series in English Fiction, 1850–1930*. Ithaca and London: Cornell UP, 1999.

———. "Absolute Commonplaces: Oliphant's Theory of Autobiography." *Margaret Oliphant: Critical Essays on a Gentle Subversive*. Ed. D. J. Trela. Selinsgrove: Susquehanna UP, 1995. 124–34.

Lather, Patti, and Chris Smithies. *Troubling the Angels: Women Living with HIV/AIDS*. Boulder, CO: Westview P, 1997.

LeFevre, Karen Burke. *Invention as Social Act*. Carbondale: Southern Illinois UP, 1987.

Lensink, Judy Nolte. *"A Secret to be Burried": The Diary and Life of Emily Hawley Gillespie, 1858–1888*. Iowa City: U of Iowa P, 1989.

———. "Expanding the Boundaries of Criticism: The Diary as Female Autobiography." *Women's Studies* 14 (1987): 39–53.

Long, Judy. *Telling Women's Lives: Subject/Narrator/Reader/Text*. New York: New York UP, 1999.

Mallon, Thomas. *A Book of One's Own: People and Their Diaries*. New York: Ticknor and Fields, 1984.

Mathews, William. *British Diaries 1442–1942*. 1950. Gloucester, MA: Peter Smith, 1967.

McCarthy, Molly. "A Pocketful of Days: Pocket Diaries and Daily Record Keeping among Nineteenth-Century New England Women." *New England Quarterly* 73.2 (June 2000): 274–96.

Meese, Elizabeth A. "The Languages of Oral Testimony and Women's Literature." Hoffman and Culley. 18–26.

Miller, Susan. *Assuming the Positions: Cultural Pedagogy and the Politics of Commonplace Writing*. Pittsburgh: U of Pittsburgh P, 1998.

Miner, Earl. "Literary Diaries and the Boundaries of Literature." *Yearbook of Comparative and General Literature* 21 (1972): 46–51.

Moffat, Mary Jane, and Charlotte Painter, eds. *Revelations: Diaries of Women*. New York: Random House, 1974.

Norris, Kathleen. *Dakota: A Spiritual Geography*. New York: Ticknor and Fields, 1993.

Nussbaum, Felicity A. "Toward Conceptualizing Diary." *Studies in Autobiography*. Ed. James Olney. Oxford: Oxford UP, 1988. 128–40.

Pascal, Roy. *Design and Truth in Autobiography*. Cambridge: Harvard UP, 1960.

Patterson, David. *Along the Edge of Annihilation: The Collapse and Recovery of Life in the Holocaust Diary*. Seattle: U of Washington P, 1999.

Podneiks, Elizabeth. *Daily Modernism: The Literary Diaries of Virginia Woolf, Antonia White, Elizabeth Smart, and Anaïs Nin*. Montreal: McGill-Queen's UP, 2000.

———. "'Keep out/Keep out/ Your snooting snout': The Irresistible Journals of Elizabeth Smart." *a/b: Auto/Biography Studies* 11.1 (Spring 1996): 57–81.

———. "The Theater of 'Incest': Enacting Artaud, Mirbeau, and Rimbaud in the Pages of the Diary." *Anais* 13 (1995): 39–52.

Ponsonby, Arthur. *English Diaries*. London: Methuen & Co., Ltd., 1923.

———. *More English Diaries*. London: Methuen & Co., Ltd., 1927.

Raoul, Valerie. "Women and Diaries: Gender and Genre." *Mosaic* 22.3 (Summer 1989): 57–65.

Ray, Annie Pringle. Manuscript diary, 1881–1884. Author's collection.

Rogers, Annie G., Mary E. Casey, Jennifer Eckert, James Holland, Victoria Nakkula, and Nurit Sheinberg. "An Interpretive Poetics of Languages of the Unsayable." Jossleson and Lieblich. 77–106

Rosenwald, Lawrence. *Emerson and the Art of the Diary*. New York: Oxford UP, 1988.

Schlissel, Lillian. *Women's Diaries of the Westward Journey*. New York: Schocken Books, 1982.

Schuneman, Billie. Personal interview. August 28, 1998.

Seitz, James. "Roland Barthes, Reading, and Roleplay: Composition's Misguided Rejection of Fragmentary Texts." *College English* 53.7 (November 1991): 815–25.

Sherman, Stuart. *Telling Time: Clocks, Diaries, and English Diurnal Form, 1660–1785*. Chicago: U of Chicago P, 1996.

Shumaker, Wayne. *English Autobiography: Its Emergence, Materials, and Form*. Berkeley: U of California P, 1954.

Shuman, Amy. *Storytelling Rights: The Uses of Oral and Written Texts by Urban Adolescents*. Cambridge: Cambridge UP, 1986.

Simons, Judy. *Diaries and Journals of Literary Women from Fanny Burney to Virginia Woolf*. Iowa City: U of Iowa P, 1990.

Sinor, Jennifer. "Reading the Ordinary Diary." *Rhetoric Review* 24.2 (Spring 2002) 123–49.

———. "Inscribing Ordinary Trauma: The Diary of a Military Child." *Arms and the Self: War, Military, and Autobiography*. Ed. Alex Vernon. Forthcoming from Kent State University Press.

Smith, Sidonie. *A Poetics of Women's Autobiography: Marginality and the Fictions of Self-Representation*. Bloomington: Indiana UP, 1987.

Smith, Sidonie, and Julia Watson, eds. *Getting a Life: Everyday Uses of Autobiography*. Minneapolis: U of Minn P, 1996.

———. *Women, Autobiography, Theory: A Reader*. Madison: U of Wisconsin P, 1998.

Spengeman, William C. *The Forms of Autobiography: Episodes in the History of a Literary Genre*. New Haven: Yale UP, 1980.

Spivak, Gayatri Chakravorty. "Three Women's Texts and a Critique of Imperialism." *Feminisms: An Anthology of Literary Theory and Criticism*. Ed. Robyn Warhol and Diane Price Herndhl. New Brunswick, NJ: Rutgers UP, 1997. 798–814.

Stewart, Kathleen. *A Space on the Side of the Road: Cultural Poetics in an "Other" America*. Princeton, NJ: Princeton UP, 1996.

Temple, Judy Nolte. *See also* Lensink, Judy Nolte.

Temple, Judy Nolte. "Fragments as Diary: Theoretical Implications of the *Dreams and Visions* of 'Baby Doe' Tabor." Bunkers and Huff. 72–85.

Temple, Judy Nolte, and Suzanne Bunkers. "Mothers, Daughters, Diaries: Literacy, Relationship, and Cultural Context." *Nineteenth-Century Women Learn to Write*. Ed. Catherine Hobbs. Charlottesville: UP of Virginia, 1995. 197–216.

Thomas, Trudelle. "The Diary as Creative Midwife: Interviews with Three Writers." Bunkers and Huff. 169–88.

Ulrich, Laurel Thatcher. *A Midwife's Tale: The Life of Margaret Ballard, Based on Her Diary, 1758–1812*. New York: Vintage Press, 1990.

Visweswaran, Kamela. *Fictions of Feminist Ethnography*. Minneapolis: U of Minnesota P, 1994.

Welter, Barbara. "The Cult of True Womanhood, 1820–1860." *Locating American Studies: The Evolution of a Discipline*. Ed. Lucy Maddox. Baltimore: Johns Hopkins UP, 1999. 43–66.

Wink, Amy L. "Narratives of Resistance: Negotiating the Altering and Altered Selves in the Diaries of Henrietta Baker Embre and Tennessee Keys Embre." *a/b: Auto/Biography Studies* 13.2 (Fall 1998): 199–222.

Young, Iris Marion. *Intersecting Voices: Dilemmas of Gender, Political Philosophy, and Policy*. Princeton, NJ: Princeton UP, 1997.

Index

Adams, Timothy Dow, 202
Alcoff, Linda, 13
Alexandra (town), 66
Algona (town), 62
Alice, 136, 140, 141
Anderson, Mr., 59, 64
Arendt, Hannah, 197, 214 n19
Arnold, Matthew, 32
Art (name), 82
"August 23, 1881," 35, 76–77, 88,
    169–70, 176
autobiography, 17, 199, 216 n37,
    217 n43; diary as, 26–27, 32, 44–
    57; and gender, 44–48; and life-
    writing, 202–3; as literary, 35,
    49–53, 55–57, 196; military, 203–
    7; proper, 44–46, 49, 50, 52–53,
    54, 203; resisting, 54–55. *See also*
    lifewriting

Babcock, Miss, 69
Babcock, Mr., 164, 174
Babcock, Mrs., 9, 69, 72, 164, 174
Bashkirtseff, Marie, 29
Behar, Ruth, 13
Bernstein, Basil, 158–59
Berthoff, Ann, 181
Bettelheim, Bruno, 90
Blodgett, Harriet, 32, 45, 48, 215 n23,
    216 n39
Bloom, Lynn Z., 41–42
Bloomington (town), 74
Boswell, James, 29, 31, 95
Brady, Margaret, 107, 158–59,
    221 n21
Bridgewater, South Dakota, 43, 58,
    65, 66, 103, 123, 144, 149, 188

Bullard's (store), 80, 82
Bunkers, Suzanne L., 29, 37, 38, 39,
    46, 215 n26, 216 n35
Burney, Fanny, 29
Buss, Helen, 222 n6
Byron, Lord Gordon, 31

Captain, Esther, 212 n4
Carson, Anne, 160
Carter, Kathryn, 36, 37, 212 n3
Chandler, Miss, 133
Chandler, Mr., 141
Chandler, Mrs., 133, 136, 140, 141
Chestnut, Mary Boykin, 12, 31, 42
Child, Jennie, 66, 80, 81
Child, Mrs., 135
Cintron, Ralph, 19, 21, 151–53, 180,
    190, 212–22 n5
Cleaveland, Miss, 82
Cobb-Moore, Geneva, 49–52
Cogan, Frances, 222 n6
Cook, Kay, 199
Coolige, F., 142
Coolige/Coolage family, 140, 141,
    142, 143
Cotie, Mrs., 127
Croop, Mr., 125
Culley, Margo, 32, 39, 40–47, 212 n3
cult of true womanhood, 155, 222 n6
cultural scripts, 199–200;
    nineteenth-century, 8, 91, 153; and
    ordinary writing, 5, 89, 187
cultural studies, 4, 12, 44, 199, 213 n9
Currier, Mr., 77, 78

dailiness, 36, 91–97, 155–58, 179,
    181; and diurnal form, 92–96,

dailiness (*continued*)
157–58; features of, 17–19, 56–57;
and gender, 95–96; historical
roots of, 18, 92–95; replicating,
97, 102–13, 118

Dapogny, James, 10–11

diaries, 17, 26, 28; as account books,
38, 103–5, 110–11; alternative
reading strategies for, 34–35, 38,
55; and audience, 38–43, 215 n23;
of author, 24–26, 27, 32–33, 53–
54, 203–7; as autobiography, 26–
27, 32, 44–57; censorship of, 4, 38–
40, 168–70, 222 n11; content of,
101, 103, 113, 162, 219–20 n12; as
devalued form 27; and domestic-
ity, 28; early scholarship on, 28–
32; and economy, 105, 108–9, 118;
editing of, 42–43, 89–90; encoding of, 38, 119–21, 155; as female
form, 26, 44, 47–49, 95–96, 119,
157; as fragmented, 13, 34, 43, 44,
47, 49, 51–52, 55, 217 n52; as keepsakes, 38; as lifewriting, 26, 202–
7; as literary form, 12, 17, 27, 29,
31–32, 33–35, 40–43, 49–52, 55–
57, 95–96, 179, 216 n39; and maps,
91–92, 101–2, 148–50; and middleness, 14, 17, 18; and New Criticism, 30, 33; preprinted, 38, 100–
3; as public or private, 26, 36–43,
214 n18, 214–15 n20, 215 n26; as
raw material, 29, 52; reading of,
28, 38, 39, 87; recovery of, 26–27,
29; as social, 38, 215 n28, 216 n30;
and space and form, 48, 91–92,
100–9, 115–21, 171, 220–21 n19;
and time, 92–97; as tool, 94, 97,
99–100. *See also* diurnal form; ordinary diaries; Annie Ray, diary of

diarist, 25–26, 39–40, 95, 157;
agency of, 8, 153; construction of,
41, 89–90; performance of, 48–
49, 52–53, 101–2, 110–11, 120–22;
positions of, 45, 105–6; as strategic writer, 109–11

diary discourse, 26, 50, 51, 101, 107,
151

diary literature, 12, 29, 212 n2,
212 n3

discourse of measurement, 150–51,
152, 156, 221 n4, 221–22 n5

diurnal form, 26, 27, 55, 116; and
dailiness, 56–57, 91–97; definition of, 212 n2; features of, 18, 92;
and measuredness, 92–97, 121–
22, 150–51, 154–56; as narrative
of self, 95–96; and the pendulum,
92–93, 145; rhetorical work of,
18–19, 153, 156–79; rise of, 92–
93; and self knowledge, 94, 110,
122; and usefulness, 94–97, 99–
100, 104–5, 107, 110, 120, 121–22,
156, 174. *See also* diaries; ordinary
diaries

diurnal lens, 17–19, 55–57

domestic, 3, 28, 37, 47, 95–96, 102,
121, 153–56, 198–200, 211 n3

dreams, 110, 176–79

Dudley, B., 135

Emma, 71

ethnography, 190–91, 199

everyday, 5, 10, 18, 19–20, 185, 196–
200, 206

Felman, Shoshana, 13

Felski, Rita, 189, 197, 200

feminist theory, 4, 13, 30; and diaries, 31; and identity, 8

Fisher, Philip, 149

Flint, Mr., 132, 139

Flint, Mrs., 116, 133, 136, 137, 139

flower symbol, 76, 77, 78, 120, 124–
31, 133–39, 141–43, 144, 220 n19

Foss, Mrs., 83

Fothergill, Robert, 23, 30–31, 33

fragmented texts, 51–55, 191–92,
217 n52

Frank, Anne, 31, 42, 112

Frank, Otto, 89–90

Freedman, Diane, 212 n4

Gannett, Cinthia, 214–15 n20, 219 n8, 221 n4
Garner, 71
Gere, Anne Ruggles, 39
ghost, 168–69, 170, 172, 174, 175, 179
Gilmore, Leigh, 188
Gramegna, Lorenza, 167
Granger, Mr., 14, 58, 61, 62, 64, 65, 165–66
Granger, Mrs., 61, 62, 64, 65, 114, 165–66
Granger's Boarding House, 78
Grimké, Charlotte Forten, 12, 49–52

H., Ida, 69
Hampsten, Elizabeth, 21, 32, 38, 113, 155, 158, 222 n6
Hasselstrom, Linda, 22
Haverstroh, Mrs., 67
Heath, B., 135
Hogan, Rebecca, 157
Holmes, Mrs., 59
homestead claim, 8, 43, 71, 73, 74, 85, 102, 105, 110, 111, 123, 127, 140–50, 165, 173, 175
Huff, Cynthia A., 12, 29–30, 34, 36, 38, 48, 219 n11
Hunt (name), 125
Hunt, Frank, 132, 137
Hunter, Jane, 38
Hynes, Samuel, 204

identity, 8, 48–49, 110–11, 188–89, 192–93, 199, 202
ideologies, 155, 220 n16

Jane, 73, 143
Jelinek, Estelle, 44–45
Johnson, Alexandra, 34, 41
Johnson, Samuel, 95
Juhasz, Suzanne, 47, 217 n52

Kadar, Marlene, 203
Kagle, Steven, 32, 167
Kaplan, Caren, 54–55

Kaufman, Rona, 88–89, 218 n1
Kemble, Frances Anne, 31
Kennedy, B. E. B., 135

Land Ordinance of 1785, 149
Langbauer, Laurie, 5, 6
language, 179, 190; and class, 158; imprecise, 168, 172–74; metaphor, 160, 174–76; and parataxis, 158–61; precise, 154–61; restricted code, 158–59; and routine, 159
Larkins, L., 74
Lather, Patti, 13
Leadville, Colorado, 58, 64, 65, 66, 67, 68, 108, 142, 143, 163
LeFevre, Karen Burke, 39
LeMars (town), 141
lifewriting, 20, 182, 202–7; and the literary, 47, 49, 203. *See also* autobiography
literary, 6–7, 8, 15, 182, 184, 189, 191, 193, 196, 208; and autobiography, 44, 49–52, 55; and the diary, 12, 17, 26–27, 29, 30–32, 33–36, 40–43, 55–57, 95–96, 162, 179, 216 n39; lens, 6, 17, 33; and lifewriting, 203–7; limits of, 182. *See also* story
Lizzie, 74

Mallon, Thomas, 15, 32, 183, 184
Manahan, Mr., 141
Mansfield, Katherine, 54
manuscript diaries, 12, 13, 129–30
Matson family, 80
May, Lea, 64
McAllister, Miss, 61
McCarthy, Molly, 34, 36, 38, 48, 103, 219 n11
McKemmie, Miss, 126
McKinnan, Mrs., 75
measuredness, 18, 19, 56, 92–97, 102, 122, 150–51, 154, 156, 157, 162, 171, 172, 173, 175, 176; and ordinary writing, 184–87, 200
Menchu, Rigoberta, 202

menstruation, 47, 119–20
middleness: and ordinary writing, 14, 17, 56, 106
Miller, Susan, 89, 183
Milt, 79
Milwaukee house (in Mitchell), 65
Miner, Earl, 33
Mitchell, South Dakota, 60, 61, 62, 64, 65, 66, 73, 74, 74, 165–66
Moffat, Mary Jane, 31–32, 33, 45, 47
Morse, 76

Nelson, Mr., 75
Nin, Anais, 12, 31, 42, 54
Norris, Kathleen, 145, 146
Nussbaum, Felicity, 48–49
Nye, Mr., 64

occasion, 92–97, 102, 105, 113, 122, 155–56, 171, 178, 207; dismantling of, 163–67
ordering, 151–52, 156–79, 192; explicit, 152, 154–56; failure of, 167–68; and language, 158–61; outcomes of, 152–53; in sentences, 161
ordinariness, 3–5, 19–20, 182, 184, 185, 196–98, 205–7, 210; evaluation of, 5; and the military, 205–7; as river, 7; and subjectivity, 198; as term, 196–97; as unremarkable, 6; as white space, 182
ordinary diaries, 31–32, 35, 40, 44, 51, 55; and content, 219–20 n12; conversational strategies in, 112–22, 221 n20; and cultural scripts, 89, 155; and dailiness, 96, 155; editing of, 35–36; features of, 17–19, 56–57; and margins, 115–21, 220 n18; and measuredness, 11, 163; reading of, 14, 17, 18, 87–91, 110; and usefulness, 99–100, 102, 121–22; as vulnerable, 88, 218 n3. See also diaries; diurnal form; Annie Ray, diary of
ordinary writers, 92; agency of, 7–8, 16, 17, 153, 187; as lifewriters, 207;

as makers of text, 8, 19, 192–93; positions of, 15, 16, 89–91, 187–89; skill of, 7, 19–20, 96–97, 102, 211 n5; and use 14, 96–97. See also diarist; Annie Ray, as writer
ordinary writing: Annie Ray's diary as example of, 7, 10, 11, 179, 184; benefits of, 200; content of, 13, 184, 211 n5; as devalued, 7, 183; as discarded, 4–5, 9, 182–83; and everyday, 19, 185–87; failure in reading, 10, 189, 209; as fragmented, 13, 185, 187, 190–93, 204; as lens for nonordinary, 188–89, 209; as made text, 183, 190–93; making of, 15, 181–83; outcomes of reading, 10, 19–20, 182, 183–84, 187; qualities of, 5–7, 13–16, 19–20, 182–89; reading of, 5–7, 8, 12, 89, 184; and story, 16–17, 36; and temporality, 184–85; as testimony, 13; transience of, 9–10, 182–84, 189

Painter, Charlotte, 31–32, 33, 45
parataxis, 156; between entries, 163–67; in sentences, 161–62; and vocabulary, 158–61; within entries, 162–63
Pascal, Roy, 45–46, 49
Pease, Mr., 76, 77
Pepys, Samuel, 29, 31, 93–96, 184
Pete, 77
Pierce, Mrs., 83
Plankington (town), 65
Plath, Sylvia, 54
Podneiks, Elizabeth, 34, 41, 52–53, 215 n23
Potter, Beatrix Webb, 46
Pringle, Bettie, 84
Pringle, David, 58, 69, 77, 79, 80, 84, 112, 126, 128, 135, 175
Pringle, James/Jim/Jimmie, 72, 73, 77, 79, 81, 129, 131, 132, 133, 134, 136, 143, 144
Pringle, Joan Ormiston (mother), 74, 82, 101, 139, 140, 158, 164, 187

Pringle, Johnnie, 66, 68, 72, 76, 78, 80, 81, 82, 83, 123, 124, 127, 128, 133, 140, 162, 164

Pringle, Robbie, 8, 14, 58, 59, 60, 61, 62, 64, 65, 66, 67, 71, 74, 77, 78, 79, 81, 82, 83, 84, 124, 135, 138, 143, 174

Pringle, Robert (father), 9, 67, 72, 74, 75, 76, 78, 80, 83, 102, 111, 118, 123, 124, 126, 140, 159, 162, 163, 164; deceased mother of 84

private writing, 214 n18; and nineteenth-century women, 37–38; as space of deprivation, 37, 197, 214 n19. *See also* diaries, as public or private

protodiaries, 30–31

public, 40–43, 197. *See also* diaries, as public or private

puppy, 78

Ray, Annie: class, 158; diary of, 10–11, 14–15, 16, 20–22, 27–28, 32–33, 35–36, 43–44, 53–54, 87, 95–96, 100–9, 113–22, 153–56, 159–79, 181, 218 n57, 220 n13, 220–21 n19; education, 158, 161; and loneliness, 111–12, 118, 160–61, 167; neuralgia of, 36, 84; obituary, 188; uterine inflammation of, 84; as writer, 18–19, 91, 106–7, 108, 153, 192–93

Ray, Charley, 15, 36, 43–44, 54, 58, 101–2, 108, 110, 120, 121, 149, 154, 159, 160–61, 163–65, 168–69, 178–79, 198–99, 207; mentioned in Annie's diary, 58–85, 123–44; unnamed sister of, 79

Ray, Gus, 72, 74, 75, 143

Ray, Walter, 58, 72, 73, 74, 75, 76, 77, 79, 80, 90, 126, 143, 170, 174, 175, 222 n11

recovery, 4; accountability, 13, 15, 16–17, 21, 26; challenges of, 10–11; failure of, 26–27; role of researcher in, 12, 16–17

Redcloud, 64

rhetorical strategies: ordering in, 156–67; ordering out, 167–79

Robinson, John, 6

Rodgers/Rogers (name), 126, 127, 129, 135

routine, 159, 154, 156, 171, 195, 198

Sacks, Oliver, 203

Sand, George, 86

Sarton, May, 12, 54

Schlissel, Lillian, 38

Schuneman, Billie, 3, 10, 27–28, 194–96

Scott, Walter, 31

Scott-Maxwell, Florida, 31

Seitz, James, 191–92

Seville, Mr., 65

Sheldon (town), 65, 79, 80, 83

Shepard, Sarah, 128

Sherman, Stuart, 18–19, 21, 23, 27, 92–96, 110, 152, 214 n11, 219 n6, 219 n7

Shiffler, Mr., 64

Shipton, Mother, 63

Shuck (name), 124

Shumaker, Wayne, 46

Shuman, Amy, 6

Simons, Judy, 39

Sioux Falls, South Dakota, 79

smallpox, 137

Smith, Dr., 70, 71, 75, 81, 82, 83, 84, 124, 125, 126, 127, 128, 129, 131, 133, 143, 162, 163

Smith, Emma, 69

Smith, Sidonie, 199, 213 n9

Sophie (hired girl), 58, 66, 67, 68, 69, 70, 159, 163–64, 172, 178

space, 115–16, 148–50, 152

Spivak, Gayatri, 26

Stauffer, Donald, 28, 31

Stein, Gertrude, 42

Stewart, Kathleen, 115

Stiffler, Mrs., 61

Stitz, 76

story: and Annie's diary, 166–67, 192–93; and diary, 17, 25, 41, 50–51, 217–18 n54; and lifewriting,

story: and Annie's diary (*continued*)
202–4, 207; and ordinary writing,
5–7, 13, 16–17, 20; privileging of,
12, 13, 194–95, 223 n12; pull of, 14,
15, 33, 36, 44, 56–57, 87, 90, 187;
and temporality, 219 n6; use of,
16, 209–10. *See also* diaries, as
public or private

Tabor, Elizabeth "Baby Doe," 51–55
Temple, Judy Nolte, 34, 37, 48, 49,
51–52, 218 n3
time: diurnal, 18; and diurnal form,
93–97; and gender, 95–96; and
measure, 92–97; and occasion,
92–97; and pendulum, 18, 92–93,
145; and written form, 93
Thrale, Hester, 112
trauma, 25, 205–7

Ulrich, Laurel Thatcher, 13, 34, 51

Virgile, Miss, 66
Visweswaran, Kamela, 13, 190–91

Walker, Alice, 1, 201
Ward, Mrs., 17, 66, 126, 175
Watch (dog's name?), 73, 78, 135,
137
Watson, Julie, 199, 213 n9
Wilkomirski, Benjamin, 202
Wilson, Mr., 135
Wink, Amy, 36, 223 n4
Women's Christian Temperance
Association, 82
Woolf, Virginia, 12, 31, 42, 54
Wordsworth, Dorothy, 31
writing, 153; making texts, 16, 21,
190–93, 208–10; social nature of,
39, 40

Young, Iris Marion, 197